Estelle Buck

oretta
pr 2 - 1960

Best wishes

Paula Illasta

PERLE

Perle

MY STORY

BY PERLE MESTA

WITH ROBERT CAHN

McGRAW-HILL BOOK COMPANY, INC.

New York   *Toronto*   *London*

To the memory of
my beloved
mother and father

CONTENTS

P E R L E

ONE: *The Mostes' What?*

AT TIMES in recent years I have been referred to as "The Hostess with the Mostes'," a title which has always puzzled me. The mostes' what? Some people seem to think it is the mostes' money, but it isn't. It's certainly not the mostes' glamour or beauty. Nor is it the mostes' *savoir-faire*. And I hope that those who call me Hostess with the Mostes' are not referring to my weight!

Once when I was visiting in a shop in Florida, the salesgirl looked at me and commented, "You certainly do look like Perle Mesta."

"A lot of people have told me I look like her," I said matter-of-factly. Of course, I should have identified myself immediately to save the salesgirl embarrassment. But curiosity led me on. I wanted to hear what else she might say.

The salesgirl looked me over more closely.

"But no," she added with finality. "You couldn't be Perle Mesta. You don't have all those chins she has."

I admit that there have been periods in my life when press descriptions of me as "plump" or "pudgy" were reasonably accurate. But since 1957, when I went on the Swedish Milk Diet and lost twenty-six pounds, I have managed to keep a figure that lets me wear some of Marusia's best creations. Maybe I'm not slim—but at least I'm not fat.

Of course, this Hostess with the Mostes' business all started with one of Irving Berlin's hit tunes in the musical comedy *Call Me Madam,* "The Hostess with the Mostes' on the Ball." The heroine of *Call Me Madam,* Sally Adams, was an avid Democrat and a close friend of a President of the United States called "Harry." Sally Adams was also a party-loving Washington hostess and the ambassador to a tiny European duchy, and these circumstances

1

were so strikingly similar to my status in 1950 that some suspicious souls insisted the Howard Lindsay–Russel Crouse comedy was a satire on my life. While it would be presumptuous of me to claim for myself any such title as Hostess with the Mostes', let's not kid ourselves, the musical comedy *was* based on some of my experiences—I don't deny it.

In the fall of 1950, when *Call Me Madam* was all set to open, a few of the striped-pants boys in Washington were worried about possible similarities between the play and real life. I guess they thought it beneath the dignity of the State Department to have one of its representatives made the subject of satire. I was aboard the *Liberté,* returning to Washington for briefing after my first year in Luxembourg, when I received a cable from Dean Acheson's assistant, Undersecretary of State James Webb, ordering me not to attend the Broadway opening but to come posthaste to Washington.

Although I had been invited by the star of the play, Ethel Merman, to attend the opening, and had even had a special new dress made for the occasion, I hurried off the ship and took the first train to Washington. That night, while the New York press looked for me on Broadway, I accompanied Mrs. Truman to a benefit concert at Constitution Hall.

When I reported in to the State Department the next morning, I tried to find out just what was so wrong about my going to see *Call Me Madam.* I wasn't mad. But when I'm ordered not to do something, I like to know the reason why. Such an attitude is not particularly welcome in the State Department. After several days, I still hadn't received a satisfactory answer to my question.

"Your presence would tend to dignify a burlesque on a State Department official," I was told when I pressed the question.

"But, how do you know it's a burlesque?" I countered to the Department official who handed down the edict. "Have you seen it?"

"No," he replied. "But we have heard disturbing reports regarding its political innuendo."

All this highfalutin talk only made me more determined to see the play. During an interview I had with President Truman a few days later, I brought up the subject of the new musical. I had already mentioned to Mrs. Truman that it might be fun to sneak up to New York and take in a matinee, and have Margaret (who was there studying singing) join us, and Bess was all for it. I asked

2

the President if he had any objections either to my seeing the show, or taking Mrs. Truman and Margaret with me.

"Go ahead," he told me. "I'd go with you if I could spare the time. But remember, don't be offended at any of the lines. It's just a play and they've got to make up things or it wouldn't be funny."

Columnist Leonard Lyons had invited us to see the show with him, so I phoned Leonard and asked him to get the tickets secretly and not let anyone, not even Ethel or the theater management, know we were coming. I had found from experience that I could trust Leonard with a secret.

Bess, Margaret, Leonard, and I timed our arrival so we would enter just as the house was darkened for the opening curtain. We would have slipped in completely unrecognized except that the theater manager, Norman Light, saw us in the lobby and gave us a somewhat startled look as we rushed by to our seats. He had suddenly realized why Leonard had been in such urgent need of four choice seats up front, with a few singles immediately behind and in front (for the Secret Service men who always accompanied the First Lady and her daughter).

Well, I thought it was a wonderful show even though it contained some pretty sharp gibes. When the curtain went up on the second scene at Sally Adams' party to celebrate her swearing in as Ambassador to the "Grand Duchy of Lichtenburg," and one of the chorus sang about how Sally "Makes 'em sing at her parties and each guest becomes a ham, giving all that he's got," Bess nudged me and said, "Just like you do." When Mrs. Truman's turn came, she was a good sport about the satire aimed at the President. And when there was a joke about "Harry's daughter" getting a bad notice for her singing, Margaret laughed goodnaturedly and was very diplomatic about it. I am sure, though, that it hurt her deeply to have her singing career treated as a joke.

I winced once or twice myself, but most of the time I was so taken up with Ethel Merman's marvelous performance that I managed to forget it was supposed to be a satire on me and my job. A lot of it was, of course, pure fiction. I didn't fall in love with the Foreign Minister the way Sally Adams did. And Luxembourg never asked for a single penny from the United States, unlike the "Lichtenburgers" in the play who asked for a hundred million dollars. But when Ethel fell on her *derrière* while curtsying before the royal

3

court, I was brought back to reality, remembering how I had practiced and practiced so as not to fall while backing out of the room after presenting my credentials to the Grand Duchess Charlotte. And when Sally Adams ventured forth on her duties saying, "I want Harry to be proud of me," Lindsay and Crouse could have been reading my innermost thoughts when I first became Minister to Luxembourg.

Like the musical comedy ambassadress, I earned my diplomatic post through service to the Democratic party rather than through apprenticeship in the State Department; and I by-passed channels and went to the President when I wanted to get things done. And also like Sally Adams, I seem to have a reputation as a party giver. It's no secret that I love to give parties—lots of them.

My parties seem to fit no pattern, either in how often they are held or in who is invited. I may give three in one week or none in three weeks, depending on what I think is the best timing for the particular purpose I have in mind. A few months ago at one of my parties, Dr. Wernher von Braun held my guests spellbound as he told what we could expect in space travel in the next few years. At another party I gave, Eric Johnston was able to tell us his firsthand impressions of Khrushchev, shortly after he came back from spending a weekend with the Soviet leader near Moscow.

I have been privileged to entertain old friends like the Truman family, Ike and Mamie Eisenhower, Sam Rayburn and Joe Martin; to introduce new political figures such as Nevada's Governor Grant Sawyer; to recognize people in government, industry, or science who have done important things; and to honor the representatives of foreign countries. And I enjoy giving parties for show people; recently I have given parties for Judy Garland, Shirley Booth, Carol Channing, Celeste Holm, Fernanda Montel, and ballerina Maria Tallchief.

At times I have hired entertainers, but my most successful parties have been the ones at which the entertainment has sprung up spontaneously. I always provide live music—these days usually a five-piece combo. I never ask guests to perform. When the atmosphere is right, though, they frequently volunteer.

At one party, Edgar Bergen, who had left Charlie McCarthy at home, transformed his left hand into a delightful lady named Ophelia, supplied her with the voice of a tired vixen, and kept us

4

laughing for half an hour. Judy Garland once gave a whole show in my living room at three o'clock in the morning. The great opera star Rosa Ponselle more than once has filled my drawing rooms with her glorious music. And often my guests and I have been favored by a performance from that distinguished Missouri pianist, Harry S. Truman.

Sometimes our entertainment comes from unexpected sources. One balmy summer evening in Washington the wife of Korean Ambassador Yang kicked off her shoes and danced a graceful hula on the terrace. At my home in Newport, Rhode Island, Mrs. Cornelius Vanderbilt once performed a whistling duet with Washington columnist Betty Beale. And a General called Ike, who was soon to become President, is memorable in my party annals for his stirring baritone solo rendition of "Abdul Abulbul Amir."

People often ask me why I give so many parties. Am I lonely and do I crave company? Is my party-giving the outlet for some suppressed desire? Am I making up for a deep scar left on me as a little child when no one showed up for my first party—as was once portrayed in a television version of my life? Or do I give parties for some Machiavellian purpose, secretly trying to sway the course of history?

I have never been a great one for stopping to figure out such matters. I would discount most of these points, although I do like to have people around me and it is certainly true that most of my parties have a purpose. Socializing brings people together and getting people together promotes better understanding of common problems. And since men first began to associate with one another, feasting has always been one of the most pleasant methods of finding out what is going on.

Whether I give a party in New York or London or Hollywood or Washington, I like to have guests who are in the thick of things. Whether or not they are in the *Social Register* means nothing to me. In Washington, I like to mix government officials, diplomats, businessmen, and professional people. In an atmosphere of good food, music, and gracious women, differences sometimes can be settled or important matters of policy worked out. A Cabinet member who might not want to be seen going to call on a senator at his office may be able to settle a problem with him off in a quiet corner at a party. Or a legislator can say to a colleague over a demitasse,

5

"What's wrong with my bill?" and get a forthright, unrestrained answer that would not be possible if the two men were clashing on the floor of the House or Senate.

Of course, the first requirement of any party is that every guest have a good time. But while I try to make sure that no one goes home unhappy, I nearly always have some specific reason for bringing together certain combinations of guests. For example, take the party I gave last year for Clare Boothe Luce.

I have known Clare for years and, while we are often at odds politically, we are good friends. When I heard of her appointment as Ambassador to Brazil and knew she would be coming to Washington to appear before a Senate committee, I telephoned her in Arizona. I asked if she would like to come to a dinner where she could talk informally with some of her old friends and others who might have information helpful in her new undertaking.

I wanted especially for Clare and Henry to get better acquainted with Brazilian Ambassador Peixoto and his wife. I also invited Senator and Mrs. Bourke Hickenlooper (he is on the Foreign Relations Committee, which passes on ambassadorial appointments), Senate Majority Leader and Mrs. Lyndon Johnson, Congressmen Joe Martin and Paul Rogers, the Wiley Buchanans (Chief of Protocol), the Charles Finucanes (Assistant Secretary of Defense), Bob Gray (Secretary to the Cabinet), and a few of the Luces' close friends including Alice Roosevelt Longworth and Margaret Case, of *Vogue* magazine.

About six o'clock the evening of the party, Lyndon Johnson phoned to say he might not be able to come because the Senate was still in session on the Kennedy-Ervin labor bill and it looked as if it would go on far into the night. I told him not to feel embarrassed; that what he was doing was far more important than my dinner. But both Senators Johnson and Hickenlooper managed to break away from the Senate session just before eight o'clock when many of the other senators were ducking out for dinner. While we were at the table, Senator Johnson was called to the phone and was informed that a roll-call vote was being held on an amendment to the bill. He and Senator Hickenlooper, who were on opposite sides of the issue, agreed to "pair" their votes (one for and one against the amendment), and they managed to stay long enough to finish the main course. Then they excused themselves and went back to work while the rest of us had dessert.

A hostess has to be prepared for anything, but I must admit I was surprised when Alice Longworth, who is one of Washington's most august social figures, asked me where I kept my television set. She said there was a program at ten o'clock she didn't want to miss. You don't say no to Alice Longworth even when you have known her for thirty years, as I have. It happened that my set was out of order, so I borrowed my maid's and soon Alice and three of my men guests went to another room to watch a prize fight. An hour later when they rejoined us, Alice looked disgusted. The fighter she had been pulling for had lost and Alice had lost a dollar bet to Wiley Buchanan.

While the boxing fans were glued to the television set, the rest of us had started dancing. I got Henry Luce to rumba with me, although he said he hadn't danced in years. He turned out to be a wonderful partner. And Clare ended up the evening being taught some new samba steps by Washingtonian Jack Logan—she thought they would come in handy in Brazil. And even though Clare later declined her ambassadorship so that the purpose of my party was largely lost, I'm sure that all of my guests at least had a memorable evening.

It is almost impossible to keep a Washington social event, no matter how nonpolitical, from being linked to partisan politics. A few days after the Clare Luce party, Republican columnist Fulton Lewis, Jr., commenting on the Senate debate on the Kennedy-Ervin labor bill, wrote: "Both Republicans and Democrats were angry because Majority Leader Lyndon Johnson had kept them on the floor all night while he partied it up at Mrs. Perle Mesta's."

"Partied it up at Perle Mesta's"! How many times I've heard that line. Some people seem to think that my life has been one long party. As noted before, I love to give parties and I am flattered if I am sometimes referred to as the Hostess with the Mostes'. But even so, I like to think I have done something more in my life than just give parties, and I hope this will be evident to readers of these pages.

TWO: *No Kilts for William*

MY STORY would undoubtedly be more fascinating if I could say that I started out as a homeless waif selling violets on a street corner. But too many people in Oklahoma City know me as the oldest child of Bill Skirvin, who owned all those oil wells and the Skirvin Hotel. Father wasn't so rich that you could say I was born with a silver spoon in my mouth, but we certainly never knew want in the Skirvin household.

My father, William Balser Skirvin, was ordinarily easygoing, although at times he showed his quick temper. He was also kindhearted, persuasive, a shrewd businessman, and very much an individualist. He had been reared on a farm in Michigan and was selling farm machinery in the Midwest when he met and married Harriet Elizabeth Reid, one of eleven children of the best cook in Wyandotte County, Kansas—or so we children were told. Hattie, my mother, was born in a log cabin in Kansas, yet her simple beginning did not keep her from getting a sound education. She graduated from the University of Kansas before being married. In fact, all seven Reid daughters had a college education, each one helping out the next one financially.

For a while, Father and one of his brothers-in-law, Orrin W. Shepherd, had a real-estate business in Kansas City. When the Oklahoma Territory was opened to settlement, he and Orrin were on the first train in. They were literally "on" the train, because it was completely filled and they had to ride on top of a car. They got off in Guthrie, and staked out some lots in the new town that later became the first capital of the state.

Father used to delight in holding me on his knee and telling me how he got his start selling lemonade at fifty cents a glass to thirsty

Easterners heading west to stake out a homestead. I believed him. It never occurred to me to wonder where he got the lemons. Later I found out that he had shrewdly bought and sold real estate and made quite a bit of money in Guthrie before moving on to Texas, where he and Orrin started another real-estate business in Galveston. Orrin moved back to Kansas City and became a banker, but Father laid out a new town, Alta Loma, across the bay from Galveston, on the mainland. He drilled and discovered the first deep water wells in the area, and soon had a profitable development under way. Some of his earnings went into oil prospecting, and Father was in on the second gusher at the famous Spindletop field near Beaumont. That's why we children never lacked for anything.

There were three of us Skirvin children. I'm the oldest, then comes my sister, Marguerite, and my brother, William. We are not a bit alike. Marguerite, who is now Mrs. George Tyson and lives in Nevada, is blond and blue-eyed—the real beauty of the family. She is of an artistic nature, and is never happier than when in the midst of decorating a house. Marguerite likes the formal way of doing things and is much more proper than I am—sometimes I think she is a little shocked at me when I dance all night or badger a senator for his vote on women's rights. She has great tact, and when we are together she helps to keep me from letting my temper flare up, which it does on occasion. My family says I'm like my father on that score. Marguerite loves to read books, has great powers of concentration, and is an expert at bridge. Canasta is more my speed, and I never can find the time to read. I like to get my information from talking to people and watching things happen.

William, a confirmed bachelor, is in the oil business in Oklahoma. He is the stabilizing influence in our family and is also the brightest one. William has better judgment than Marguerite and I together. He loves the outdoors and, oddly enough, considering the sisters he has, he hates parties. Marguerite and I are great talkers, but William is close-lipped and when he does have something to say, he says it in few words. I depend a great deal on him for financial advice. He is a stickler for detail, and I hate detail.

Of course the three of us have our disagreements about politics and other things, but when any really important decision comes along, we work as a team, pray over the outcome, and are of one mind. If you touch one, you touch us all, and anyone who starts something with one of us had better watch out because he'll soon have all three to contend with.

We children were told we had a bit of Irish, Scotch, and English from Father's side, and a background of French from Mother. We believed what we were told. In Oklahoma folks never went in much for tracing ancestry. Recently I was made acutely conscious of my lack of knowledge about my ancestry when I was asked to be guest speaker at a meeting of the Daughters of Founders and Patriots of America. This is an organization even more selective than the Daughters of the American Revolution. To be a member, you have to have an ancestor who traces directly, not only from a patriot of the Revolution, but also from one of the early founders who came to America in the seventeenth century. After dinner, one after another of the ladies got up and introduced herself, telling how this ancestor did this and another did that. When it came my turn to speak, and the woman who introduced me had gone into my background only as far back as my being Minister to Luxembourg, I felt a brief explanation was in order.

"It is just marvelous to hear about all the wonderful ancestors you people have," I said, "and I wish I could tell you about mine. Unfortunately, I never checked back because I'm sure I would find at least a horse thief before I had gotten back to 1800." And do you know? No one so much as cracked a smile.

Actually, I did make one attempt to determine my origin. When my sister had a house in England in 1953, and I was with her for a short time, my brother-in-law kept bragging about his wonderful ancestors. George Tyson comes from an old-line Boston family, and tracing ancestry back to kings and dukes is old sport for those Back Bay people. One day I slipped off to Scotland and went to a place where they keep the histories of all the British royal families. I told the old fellow who kept the records that my father was named Skirvin. He went back into his archives and came out a short time later with a dusty volume.

"Let's see, Skirving . . . Skirvine . . . Here it is: Skirvin." The Scot traced with his fingers across the page. His eyes brightened. "Why, you've got a wonderful background. You belong to the same clan that the Queen Mother belongs to." Then he asked if I had a brother.

"Yes," I replied. "His name is William."

"Look right here on this family tree," the old fellow said, and he showed me the name of William. "Why, your brother has the right to be an earl." Then he showed me the tartan of our clan and offered to trace our family tree and give me a copy of it, and also a copy of our family crest.

"How much?" I asked.

"Three hundred dollars," he replied.

I went back to my hotel, called Marguerite in London, and asked if she would pay one-third of the cost. It ought to be worth that, I told her, to be able to have something to show George every time he started talking about *his* family. Marguerite wasn't enthusiastic —family trees didn't seem to impress her—but finally said if William would agree, she'd pay her third. So I put in a call to Oklahoma City.

"Just think, William, you could be an earl," I told him when I got through to Oklahoma and explained why I was calling.

William didn't answer for a moment. He likes to think matters through before making a decision. At four dollars a minute, I wasn't very patient, and kept pressing him for an immediate answer.

"Being an earl won't do me any good in Oklahoma," he answered at last. "But if you can find anything on that family tree that says I'm an Indian chief, I'll pay for the whole thing."

The records keeper had assured me that I had authentic Scotch ancestry, and I acted as if I had, for I gave up the idea of having our family tree traced. It struck me that three hundred dollars was too much for a list of names that really didn't mean anything. I did buy a few yards of the tartan of "our clan," however, to have some kilts made for William. But he said he would burn them, so William never got his kilts—and that was the end of my excursion into ancestry.

I happened to be born in Sturges, Michigan, where Mother had gone to escape the summer heat of Texas, but my earliest recollections of childhood were in Galveston. Mother, despite her chronic ill health, was the dominant influence in our family. She had light brown eyes that sparkled when she talked. If she had something serious to tell us, she would often end it with a little story. That way we would remember. Mother spoke in a well-modulated voice and with rather precise diction. She had studied elocution in college and taught all of us to recite even before we were old enough to go to school. She played the piano beautifully and I guess I inherited my love of music from her.

Our house was a warm, gay place, and our playmates were always welcomed. Mother was a good organizer and could always have a lot of children around without having them get out of hand. She encouraged us to have little parties at the least excuse and was always thinking up new games for us. It's no wonder that party-giving comes easily to me, for parties were as natural as breathing in our home.

Mother was very religious and tried to teach us principle. Every meal was started with a blessing, and after breakfast each morning we would all stay at the table while she read a few passages from the Bible. All of us children went to Presbyterian Sunday School. Mother was quite strict about some things—we weren't allowed to play cards and no swear words could be used. Father went along with all of this and attended church with us, but only because of Mother. He wasn't very religious. Like lots of men, he more or less carried his religion in his wife's name.

Mother was quite intellectual and came from a family where education was the most important thing. Father had a great zest for living. He believed in having a good time and making money, and always had some promotion scheme going. But unlike many promoters, he prepared ahead for the possibility of lean times. We always had money because when Father made his first big profit in oil, he put half of it in Mother's name. "Some day I might go broke," he told her, "and I want to make sure the children are educated." And Father kept on putting large sums in Mother's name.

Mother and I were very close and I adored her, but the bond between my father and me was even closer. I was his favorite. I guess Father and I were cut out of the same piece of cloth. Father had counted on his first child being a boy, so when I came along he treated me like a boy anyway. He taught me to play baseball, to pitch horseshoes, and to ride horseback. For a while I was a tomboy. Once when I was eight, and Mother and I were visiting in Kansas City, I disappeared from the living room where she and her friends were talking. She glanced out the window and there I was, high on a tree branch twenty feet above the ground. Mother was terrified. But I got down all right—just the way I got up.

From the time I was a tiny child I would stand right up to Father and talk back. When his temper rose, the others were usually a little scared of him. But I always stood my ground and gave it right back. If I did something wrong and he scolded me, I would demand: "Why can't I do it?" And most of the time I could win him over.

I loved to listen as he told me about bringing in oil wells or making big real-estate deals. There is no doubt that I was "Father's girl" and that he spoiled me and made discipline very difficult for Mother. She always said I was the worst child. When I was very young, if she tried to spank me, I would lie down and bang my head against the floor. And when I got a little older, I would use every trick I knew to get what I wanted. Mother never knew what I was going to try next.

From my earliest days, I wanted to be the leader in our neighborhood projects. If I couldn't be the leader, I wouldn't play. The first real party I remember giving on my own was when I was about eleven. I organized it all myself and invited a dozen or so playmates. We played games and when everyone was ready for a rest, I introduced my star performer of the afternoon—a missionary friend of the family who showed magic lantern slides of Japan. As the *pièce de résistance* I served some nasturtium sandwiches. I had picked some nasturtiums, mixed the seeds with mayonnaise, and then topped each sandwich with a nasturtium flower. My playmates thought the sandwiches were somewhat bitter, but they ate them, flowers and all. The party was a great success, and I decided then and there that giving parties was even more fun than going to parties. Although it made a good story for television's Playhouse 90 to portray this first party as a pathetic event where no one showed up because my father forgot to mail the invitations, the above is what actually happened.

During these years Father was frequently away in the oil fields and our close family spirit began to fade. Father liked to have his drinks and good times, and stayed away more and more often. I will never forget the Christmas Eve when we went down to the station to meet Father. We were all full of the cheer of Christmas and could hardly wait to give him a rousing welcome home. The train pulled in and all around us people were gaily greeting their loved ones. But Father wasn't on the train. He didn't come home for several days. Mother did her best to make our Christmas gay and happy as if nothing were different. But it hurt her very much.

During the early 1900s we moved to Oklahoma City and Father bought a house on Northeast Eleventh and Geary Streets. One of the first things he did was to drill a 300-foot water well in the back yard. When he finished it, I remember he said, "I think there's an oil field right here." Everyone laughed at him, because there had never been oil anywhere near Oklahoma City. But years later, long after Father had sold the property, Phillips Petroleum Company drilled a 6000-foot oil well just fifteen feet from that old water well and it has already produced more than a million dollars worth of oil!

There was always a menagerie around our house in Oklahoma City. We children had Shetland ponies when we were little and then graduated to horses. We made great pets of the horses. Of course, it was our duty to take care of them—that was all part of owning a horse. I took great pride in keeping my horse, Rex, shining and well curried. With a big pair of shears I would even up his mane so it was all nice and neat. I loved to ride. It was always a great thrill to me to feel the power and challenge of controlling a horse.

Marguerite always had a small pedigreed dog, usually a poodle, but William was the real animal lover and had no less than a dozen hound dogs as well as raccoons, owls, squirrels, and whatever else he happened to have brought home for shelter.

Among William's pets were two monkeys. Those little rascals were into everything. One morning Father heard sobs coming from the basement and went down to investigate. There was William, kneeling beside a lifeless monkey. The poor thing was stiff as a board. It had gotten into the laundry starch and gorged itself to death.

Nothing would comfort William until Father arranged a funeral service in the yard. He found a box and Marguerite lined it and decorated it and Father read a little eulogy before the "casket" was lowered into the grave. The "funeral" seemed to make it all right for William.

When William was fourteen he became famous—well, at least he got his picture in the local newspaper. He had dreamed up a design for a glider and spent his summer vacation building it. It was a surprisingly professional job. We were all on hand the day he tested it. William took it up a small hill just outside of town and when the wind was strong enough, he ran down the hill into the wind. He got about seven feet off the ground and flew for about 200 feet. His longest flight was almost 400 feet. Then the glider flipped over. William wasn't hurt badly, but his glider was ruined. And Father wouldn't let him build another one.

Mother's health failed steadily after we moved to Oklahoma City. I was getting old enough to have a little sense of responsibility and when Mother would have a bad spell, I would stay with her and try to comfort her. One night she called me into her room.

"It doesn't look as if I'm going to be here much longer, dear," she said. "You are the oldest one and you soon will be a young lady. When I go, I want you to look after Marguerite and William and your father. I've tried to give you the best training I could, and I'm going to trust to God that you will carry on."

"Oh, Mother! Don't talk like that," I said, hiding my anxiety. "You've come through these bad spells before and I just know you're going to get well," I added, trying to reassure her.

"No, dear," she insisted. "You listen and remember what I've said."

"I'll try, Mother," I said. "I'll do the best I know how." And then I left the room quickly so she wouldn't see me crying.

She got better and was up and around the next week. But one Sunday in March, after we had been for a ride in the country, Mother had a severe chill. We put her to bed and Father went to get our good friend and neighbor, Dr. Lea Riely. It was pneumonia, the doctor said, and it was serious. From then on, either Father or I was with her every minute. She passed away a few days later.

The night after Mother's death, I didn't sleep at all. I just couldn't seem to face what was ahead. It was Mother who had kept the family together. And with her gone, I felt all the stability of the family had gone, and I didn't know what was going to happen. But I prayed as best I knew and tried to remember what Mother had taught us from the Bible about putting our whole trust in God. I

15

recalled what Mother had told me about death—that it was only passing on to a better existence, and I opened my Bible to the Twenty-third Psalm and read:

> Yea, though I walk through the valley of the shadow of death, I will fear no evil; for thou art with me; thy rod and thy staff they comfort me.

And I was comforted. The next morning, I seemed to have some inward strength from somewhere that helped get Father and all of us over this difficult period. I began to run things around the house, and give the orders. And I guess I took my responsibilities rather seriously, because pretty soon Marguerite and William began calling me "The General."

THREE: *Father's 300-Room Hobby*

ABOUT A YEAR after Mother's death, Father became involved in a project that changed the course of our lives considerably. One afternoon in 1909 a Col. Ned Green called on Father. He proved to be the son of Hetty Green, the famous New York financier, and he had been sent by his mother to Oklahoma City to purchase some property. After looking all over town, Colonel Green decided he wanted four lots at the corner of First and Broadway. Father happened to own these four lots. The offer was substantial and Father was almost ready to agree to the sale when Green happened to mention that his mother planned to build the biggest hotel in Oklahoma City on the land. When Father heard this he immediately turned down the offer.

"That Hetty Green is no dumbbell," Father said to me that night. "If she thinks that's a good site for a hotel, then it probably is." Father called in his pal, S. A. (Sol) Layton, the best architect in the state of Oklahoma, and within a week they were working out plans for a six-story hotel. Early in 1910 the Governor of Oklahoma, Charles N. Haskell, helped Father turn the first shovel of earth at the ground-breaking ceremony.

One night in September, Father went over to Sol Layton's office to celebrate the completion of the fifth floor framework. One drink led to another, and Sol kept insisting that at the rate Oklahoma City was growing, a six-story hotel would be far too small. By 3:00 A.M., Father thought so too, and the next day he increased his order to obtain enough of the Malakoff brick to cover eight stories.

Several weeks later, Father and Sol celebrated the completion of another two stories of framework, and that night the plans were again altered upwards. In September, 1911, when the Skirvin Hotel was ready for occupancy, it was ten stories high, had two wings

17

and three hundred rooms, and was the biggest hotel in the state. It was also the most de luxe hotel in the entire Southwest, featuring all outside rooms, running ice water in every room, a ballroom that could hold five hundred people, and a sumptuous main dining room where every evening Professor Kachelski conducted the nine-piece Skirvin Orchestra.

Father was like a feudal baron with his hotel and didn't want to be dependent upon anyone for its operation. Finding that the local gas company had an exclusive franchise, he used his political influence to obtain a permit to build his own gas pipeline. He did the same thing with water, putting down three of his own wells. Having the water and the gas to generate steam, he put in his own electric plant. Father set up a laundry in the hotel and not only did his own but the laundry of other hotels in town. The Skirvin Hotel was almost a city in itself, and later, when Father put in his own garbage disposal plant, he was practically self-sufficient—except for telephone service. He never could get his own telephone company.

Soon after the opening celebration, Father sold our house and we all moved into a five-room suite on the ninth floor of the hotel. Marguerite and I thought living in a hotel was just about the most exciting thing in the world. We thought we were terribly sophisticated. William was less enthusiastic. He owned at that time eleven dogs, two raccoons, the one surviving monkey, an owl, and a horse. Father's rigid rule for his hotel was No Pets Allowed. But in his family's case he made a slight exception. Marguerite's poodle and Russian wolfhound lived in the suite with us, and William built cages and doghouses on the roof for most of his menagerie, although six of the dogs and the horse were exiled to a friend's farm in the country.

There were occasional problems. One night a raccoon got loose from its pen and jumped off the roof to its death. A large hawk William brought into his aviary disposed of the owl. And guests sometimes complained about barking dogs. Father's reply was the guests were free to leave if they didn't like the Skirvin atmosphere.

One night, the room clerk awakened Father to tell him of a guest's complaint.

"The man swears he hears a wolf howling right on top of his room," the clerk reported. Father was convinced the guest must be drunk and was all ready to have him thrown out for causing a disturbance, when he, too, heard something oddly wolflike. He put on his robe and slippers and padded up to the roof. There in a cage were three small wolves that William had trapped and secretly brought home.

Softhearted Father let William keep the wolves for a while. But as they started growing, he became concerned, and even William realized the danger when they broke into the aviary one night and disposed of his hawk. When a rancher friend of the family offered to buy the wolves from William for five dollars each, William agreed to sell them. Not till several years later did he discover that the rancher hadn't wanted the wolves at all—that Father had paid the man twenty-five dollars to put over the deal.

Father was generally not so lenient with his paying guests in the matter of pets. Years after the wolves departed, Katharine Cornell and her troupe came to Oklahoma City to present *The Barretts of Wimpole Street*. Her manager, who had arranged her accommodations at the Skirvin Hotel, arrived a day or so before Miss Cornell. He happened to mention that the actress was bringing her two dachshunds. Father said that was all right and that an excellent kennel was provided in the basement.

"Why, Miss Cornell wouldn't think of putting those dogs in a kennel," said the manager. "They always stay in her suite."

"Well, she'll just have to go some place else then," said Father. And she did.

But Father was unpredictable. When a family named Hutchison appeared at the hotel with a full-grown lion, Father welcomed them with open arms. The Hutchisons had picked up the lion in Africa as a cub and had raised it to be a pet. Since it was far too large for the dog kennel, Father gave the Hutchisons permission to have the lion in their room. He suggested they keep the beast in the bathroom. While the Hutchisons were out at dinner, a maid entered the room to deliver some fresh towels. There was a shriek. The maid shot out of the room, towels flying in all directions. As she went running down the hall, the lion was right behind her, thinking she wanted to play. The whole hotel was in an uproar for an hour while Father got the maids calmed down and Mr. Hutchison corralled his pet. Father used the incident to advantage. In the first place, it was fine publicity for the hotel. In the second, it gave him something to hold over the help. "Now, Rosie," he'd say to one of the maids, "you just better toe the line and do your work right or I'll get a lion after you!"

Marguerite and I were away at private schools much of the time as we grew older, but we loved living in the hotel when we were back in Oklahoma. I thought it was great fun to sit in the lobby and watch all the activity, and I got my first interest in politics from eavesdropping on the lobby conversations. The official state Republican headquarters were located in a room Father donated to the Party. And at times the hotel lobby appeared to be also the unofficial Democratic headquarters. Father was a Republican, but had many Democratic friends. And although his support for local and state candidates always went to the Republicans, in national politics he was a maverick, and often sided with the Democrats.

I can almost see Father now, sitting in the lobby, usually surrounded by three or four friends, his dark brown eyes catching everything that went on. He had signals worked out with his desk clerks so that by the lift of an eyebrow he could indicate a course of action toward a prospective guest. If he saw someone he didn't like heading for the desk, Father would signal the clerk to give the "sorry, sold out" reply. On the other hand, if one of Father's oilfield cronies arrived, the clerk would be signaled to cut the price of the room in half. Often, Father would give one of his cronies a room for nothing and invite him to his suite to sample his liquor.

In 1911 Oklahoma City was still almost a frontier town. For hundreds of miles to the west, there was nothing but ranch country and a few widely separated villages. Father's hotel was a kind of melting pot: his guests included millionaires, Indians, and even the fabled Western train robber, Al Jennings, who launched his unsuccessful campaign for governor from the Skirvin lobby. Cattlemen like the millionaire Miller brothers, who owned the famous 101 Ranch, also frequented the hotel, and I loved to hear the jingle of their spurs as they walked across the gray-tiled lobby. As a gesture to the cattlemen, Father had every piece of furniture in the lobby covered with genuine cowhide leather. And he also provided numerous tall, solid brass cuspidors with wide flared tops that could hardly be missed—even at ten paces. Sometimes Osage Indians, or Cherokees or Kiowas or Pawnees, in full regalia would come into the lobby, and I was fascinated when I would see a papoose swinging from a squaw's back. When the hotel first opened, the Indians were afraid of the elevators. Father would always assign them rooms on the lower floors so they could use the stairs. And I can still picture those Indians sitting stiffly in the big leather chairs, munching peanuts, and letting the shells drop on the floor.

One of our first guests after the hotel opened was an Osage by the name of—believe it or not—John Stink. He had been a guest at the hotel three days when the housekeeper mentioned to Father that the bed in his room had not yet been slept in. Father was ready to take this as a personal affront. He had made a trip to the Sealy factory in Texas to see exactly what was going into his box springs and mattresses. He was determined that his hotel beds would be the most comfortable in the country.

When the Indian came back to the hotel that afternoon, Father was waiting for him in the lobby.

"What's the matter, John?" asked Father. "My housekeeper says your bed hasn't been slept in for three nights. Anything wrong?"

"Nothing wrong," replied the Osage. "Bed too soft. Sleep on floor."

Oilmen like Bob Galbreath, Bill Skelly, and Walter Ramsey, who became leaders in the industry, frequently came to the Skirvin. I could always tell the oilmen by their leather jackets and laced boots, usually covered with oily mud, which they would track all over the lobby. Because of the ever-present oil and the peanut shells, Father didn't put any rugs in the lobby.

The hotel was just across an alley from the Rock Island Railroad. Father figured that by being so close to the depot, he would get first crack at all the passengers as they left their trains. Later he was to rue this decision when most of his guests arrived by automobile and there were numerous complaints about the noise from the trains.

One of the small banquet rooms, called the Green Room, was on the north side of the hotel, almost directly over the railroad tracks. There were many occasions when an after-dinner speaker had to compete with a rattling, banging freight train, and would sometimes have to stand for ten minutes waiting for the caboose to pass. Finding he couldn't do anything about the noise, Father renamed the banquet room and had an electric sign placed over the door: THE ROCK ISLAND ROOM. People were so amused that the room then became very popular and Father dedicated it to the railroad. Father's sense of humor could turn any such liability into an asset.

21

The proximity to the station also made the Skirvin Hotel a favorite spot for the traveling salesmen who had to wrestle with numerous heavy sample cases. Father didn't want Marguerite or me hobnobbing with the traveling men. If he ever saw one of them talking with me, Father would refuse him a room next time he came. I wasn't supposed even to look sideways at the traveling salesmen—but I did. Even when they weren't traveling salesmen, Father resented any attentions we received from hotel guests. There was one fellow, for instance, who came to town periodically from Kansas. And I went out with him a time or two. Father saw me with him one day and then he laid down the law to me.

"I don't want you to have a thing to do with that man," said Father.

"But he's a nice man and he comes from a good family, and he knows many of our relatives in Kansas," I protested.

Father was adamant. "You will have nothing more to do with him."

"Why?" I demanded, as usual.

"Well, if you must know, your nice man was known to have had a woman in his room last night, and I'm going to put him out of the hotel."

I didn't believe a word of it. But that's the way Father was about any man in whom I took an interest. And he never let that man have a room at the hotel again. Once, shortly before Mother died, she had said to me, "I dread the day when you will want to get married because your Father will never think anybody is good enough for you."

Though Father was generally a good businessman, the hotel was mostly a hobby with him and he never worried if it wasn't making money. After his first gusher at Spindletop, Father was in on several other big oil fields in south Texas, then got in on the great Glenn Pool near Tulsa. By the time he built his hotel, he already was a millionaire.

Father never dressed like an oilman. Even when he went out to the fields, he always dressed in a business suit and wore an impeccable white shirt and a felt hat. He saw to it that the best tailor in Oklahoma City had a shop right in the Skirvin Hotel, and he took out the rent in clothes.

Once in a while when Marguerite and I were both home from

school, Father would get all dressed up in his cutaway, we would put on our best formals, and the table in the center of the hotel dining room would be decorated as if the President of the United States were coming to dinner. Even on ordinary nights, we never sat down to dinner without Father, although Marguerite sometimes would have to scout around for a couple of hours to find him, as he liked to visit friends for a few drinks late in the afternoon. Father did like his liquor, and after Mother passed on, he indulged himself more frequently.

Of course, one wonderful thing about living in a hotel was the opportunity to use the ballroom for parties. Once I wanted to have some friends in to learn a new dance, the Bunny Hug, but didn't want Father to know about it because some people thought the dance was risqué. I had my friends come early so we could have the dancing over with before we ate, and thus fool Father. But just as we started dancing, the door flew open and there he stood. We were scared to death.

"So you thought you could put something over on the old man!" Father said sternly. But he couldn't keep a straight face, and broke into a laugh. Then he joined in the fun and we taught him the new dance.

Hotel life had a few drawbacks, however. My pet peeve was the lack of privacy on the telephone. The operators thought it was their mission to listen in on my calls and report to Father. I tried to win them over to my side, but they always remained loyal to Father.

I had picked out music as my intended career, and when I finished school, I studied piano and voice at Sherwood School of Music, in Chicago. During this time I fell in love frequently with musicians. Father was always worried that I would get carried away and marry one of my boy friends, because I was pretty emotional. And he probably had good cause to be worried. When I was eighteen, I became secretly engaged to a man who had been divorced twice and had several children. He gave me two diamond rings, but I didn't wear them because I didn't dare let Father know what was going on. This romance broke up when I found out that the man had been lying to me. I gave him back his rings and went right into another romance, also with an older man.

I was always fascinated by older men. They were doing things in the world, while the young men my age were still floundering around and I couldn't respect them. When I was going to Sherwood, I had dates with college men, but they were a wild lot, and I never took them seriously.

Father's opposition to my gentlemen friends was balanced, I must admit, by my disapproval of all the women in whom he took an interest. I always insisted his women friends were not right for him and tried to discourage him from giving us a stepmother.

FOUR: *"You—That's Who"*

In 1915, deciding I had spent enough time at Sherwood School of Music, I moved on to New York. I had aspirations to become a good singer, although I did not have the desire or inclination or voice to work toward grand opera. I was a dramatic soprano, but more dramatic than soprano, I am afraid. Though I was now old enough to look out for myself, when I told Father that I intended to pursue my musical studies in New York, he insisted on coming with me to see that I got settled right. I was invited to live with my great-aunt, Mrs. Roger Wellis. She was a wealthy society woman, a widow, and had a lovely apartment on Park Avenue. Father went back home to Oklahoma City, satisfied that I was well settled and well chaperoned.

Several months after my arrival in New York, I was invited with Aunt Florence to a dinner party a friend of hers was giving at the old Waldorf. She said she had a man she wanted me to meet. I had been seeing quite a bit of a New York cotton broker, but we weren't engaged or anything, so I was always interested in meeting new men.

It wasn't love at first sight when I met George Mesta at that party, but I was immediately attracted by him. He was blond and distinguished-looking, of more than medium height, and rather slim. I guessed him to be in his forties, and from his air of authority and his conversation about places he had been all over the world, he was obviously a man of wide experience. No one had told me a thing about him, but we clicked immediately and found many common interests to talk about. For one thing, he loved music as much as I did. When he escorted me home, he asked if I would have dinner with him the next evening. I accepted.

"Let's go to the Ritz for dinner and then we'll take in some clubs," George Mesta suggested the next evening when he called for me.

Not knowing anything of his financial status and fearing that such a program might drain his pocketbook, I countered by proposing that we dine at Schrafft's and then take a carriage ride in Central Park. George looked a little puzzled, but he agreed and Schrafft's it was. During dinner he talked about orders he was getting for engines or turbines or something. I didn't know what turbines were, but I assumed that engines had something to do with railroad trains. I didn't really care, and soon switched the conversation to music. The evening was enjoyable and I remember wondering, as we parted at Aunt Florence's door: Will I ever see him again?

George hadn't made a very good impression on Aunt Florence. She said he was too old for me and had no social standing, and she also thought it terrible that he wore light tan—almost yellow—shoes with a blue suit. She said he was just an ordinary Italian—a "wop" she called him—and that he didn't know anything or he wouldn't dress like that. But Aunt Florence and I disagreed on almost everything anyway, so her strong opinions only increased my interest in George.

The next morning, the woman who had introduced us called to ask what I had thought of George Mesta. I said I thought he was very nice.

"You know who he is, don't you?" she said.

"Well, not exactly," I replied. I had pictured him as a minor executive, possibly the sales manager, of some firm that made engines for trains.

"You'd better not let this one get away," Aunt Florence's friend said, laughing. "George Mesta owns the Mesta Machine Company, which makes some of the biggest steel machinery in the world. I hear he's worth at least fifteen million," she added.

And I had persuaded him to take me to Schrafft's!

A week later George called me from Pittsburgh, saying he was going to be in town that weekend and wanted to see me. This time, when he suggested an expensive restaurant, I didn't say no. And, being frank little me, I told him right at the start what I had heard about him and asked him if it were true.

George laughed and admitted that it probably was true, although

26

he wasn't sure he was worth that much. Then he told me a little about himself. His parents had come from Germany. His father, of Italian descent and a machinist and pattern maker, had wanted George to be a doctor, although George had from childhood been interested in building things. But because of his parents' desires, George had entered Western University of Pennsylvania (later the University of Pittsburgh), to study medicine. Yet his heart wasn't in it and one day he told his father that he didn't want to become a doctor but wanted to study engineering. His father said, in the tradition of the Old Country, "You will either do what we want you to, or you will leave home." So George, in the tradition of the United States, left home. He taught night school for board and room money and studied mechanical engineering in the daytime.

After graduation, he worked for a while as an engineer, then borrowed some money to start a small company to make machine tools. Gradually the Mesta Machine Company expanded until it became the biggest of its kind in the world, making huge machines to roll out sheets of steel, great turbines for dams or electric plants, and propeller shafts for the largest ships. Unfortunately, George's father did not live to see the success of his supposedly erring son.

For several months George and I dated whenever he came to New York. I was still going with the cotton broker, but he now seemed pretty dull in comparison with George Mesta. George and I had such fun on our dates. He loved the opera, he loved to go to the theater, and he loved to dance. Friends told me he was almost as old as my father, but he was always young and vital in his thinking, and he really didn't look or act like an older man, so I was seldom conscious of our age difference.

I don't know just when it was that I began to fall in love with George. I had been infatuated dozens of times, and I had even been engaged. But this was different. It was a funny thing: as soon as I realized I was falling in love, I withdrew myself from him ever so slightly. I wasn't at all sure I wanted to be serious yet. And anyway, George had never spoken of marriage. And I had heard via the grapevine that he had left some smoldering romantic trails behind him.

He never wrote to me. I found out later that he didn't like to write letters and at his office always used the phone to avoid dictating letters. He usually phoned me once or twice a week from

Pittsburgh or wherever he was. Once there was a lapse of three weeks when I didn't hear from him at all. During those three long weeks, I began to miss him and realized how hard I had fallen for him. When he finally phoned again, he explained that his mother had died and he had not felt like talking to anyone.

George and I had been dating for several months when I heard from a friend that he was "practically engaged" to a Pittsburgh girl. I was stunned. The more I thought about it, the madder I got. The next time George came to town and we started off in a taxi I blurted right out:

"Why are you asking me out so often? I hear you are almost engaged to a girl in Pittsburgh."

George looked surprised.

"Why, I have no intention of marrying her," he said. "I know who I'm going to marry."

I said, "Who?"

And he replied, "You—that's who."

And that's the way he proposed to me. I hope the taxi driver was of a romantic nature—or that he didn't happen to look over his shoulder.

We weren't exactly engaged then, but we had a sort of understanding. I wanted to be absolutely sure this was *it*. When it came right down to marriage, I felt balky. I had always had a great fear of a marriage not lasting. The thought of having to go through a divorce appalled me.

One evening George and I were at a night club when he saw friends from Pittsburgh. He took me over to their table to meet them—a man and his wife—and they froze me out like an iceberg. I was bewildered and hurt, and when we returned to our table I was on the verge of tears. I said to George, "I don't think they liked me." Only then did he explain that these were the parents of the girl he had been going with for several years. When I met the girl later I found she was beautiful, just beautiful. I sometimes wondered why George had picked me instead. I guess he liked my forthrightness and spunk and it probably was a perpetual challenge to him to try to figure me out.

Scared to death to tell Father about George, I finally decided to get him to come to New York for a week so he could meet George before I told him. By that time I had an engagement ring, but I didn't dare wear it. When they first met, Father didn't like him. I told Father that George and I were very congenial.

"What do you do that is so congenial?" asked Father. "That man is much too old for you."

Father always found fault with men who were interested in me. The fault with George was that he was too old, but if he hadn't been too old, he would have been too young. If he hadn't been too young, he would have been too gay. If he hadn't been too gay, he would have been too sober. So I didn't pay Father's objections any real heed. I knew he just didn't want to lose a daughter. When he insisted I go back to Oklahoma with him, I did. But I returned to New York in a couple of weeks. And Father changed his opinion about George after he saw how much I was in love with him. I also think Father was impressed because George had started out with nothing and had made a fortune, just as he had done.

We were married early in 1917 in New York. I wanted the wedding in the Little Church Around the Corner, but George persuaded me to have a private wedding. The ceremony took place in Aunt Florence's apartment, and the only people there were Father, Marguerite, William, Aunt Florence, a violinist and the Presbyterian minister who married us.

We honeymooned in Havana. It was a warm and golden place and I loved the colorful abandon of the Cubans. I nearly made myself ill drinking the delicious coconut and pineapple and orange juice they served. Our suite at the hotel was sumptuous, and all would have been perfect except that George knew too many people there. We had to resort to all kinds of schemes to get off by ourselves.

Everything was so gay and carefree on our honeymoon that I was totally unprepared for the problems that confronted our marriage as soon as we got to Pittsburgh. I think I packed a lifetime of experience and understanding into that first year. We came home from the honeymoon to George's large house on the hilltop overlooking his plant in the West Homestead suburb of Pittsburgh. George's steel empire was a thrilling sight, spread over many acres on the banks of the Monongahela, but it wasn't very pleasing aesthetically. Smoke and fumes poured forth and I wondered if I could ever get used to the murky atmosphere.

The house had been run for years by Mrs. Shultz, a heavy-set, square-faced German woman. "You two will get along fine," George had said on our way to Pittsburgh when he described Mrs. Shultz. Dear George was never more wrong.

Mrs. Shultz and I were at daggers' points from the first day I arrived, when she informed me she had been running the house and intended to keep on doing so. She was efficient to the last word and kept the house immaculate. Though I really had no desire to worry about household affairs, when she challenged me, the Irish in me arose, and the battle was on.

George had three other German servants and a colored chauffeur, and all except the chauffeur were hostile toward me. I wasn't free to change anything around in the house or do any ordering or plan any menus. When I suggested we have a few lighter dishes at dinner, Mrs. Shultz bristled. "This is a German house, and I will plan the meals," she said.

She kept insisting to George that I was just a girl who had been raised with a lot of money, and didn't know how to run a house or to handle servants. And George had been a bachelor for so long that he didn't realize that a wife wants to have charge of her own household. Pretty soon, though, he became aware that something was bothering me.

"What's wrong, honey?" he asked one night when I seemed especially unhappy. And then I cried and blurted out the whole story and said I couldn't exist another day with that mean old housekeeper.

"Now, honey, listen," George said. "I want you to go with me whenever I travel. And Mrs. Shultz is very capable and runs this house perfectly. If we get rid of her, I don't see how you will be able to go with me, because you'll have to stay and take care of the house."

When he put it that way, I saw I was defeated. So I dried my eyes and said I guessed I was just being silly—that I didn't really want Mrs. Shultz fired, and would try to get along with her.

In a much lesser degree, there was also a problem with George's large family. He had eight brothers and sisters and there was quite a close family feeling. A large family can always be a problem for a new bride. I think at first they were all a little afraid I was going to be too extravagant, but they soon found out I wasn't and that

30

I had money of my own. Often when I would buy something for myself—new gloves or shoes or the like—I would also buy presents for the sisters.

I knew that whether or not George's family would become a difficult problem was really up to me. They depended on George a great deal, so I tried never to lose sight of the fact that he had been their brother long before he was my husband.

I had family dinners for ten or twelve of George's relatives at least twice a week. And even though their interests weren't my interests, I tried to become familiar with things they talked about—children and cooking and putting up preserves. All the women in George's family were wonderful housekeepers and providers. But frankly, at that time, I didn't give a hoot about cooking or jam making. They all liked music, though, so we had that in common. And always after dinner I would play the piano and we would all sing. All in all, we got along pretty well.

I was never really accepted in Pittsburgh society. The girl George had jilted managed to spread the word that I was an intruder who had married George for his money and that I didn't deserve to be included. There is no way to combat such lies, and I didn't try.

I had had a taste of New York society through Aunt Florence, and it was sparkling compared to the Pittsburgh society of that day. In Pittsburgh everyone had known everyone else for years and all they talked about was their own doings and their friends. I'm happy to say that George considered such society a bore. About the only social leader I became well acquainted with was Mrs. William Thaw. George and I often went to her house or had her to dinner at our home or at the Duquesne Club.

George's life was wrapped up in his business. Every Sunday when we were in Pittsburgh I would go to the plant with him and we would walk all through the buildings. We could stand on a balcony and look down on the huge flaming furnaces. He tried bit by bit to teach me something about the business.

We hadn't been in Pittsburgh very long before George was called to Washington, and, of course, I went with him. With the United States' entry into World War I, George's plant had begun making huge naval gun barrels and other war machinery. He was frequently needed in Washington and was asked by President

31

Wilson to serve as a dollar-a-year consultant. We took a four-room suite at the Willard Hotel in Washington and kept it all during the war.

On this first trip to Washington, George was asked by Samuel Gompers, head of the American Federation of Labor, to serve on a labor-management committee that became known as the Gompers Committee. At first George was going to refuse, because of personal convictions against unions. He was very fair with his help, paid well, and gave bonuses, but he was dead set against unions and didn't feel labor should tell management what hours would be worked, and how much should be paid. Until George's decision to refuse the committee appointment, I had not expressed myself about my husband's affairs. But this was too much for me.

"George Mesta, you just forget some of your antiunion ideas and accept that appointment," I told him. "It's really an honor, and your country needs you. And besides, isn't it better to be on the committee and know what's going on than to be on the outside?" Surprisingly (to me at least), George admitted I was right and accepted the appointment.

I had been to Washington several times previously with Father, especially when Marguerite was at a finishing school in Forest Glen, Maryland. And because of Father, I had always been taken in tow and toured around by Oklahoma's Senator Thomas Gore. I was therefore not a complete stranger to the city and, as Mrs. George Mesta, I had my husband to lean upon, and he knew everybody worth knowing. I was suddenly somebody and was invited to many social functions.

One of the first people I met was Mrs. Thomas Marshall, the wife of the Vice-President. The Marshalls also lived at the Willard in a small suite placed at their disposal by the management. George and I got to know them quite well and we frequently had dinner together. Mr. Marshall was a tobacco-chewing Hoosier and had the homespun quality of the Oklahomans. He was short of stature, with gray hair and a huge mustache that drifted down over his lip. Mrs. Marshall always had a ready smile even though things were sometimes difficult for them. They had very little means and Mr. Marshall had to supplement the modest vice-presidential salary by giving lectures. George, a very conservative Republican, didn't agree with the President's policies, so at dinner we wives would always try to shift the conversation away from politics. But our dinners were never tense because the Vice-President was so friendly —I felt as if I had known him all my life.

I recall only one small crisis. The first time we four had dinner in our apartment, Mrs. Marshall looked around after dinner at all the expensive things we had, and commented, "It must be a wonderful, wonderful thing to have all the money you want and to be able to buy all these nice things."

I was proud of the way George handled this situation.

"Mrs. Marshall," he said, "it is far more wonderful to have the honored position your husband has than to have all the money in the world."

During our first stay in Washington, one of the Administration officials invited me and two other businessmen's wives to luncheon. The service was slow and both the other ladies had to leave before the dessert course to attend a meeting. I found myself alone with the official, who was quite a dashing figure about town. He gave me a searching look.

"I know your husband has meetings quite often at night," he said. "How about going dancing with me some time when George is busy?"

I realized I was in a very touchy situation because George was about to get a large contract through this man. When he saw me hesitate, he laid his cards on the table.

"Oh, come on. I'll fix it right if you do."

"Just what do you mean?" I asked guardedly.

"I'll fix it so your husband will get the contract," he said. "And I'll have you home before he gets back."

Then I lost my tact.

"Whether or not George gets the contract, I want to tell you something," I announced furiously. "I adore my husband and if I have to double-cross him in order for him to get a contract, then he just won't get it."

The man, obviously an old hand at such things, just smiled, and I got up and left.

That evening George greeted me with a puzzled look. "Have you been seeing Mr. ——?" he asked. I immediately told him about the conversation over lunch.

"Now I understand what he meant," George said. "Just an hour

33

ago he told me, 'I'm giving you this contract. And I want to tell you that you have one of the finest wives I have ever met.' "

When my sister came to visit us in Washington I tried to make a match for her with the best catch in town: Kenneth McKellar, the well known senator from Tennessee. He was a good deal older than Marguerite, but he was a very important man in the Senate and a bachelor. I invited him to dinner; he fell for Marguerite and immediately started paying court to her. At first Marguerite loved being seen with a senator and having lunch in the Senate dining room. After the first few days, however, the glamour wore off for her, and she went back to New York. For a while, Senator McKellar sent Marguerite roses. But my first attempt at matchmaking was a failure.

Washington offered so much fun and was so full of activity that I dreaded going back to Pittsburgh. But George had to return, and wherever George went, I went. One of my problems of those first married years was my own adjustment to being a wife. I had been accustomed to having my own way, being around a lot of people all the time, and going to a party almost every evening and sometimes dancing half the night. But once we got to Pittsburgh, George turned his full attention to his plant. I spent long days alone at home because I knew very few people in Pittsburgh except George's family. When George would come home, I would be rarin' to go, but after perhaps ten hours at the plant, George would be too tired to want to go out.

I was determined that I was going to find things to occupy my time instead of just wasting away with boredom and loneliness. I felt if I could just get out and go horseback riding once in a while, it would give me a sense of freedom. George, however, did not want me to ride for fear I would get hurt. He was so protective that he hardly would let me cross the street alone. I started going to a riding academy where I wasn't known. And when I learned about a beautiful chestnut thoroughbred that was for sale, I bought it with my own money—all this without telling George.

Once I decided to take a little revenge on my nemesis, the housekeeper. There were shelves and shelves of jams and preserves stored in the cellar—more than we could eat in a century, it seemed to me. One afternoon on Mrs. Shultz's day off I went down and loaded a big laundry basket with the stuff and had the chauffeur

34

drive me to a couple of orphanages where I distributed the jars, feeling like Lady Bountiful herself.

When Mrs. Shultz noticed the empty spaces among her precious preserves, she marched up the stairs and demanded: "Where are my jellies and jams?"

"Why, Mrs. Shultz," I said, "I think it's my business what I do with the preserves in my own basement. But since you ask, I took some of them and gave them to the needy. I think they will serve a better purpose there than simply decorating our cellar shelves."

She glared at me. "Mr. Mesta will hear about this," she said.

"I'm sure he will," I replied as she left the room. Sure enough, George had heard all about it by the time he came upstairs to change for dinner.

"Now what's all this nonsense about taking Mrs. Shultz's preserves?" he demanded.

"That's what I'd like to know," I answered tartly. Then I decided to kid him out of it. "Oh, honey, what difference does it make?" I said. "We can't eat all that stuff anyhow. And besides," I added, "I had a wonderful time visiting the orphanages." George mellowed at that, and the whole affair was soon forgotten.

The long days and weeks dragged by and I tried to amuse myself by practicing the piano and singing; I made efforts to write letters to Father and William and Marguerite. But none of this really did any good. Once in a while, when I would get really down in the dumps, I would put in a long-distance call to Helen McLean in Fort Smith, Arkansas. Helen had been a boarding-school chum of Marguerite's and has been our closest friend through the years. One day I impetuously invited Helen to Pittsburgh for a visit, and she said she would love to come. I kept putting off telling George that Helen was coming. I had not confided my loneliness to him because I didn't want to worry him, and I was afraid he would not understand. By the time Helen arrived, I had convinced myself that the best thing to do was keep her visit a secret. I hid her out at the Schenley Hotel.

Helen and I had such fun. I would sneak into town each day and Helen and I would go horseback riding, take in shows, or have luncheon and go shopping. I wasn't quite as smart as I thought I was, though. The fourth morning when Helen and I were in her room at the hotel cooking up our day's mischief, the phone

35

rang. Helen picked up the phone and it was George. He said we would be most happy if Miss McLean would come to our house for dinner, and wouldn't she plan to stay with us?"

I had no idea how he found out, and I was really shaking in my boots when I got home. Helen was shown to a guest room and I went to our suite to change. George came in, and I faced him ashamedly.

"Oh, George," I wailed. "How can I ever explain?"

Then he took me in his arms and said, "My little darling, why didn't you just tell me you were lonely? You have to understand that I'm too busy to think about these things. And I can't make you happy if you don't confide in me."

He was so dear and so kind about it that all I could do was cry on his shoulder.

Even after he was so sweet and understanding about Helen, I still didn't tell him about our horseback riding. One night at the dinner table, Helen started to report something that had happened on our afternoon's ride. I gave her a kick under the table, but she kept right on talking. Then I commenced to sing: "Tral-la-la-la-la!"

George and Helen both looked at me as if I were crazy. Helen finally got the idea and shut up. I don't think George figured it out even then. He probably thought Helen was talking about a "ride" in the car. But a short time later I took a bad fall and sprained my ankle. Then I had to tell him about my horse.

Poor George. I'm afraid I gave him a rough time that first year or so of our marriage. With my hot temper I would often get mad at him (although I never stayed mad very long). He loved my long hair—when I brushed it out it fell below my waist—and he begged me not to cut it. I cut it anyway. When I'd do things he told me not to do, he'd just laugh. And the more he'd laugh, the more I'd do—just crazy little things.

George knew I loved jewels, so he was always surprising me with gifts. My wedding present had been a diamond necklace, and the first Christmas he bought me a twenty-five-thousand-dollar strand of real pearls. He would give me a ring or bracelet or necklace at the least excuse: to celebrate Thanksgiving, Easter—even Columbus Day. He used to say, "I want you to be the best-dressed woman in America, with the most beautiful jewels." He loved to

36

show me off. I may have given him a rough time, but he loved it. I was high-spirited, forthright, and gay. If he had married somebody who was docile and who kowtowed to his every whim, he probably would have taken up with some other woman. But he was my George, and he didn't dare look at anyone else—any more than his "darling" could have looked twice at another man.

Toward the end of our first year of marriage, I began to channel my overflow of energy into more worth-while things. I became interested in the welfare of the workers at the plant. It first started when I asked if I could have a Christmas tree and party at our house for the children of all the foremen and subforemen. George told me to spend what I needed and to be sure to get enough presents for everyone. What fun I had preparing for a real party! I had a beautiful tree set up in the big music room and decorated it lavishly. The servants helped me put bowers of holly and spruce all over the room. I used lots of tinsel and many candles and when I had finished, the room looked like something out of fairyland. It was quite an innovation for the children and their mothers to come to the home of the owner of the plant. More than two hundred children came, and we had cookies, cakes, punch, and ice cream for all. Each child was given a toy and a bag of candy. Music was provided by our electric player piano, and the youngsters couldn't take their eyes off the keys as they magically played without hands.

Those children were so sweet and appreciative, and their mothers so warm and friendly, that I felt an increasing desire to be of help to them. A few months later, I prevailed upon George to start a cafeteria at the plant, and followed that up by pestering him to start a hospital—which he did.

When I found out that many of the fifteen- and sixteen-year-old apprentices at the plant had never had an opportunity to finish grade school, I suggested to George that they be given two hours a day schooling and be paid for the time. George resisted this at first, but later came around and even provided the classroom and teacher. Another project of mine was a nursery, which I organized so that some of the workers' children could have better care.

My ideas about unions and workers' rights always struck George as radical. He called me his "little liberal"—not always approvingly. One day early in the second year of our marriage, things came to a head. George discovered that I had been talking to some of the workers' wives about getting more benefits for their husbands.

"Honey," he said, "I don't mind it when you talk to me about your liberal ideas, but I can't have you spreading such ideas among my workers. It has got to stop!"

I could see he wasn't fooling. And it really didn't mean enough to me to make an issue out of it. However, I did see an opportunity to use this disagreement as a wedge.

"All right, George," I answered. "I'll make a bargain with you. I'll stop meddling in your plant if you will stop meddling in something which I feel is my domain. I want you to let me have full management of our house."

I think this caught him by surprise. But my bargaining was successful and we made a pact. I stayed out of plant affairs, and within a month we had a new housekeeper, cook, and maid—all hired by me.

Arranging things so that I was mistress of my household, yet could leave it and go on trips with George, was a major accomplishment. George and I both relaxed and began to take things easier. I think a lot of people were surprised to see how well our marriage was working, considering that I was a self-centered, party-going girl and George was a set-in-his-ways bachelor type, and both of us were opinionated and accustomed to having our own ways.

Not that we didn't continue to have arguments—we had some humdingers. All the dramatics were on my side in those spats. George never raised his voice: it was only by his tone and his look that I could tell how mad he was. I remember one time I picked up a basket of fruit and threatened to throw it at him. Oh, that man could make me so mad! He was so darned lordly and all-knowing. The trouble was, he was usually right—and the more I realized how right he was, the madder I would get. But we could never stay angry at each other, and once I cooled down, I was quick to admit I was wrong. I have never been too proud to apologize. And he continued to treat me like some precious ornament, worrying about me all the time, lavishing presents on me, and putting up with all the crazy things I did.

Even when I did certain things he had asked me not to, he wouldn't rebuke me. For a party I planned to give in the Willard ballroom in Washington, I wanted to have two orchestras and lots of flowers. George said he thought one orchestra was enough, and not too many flowers. He didn't mind the expense, but he thought what I was planning was too ostentatious, especially during wartime. But I went right ahead and ordered the two orchestras and even more flowers than I had planned. When George found out, he just laughed some more at his incorrigible bride.

Sometimes, on the cook's night off in Pittsburgh, I would go out to the kitchen and try to prepare supper. I couldn't any more fix food then than I could fly to the moon, and everything would go wrong. Ordinarily George was very finicky about his food, and more than once he would send back his order at a New York restaurant because the vegetables weren't seasoned quite right or the steak was a mite too rare. But he would eat my leathery eggs with gusto. No doubt about it, George loved me.

George got along fine with my family. When my brother was going to Cornell, he would visit us occasionally, and after he transferred to the University of Pittsburgh to study petroleum geology he was at the house often. Once in a while, Father would come up to Pittsburgh and spend a few days with us. He and George grew to enjoy each other very much. Father was always interested in what George was doing at his plant, and loved to spend all day poking around there. At dinner they would discuss national events and politics. They usually were in agreement politically, although George was much more conservative than Father—I would say George was really a reactionary Republican. They both liked to take rides in our Packard limousine, and the three of us and the chauffeur would drive all over western Pennsylvania. On those rides neither George nor Father would talk much, but just sit back and notice everything that was going on.

We didn't see much of Marguerite, who spent a great deal of her time in New York. In 1919 she surprised us by marrying a very handsome Army officer, Robert Adams, and settling down in Connecticut to raise a family.

Whenever things weren't too busy around the plant, I would persuade George to go to Washington. I spent quite a bit of time there in children's welfare work, having become interested in it through the wife of the Vice-President. I frequently went with Mrs. Marshall into slum areas, seeking to help children who were getting improper care. Once, I remember, we were horrified to find a child of three tied to a bed, where his parents had left him while they went off to work.

After the Marshalls adopted a child, George and I talked about adopting a baby. We both wanted children and had always hoped for one of our own. But whenever I brought up the matter of adoption, George would say, "Let's wait and hope a little while longer, because when you adopt a child you almost certainly have one of your own soon afterwards."

When Harding became President in 1921, Vice-President and Mrs. Calvin Coolidge kept an apartment on the fifth floor of the Willard, just above our suite, and we became quite friendly with them. Shortly after the inauguration, I gave a big luncheon at the Willard for Mrs. Coolidge. Grace Coolidge was warm and gracious and I liked her very much.

Calvin Coolidge and George Mesta were such look-alikes that sometimes people mistook George for the Vice-President. They were about the same build and had somewhat similar facial characteristics. Also, they were both quiet and conservative. For years, I have been hearing people say that Calvin Coolidge was humorless and silent. Those people just didn't know him. It's true that in a big group he would clam up, but with those he knew he would talk freely, once he got started. And he had quite a dry wit. Sometimes George would say to me before a dinner to which the Coolidges were invited: "Now, darling, use your charm on him." And I knew what he meant, for I had found out how to make Mr. Coolidge talk. I would say something like, "Goodness, I'm so sorry I haven't got any boys. If I just had a son . . . Now, tell about your Calvin and John." And that would get him started. I would soon change the subject and by that time he was in the mood and would go ahead and talk about other things.

George later backed Coolidge in the 1924 election and contributed a hundred thousand dollars to the campaign. I don't suppose George's big donation was entirely a matter of brotherly love. George didn't confide in me about such things as political contributions, but we women aren't quite as naïve as some men think we are. I knew it was to George's advantage for the Republicans to stay in power. After all, he got millions of dollars worth of government contracts each year.

George and I dined several times at the White House after Mr.

Coolidge became President. The Coolidges didn't keep up the country-club atmosphere that had been evident at the White House during the Harding administration. Instead, they had small, intimate gatherings. Grace Coolidge was a lovely hostess and very good at keeping the conversation sprightly. The food was simple, but well prepared, and the story went around that the ever-frugal President kept close tabs on the kitchen budget.

I gave few parties in those days, although I went to many. One of the most important rituals of the social system of that era was the formal calling procedure. Whether you were a government official or not, you went around at the beginning of each season and left your card and your husband's card at the White House, the homes of the Cabinet members, the Supreme Court justices, and at the embassies.

There was a special day of the week for calling at the homes of various officials. The wife of the Chief Justice and the wives of the other justices would have tea and open house on Monday; the wives of representatives on Tuesday; Cabinet wives on Wednesday; Senate wives on Thursday; and wives of the diplomatic corps on Friday. They really had teas in those days—not the lavishly laid out and crowded cocktail parties they have nowadays. We would go at five o'clock and have tea or coffee, little finger sandwiches, cakes and cookies, and then visit, and sometimes the Cabinet member or justice or senator would come home early to say hello before we left.

An institution of those days was the late afternoon dancing at the huge, ornate home of Mrs. Thomas Walsh. The mother of famed hostess Evalyn Walsh McLean had her big house at 2020 Massachusetts Avenue (it is now the Indonesian Embassy), and she loved to dance. George and I had a standing invitation to attend any time we could, and we frequently did so.

At first I was very much in awe of Mrs. Walsh because she was a rather imposing figure and seemed quite cool and distant. Gradually, though, as I got to know her, I found that her coolness was only a reserve and that she was actually warm and friendly.

I'll never forget the day we were dancing at her house and my pearl necklace broke. Everybody (except Mrs. Walsh, of course, who was much too proper) got down on the floor to help me find the scattered pearls. George thought I was worried because I didn't

41

want to lose a single pearl. But the real reason I was so concerned was that I didn't want him to find out they weren't real. I did have my single strand of real pearls, but the dress I was wearing that day needed a triple strand, so I had worn some Técla simulated pearls. George wouldn't stand for my wearing any imitations, and I was in a panic lest he would discover my deception.

Another popular place for dancing was the home of Mrs. John Henderson, the widow of a famous Missouri senator. She had been one of the *grandes dames* of Washington society for thirty years or more before George and I came to Washington, and she was still going strong in the early twenties. She lived in an immense stone house, known as the Henderson Castle, on Sixteenth Street, and she gave frequent parties as well as regular Monday afternoon dances. Impressively wealthy, Mrs. Henderson built many residences in Washington and sold several to foreign countries for use as embassies. She built one large white building on Fifteenth Street that cost half a million dollars, and then tried to get the Government to buy it as a home for our Vice-Presidents. There was even talk that she offered to give it to the nation free. Nothing came of her proposition (or offer), and she finally sold the building to Spain for use as an embassy.

Both a vegetarian and teetotaler, Mrs. Henderson was a follower of Dr. Kellogg, the health fadist, and of course no liquor or meat was served at her parties. Instead, her exquisite crystal wine glasses brimmed with special fruit drinks, in various colors, and guests were offered concoctions of Protose or Nutaline that somehow never quite looked convincingly like meat loaf. Her "caramel coffee" was brewed from wholesome grain. In spite of all this, an invitation to her home was considered a signal honor.

By the time I knew her, Mrs. Henderson was in her eighties. She still liked to dance but most of all she liked to sit like a queen in a big throne-like chair with her feet (usually clad in bedroom slippers adorned with large pompons) on a little stool. I never failed to see senators, Cabinet officials, and ambassadors gathering around her as she held court.

It was at these parties that I began to understand how a Washington hostess could be a factor in politics by having the right people present at the right time. Mrs. Henderson's affairs were dull to many people because of the specialized provisions and refreshments she set forth, but nevertheless the important people were always there. George told me that Mrs. Henderson had a great deal of political influence. To the eye she was just a dainty, blue-eyed, white-haired, completely feminine-looking person, but back of all this gracious appearance was a dominating, powerful woman.

Though I loved being in Washington more and more, we never could stay there as much as I wanted. Periodically, George had to return to his plant. He knew how uncomfortable I had felt in his house in Pittsburgh and he wanted to build a new home for me. I would much rather have built in Washington, but George felt he owed it to Pittsburgh to build there. We went over every foot of every piece of available ground in the Pittsburgh area before we finally found the property we felt was just right. It covered almost half an entire city block. When the building plans were complete, George had a scale model made of the house. We spent many delightful hours dreaming over the model, deciding how we would furnish it and how we would landscape the grounds. We started building late in 1923. Since much of the material was to be imported from Europe, we did not expect to be living in the completed house until 1925.

Meantime, George's business took us often to Europe. After the war, just about every country wanted the steel rolling mills and other heavy machinery produced by Mesta Machine Company. On our trips I saw much of Western Europe. We were never any one place for very long, and our trips were primarily business with a little pleasure thrown in. In the summer of 1924, we spent three weeks at the famous spa at Bad Nauheim, Germany. George's doctor had told him he had a touch of heart trouble—an extra beat or something—nothing serious, really. It was his suggestion that George might enjoy taking "the cure" at Bad Nauheim. It was a funny old place, but the scenery was gorgeous. And George took a real rest.

When we returned to Pittsburgh that fall, our house was nearing completion. The builder thought we could plan to be in early in the spring. We began choosing lovely antiques to furnish it. George was continually busy at the plant, working day and night, so I did most of the furniture planning. But George himself ordered approximately forty thousand dollars' worth of full-grown trees and shrubs and took the time to see that they were placed in just the

43

right spots. The trees were brought in on big trucks and it took several men more than two days to plant each tree. The lot was bare when the house was built on it, but when the house was finished, and the trees were in place, they looked as if they had always been there.

In spite of our preoccupation with the house, we made several trips to New York. One evening in April, 1925, George's business dinner in New York was called off at the last minute and we took the opportunity to have a gala evening for ourselves. We had dinner at the Ritz and went to the theater. To both of us it was a very special occasion: we had thought we were going to have to spend a dull evening with business contacts, and suddenly we were free. George bought me flowers and sneaked a kiss now and then and we acted like a couple of honeymooners instead of people who had been married nearly a decade.

We got back to our hotel shortly after midnight. About 3:00 A.M., something wakened me. George had turned on the light and was sitting up in bed. He said he didn't feel well and he got up and went into the bathroom to get some soda. Then I heard a thud. By the time I reached him he was unconscious on the floor. And by the time the doctor arrived, George was dead. It had been a heart attack, the doctor said.

What happened in the following days is just a sort of a fog to me today. Even when it was happening, I was hardly aware of what was going on. Marguerite and William and Father came to me immediately and got me through those terrible days and weeks that ensued.

I had lived and breathed for George. I had made his interests my interests, his well-being my well-being. He had spoiled and pampered me like a child and I was utterly dependent upon him in every way. And now in the space of a heartbeat, I was alone.

It seems as though a woman ought to have a little time to nurse such a terrible wound. But that is not the way it was for me. There were so many practical things to be taken care of right away. But maybe that was just as well. It gave me less time to think.

I was left most of the stock in George's company and all his personal properties. The most awesome responsibility staring me in the face was management of the Mesta Machine Company. I soon discovered that the company executives expected me to sit on the sidelines and let them run things. But Father said, "George left it to you—not to them—and it is up to you to see that the company is carried on as George would have wanted it."

At first I was afraid I was going to make a fool of myself and say things that George wouldn't have wanted me to say. Father said that I should insist upon being named to the board of directors —that was the only way I could really know what was going on.

"But I'd be the only woman against all those eight men," I argued.

"Now you just stand right up to them," Father urged me. "Your stock can outvote them all."

I must have been a pretty pathetic-looking creature in my widow's veil as I took my place in George's big chair at one end of the long directors' table. I was awfully glad to sit down because my knees felt wobbly. The company executives were very solicitous as they explained that my husband's death had left a vacancy on the board and that the first order of business would be to elect a stockholder to the position. Did I wish to make any suggestion?

I took a deep breath and piped in a tiny voice: "I will take the position myself."

There was stunned silence. Then they began to argue tactfully that I would find it very taxing work. I remembered what Father had said. I remembered my majority ownership of the stock, and I remained firm. And I began to realize that these eight board members were, after all, only men.

The next order of business was the election of a new president. By this time I was gaining a little confidence. I suggested George's brother, Fred Mesta, who was then first vice-president. Fred was not considered a very good businessman, however, and most of the directors did not feel he should be made president. But George had thought enough of him to make him first vice-president and he had the Mesta name. So despite their arguments, I put my vote on Fred.

When the meeting was adjourned, I asked the men to leave me alone for a few minutes. It had been all I could do to hold back my tears. After the room was empty I sat in George's chair and looked out the window at the empire that George had worked so hard to build. I thought over the events of the past hour. I had showed the men who was boss, but was I really capable of carrying

45

on and making the important decisions that would be necessary to keep George's business empire from crumbling? I recognized that the capabilities I had were no substitute for the technical engineering knowledge needed to run the Mesta Machine Company. So I made my decision then and there not to try to run the plant. I continued to serve on the board of directors and used my voting power to the best of my ability, but I left the actual management of the company to the men who knew the steel business and had worked so long with George.

I never did furnish the new house. I couldn't even bear to go and look at it after George died. Instead, I put it on the market and it was purchased by a Pittsburgh family. As soon as I could get the rest of my affairs settled, I left Pittsburgh and went to Washington.

FIVE : *Wanderings of a Widow*

FOR A GOOD MANY YEARS after George Mesta's death I was like a ship without a rudder. I made several trips to Europe, and at various times had residences in Boston, New York, Washington, and Newport, and I frequently went home to Oklahoma City. Out of respect to George's family, who still observed a number of Old World customs, I wore black for six months, then went six months more in white mourning (white chiffon veil with white crepe around it). My long widow's veil of black chiffon—it came almost to my knees—and the black hat with a little white edging were very becoming to me, and I'm sure I was accused of wearing them just for that reason. But I truly didn't, because being dressed like that was terribly inhibiting.

I was still quite young, and having more money than I knew what to do with, I did some crazy things in those first few years. I would squander ten thousand dollars in a single season on clothes. I bought lavishly at Hattie Carnegie's in New York and Madame Chanel's in Paris. I paid twenty thousand dollars for a full-length chinchilla cape that was said to be only the second such piece in all the United States. I had kept our Packard limousine and had no need for another car, but one day I took a fancy to an expensive Auburn roadster and bought it. There I was, not even knowing how to drive, with a high-powered sports car and no one to go riding with.

But none of my extravagances filled the void in my life. I think as much as anything I missed having someone to spar with. George had spoiled me so. In the past, if I threw a fit, I could get anything in the world I wanted. I had done it with Father and my family and then I got away with it with George. But now I was all alone.

47

There was no one around to sympathize if I cried—no one to feel sorry if I threw a tantrum.

I went through a period of heavy (at least for me) gambling. I spent one summer at Saratoga and lost seventeen thousand dollars during the racing season. I didn't know a thing about race horses except that I liked them. I sometimes made a bet because of the name or the markings of the horse, or sometimes because I knew the owner. And in a few weeks at Monte Carlo during one of my European trips, I tossed away another sizable amount.

For the first few years after leaving Pittsburgh, I made Washington my base. At first, I kept our apartment at the Willard, even though I was surrounded by heartbreaking memories of George. When the Mayflower Hotel opened in 1926, I took a suite there.

The friends George and I had made in Washington were wonderful to me when I returned as a widow. My closest friend was Mrs. Lawrence Townsend, whom I called "Aunt Natalie." The widow of a former Minister to Belgium, Aunt Natalie was deeply interested in music and had started a series of Monday morning musicales in Washington, patterned after those held in New York at the old Waldorf by Morris Bagby.

Aunt Natalie took me under her wing and I was like a daughter to her. On one of my first trips back to Pittsburgh for a board meeting at the plant, she went with me because I hated to travel alone. After the meeting, I took Aunt Natalie on a tour through the plant. As we walked along we heard a glorious baritone voice soaring above the sounds of the machinery. There, operating a rolling mill, was a tall, powerful young man singing an Italian love song. In the offices we found out who the young man was and where he lived, and that night Aunt Natalie and I called on him at his rooming house. When we left Pittsburgh the next morning, the young man was with us. We went directly to New York and found him a place to live and arranged for lessons and coaching with the best voice teacher in New York. Periodically for the next year, Aunt Natalie and I made trips to New York, checking on his progress and seeing to his social training. He was a fine-looking young fellow of about thirty, but his entire life had been spent in the rugged mill district of Pittsburgh and there were a lot of rough edges to be polished off. We outfitted him in correct clothes, made him read a book on deportment, and sent him to a dancing class.

The next year we felt he was ready. I rented Town Hall and filled it with my friends for his first concert. He had a nice voice and really did quite well, but he got only lukewarm reviews. After that he got a few jobs in choruses on Broadway, but never really went further. We suggested he return to Pittsburgh and offered to help him financially until he could readjust his affairs. Thanking us for all we had done, he said he preferred to stay in New York. Having had a taste of the outside world, he didn't want to go back to rolling steel, and I can't say I blamed him. I guess Aunt Natalie and I should have minded our own business and not tried to play Pygmalion, but we did the best we could for a real talent.

I became one of the patrons for the Townsend Monday morning musicales at the Mayflower in Washington. They were quite important social events, and were often attended by Mrs. Calvin Coolidge and later by Mrs. Herbert Hoover and Mrs. Franklin D. Roosevelt when they were First Ladies. Wives of Cabinet members and senators and prominent officials were always there, as well as the leading Cave Dwellers (the term Washingtonians apply to the socialites whose families have been in the town for several generations). After the musicales, Mrs. Townsend would have a small luncheon for the performing artist, and she always included me. It was through these luncheons that I first met Rosa Ponselle, Lawrence Tibbett, Ezio Pinza, Beniamino Gigli, and many other opera stars.

Rosa Ponselle became one of my dearest friends. She had a phenomenal natural voice and had been discovered by Enrico Caruso when she was singing in a sister act in vaudeville. Within a year she was singing with the Metropolitan Opera Company.

It was always fun to go to her apartment and have some of the delicious Italian food she cooked so well. Rosa led a Bohemian life and always had an interesting assortment of characters around her. And I gained a vicarious satisfaction for the career I never had by sitting in on Metropolitan Opera rehearsals and sometimes watching from the wings. I frequently went to Rosa's dressing room after a performance, knowing she liked to have someone around to listen while she let off steam about what was wrong with the performance.

During this period, I had a large apartment at the Barclay Hotel in New York, and my Metropolitan friends came and kept bringing more and more of their friends. My apartment soon became a

49

well-known hangout for the Metropolitan Opera crowd. I guess you could call that my operatic period. I had Box No. 5 for every Monday night during the Metropolitan season for fifteen years.

In 1927, I helped Rosa Ponselle celebrate the greatest moment of her career by giving a party after her first performance in *Norma*. The Metropolitan had been waiting for years for a soprano who could handle the leading role. The opera had last been staged in the eighteen-nineties, when the famous Lilli Lehmann had sung it. Rosa, who had spent the entire ten years of her operatic career preparing herself for the role, was superb. The audience stood and cheered and some of us wept. The ovation went on for thirty minutes after the final curtain. Then I hurried to the Park Lane Hotel, where I had invited a hundred guests, including Lucrezia Bori, Lily Pons, Antonio Scotti, Beniamino Gigli, Ezio Pinza (who sang the role of Norma's father that night), and Edward Johnson, the manager of the Metropolitan.

The room was decorated entirely with orchids. I had sprays along the stairs, on the walls, and on the tables; there was an orchid corsage for each lady and when Rosa made her entrance in a beautiful white chiffon gown, I draped a lei of white orchids around her neck. Rosa turned out to be very funny that night. She had been on a strict diet for months. She really let loose and stuffed herself with caviar, salmon, and a lot of salty things. Then she got thirsty and started drinking champagne as though it were water. She seldom drank, so the champagne started her on a laughing jag. She wasn't really intoxicated and her mind was clear as crystal—she just couldn't stop laughing.

I had chosen entertainment that was a decided contrast from grand opera. Meyer Davis and his society orchestra played for our dancing and three Broadway musical comedy stars performed. Then, for a climax, I brought on Eddie Cantor. The party—which went on until 6:00 A.M.—was the biggest and most expensive I had ever given.

When Rosa appeared in *Norma* in Washington the next season while the Metropolitan was on tour, I gave another party for her at the Mayflower. I invited the entire cast and had several senators and government officials. For entertainment that night I had hired a gypsy fortuneteller who wore a wonderful costume. Fortunetellers were quite the rage at the time.

50

Rosa, who always made a dramatic entrance, paused at the doorway to the ballroom and looked all around the room, smiling and waving to her friends. Suddenly she gasped, took a step backward, and started down the hall.

"Rosa!" I cried, hurrying after her. "What on earth's the matter?"

"That woman!" she shrieked. "Get that fortuneteller out of there or I won't set a foot in that ballroom!"

I've never known anybody more superstitious than Rosa, who's a regular gypsy herself. Not until I had dismissed the fortuneteller and seen her depart would Rosa join the party. Despite her taxing operatic performance that evening, Rosa was still in a singing mood. We ended up with her getting others from the cast to join her in the sextet from *Lucia,* with Rosa taking the coloratura part.

During the twenties and thirties I gave lots of parties in Washington, but I wasn't one of the city's major party givers. Goodness, I wasn't even in the same class with Evalyn Walsh McLean and Eleanor "Cissy" Patterson, the outstanding hostesses of that era. I had quite a few good friends in the government, but mostly I went with the musical crowd. I was then interested more in fun than in politics.

Some of my parties would go on all night. Once when the Metropolitan Opera Company was in Washington for a one-night stand, I gave an after-performance supper party. I had a buffet table laden with roast beef and ham and turkey and caviar and other kinds of good food and wines. Singers all just love to eat, you know, and they are usually ravenous after a performance. At about 2:00 A.M. my guests had to leave for their train back to New York. The rest of the crowd and I went down to the station to see them off. Ezio Pinza was in fine fettle that night (it was morning by then), and as we started up the long platform toward their special railroad car, he started to sing, vying with the hissing engines. Then the other singers got started, and the few sleepy people who had reason to be at Union Station at that hour had a real treat. The greatest operatic voices in the world blended in glorious music all the way down the platform, then at the entrance to their car, and then on inside. I suppose their impromptu concert may have lasted halfway to New York.

For a time during 1929 and 1930, I had a large apartment on

51

Massachusetts Avenue across the street from the Wadsworth Mansion (now the Sulgrave Club). I gave an engagement party there for Helen Eakin, whose father was a great friend of my uncle, Orrin Shepherd. Helen's fiancé was a young man named Milton Eisenhower. Helen and Milton became my close friends, and a few years after getting to know them, I also became friendly with Milton's brother, Major Dwight David Eisenhower, and his vivacious wife, Mamie, when the young major came to Washington for a tour of duty in the War Department.

In telling about my adjustment to life without George Mesta, I have neglected one topic that occupied quite a bit of my time—men! I am often asked "Why didn't you marry again?" Although it may seem like a rather vain remark, I must admit it wasn't because I was never asked.

I had my first offer of marriage less than a year after I had left Pittsburgh, and from a man I liked very much, Stephen Porter. Steve was a congressman from Pennsylvania and he had been a close friend of my husband. When I went to Washington in 1925, after George's death, Steve was of great help to me. A widower with a lovely daughter, he was quite distinguished-looking and was an important man in Washington, being Chairman of the House Foreign Affairs Committee. Steve knew that six o'clock was a particularly difficult time for me—that was the hour when George had always come home and shared his day's experiences with me. Steve made it a practice to drop in to see me about that time every day and cheer me up. Toward the end of that year he asked me to marry him. But marriage was then the farthest thing from my thought. Steve was a dear and good friend, but I wasn't in love with him. I wasn't ready to be in love again, I guess.

A very suave military attaché at the Italian Embassy, General Augusto Villa, was much in evidence toward the end of my first year of widowhood and Aunt Natalie Townsend thought I should marry him. He was handsome and dashing and loved opera as I did. But he was never more to me than a good companion for an evening.

The first man in whom I became seriously interested was one of the White House military aides during the Hoover administration, and we went together, on and off, for several years. As he is now

52

happily married, I would rather not name him. Jack (as we will call him) was a wonderful dancer and a gay companion. We went horseback riding together almost every day when I was in Washington. Jack came to New York several times to visit me. I was in love with him, but I don't think he was ever serious about me. And when he was transferred overseas, that was the end of our romance.

Another romantic interest of mine in those days was the Metropolitan baritone, Antonio Scotti. Rosa Ponselle introduced me to Scotti and we had a rather tempestuous romance. Tony was tall, dark, and very temperamental. We used to fight like cats and dogs over every little thing. Sometimes, at the climax of an argument, he would stomp out of the apartment, slamming the door. After a minute I would open the door and peek out, and there he would be, waiting in the hall. There were other sides to him, of course. I remember that he almost never failed to bring me a little bunch of violets.

Tony dressed very flashily and drove a big yellow Isotta Fraschini. One day in New York we were strolling along, window shopping. We stopped in front of the Rolls Royce agency. Inside, I saw a beautiful beige custom-made town car. I was crazy about beige, and I said to Tony, "Oh, that car was just made for me!" When we walked into the showroom, I just couldn't resist it. The interior was all done in tones of tan and beige with lots of hand-carved wood trimming. Within an hour I had given the salesman my check for $19,500. I had a tan and beige uniform tailored for my chauffeur and I bought coats and hats and furs to match the car. Tony and I would fight over whose car we would use, and I usually won.

We often went to the Aquarium, down at the Battery, and loved to dine at little out-of-the-way Italian restaurants where Tony would sometimes sing after dinner. Every place we went, people recognized him. Tony was great fun to be with, but I knew that marriage with him would never work out. Too much temperament —on both sides.

By this time, I was spending my summers in Newport, Rhode Island. I had first gone there in 1928 at the invitation of Mr. and Mrs. Arthur Curtis James (of Anaconda Copper wealth), who were long-established Newport socialites. Mr. James had been a personal friend of my husband. My sister had three small children,

53

and our first summer in Newport I talked her into renting a house with me. Newport was reasonably near Marguerite's home in Greenwich, Connecticut, and her husband, Bob Adams, who had a cotton mill nearby, came up on weekends.

Marguerite and I knew that Newport society did not readily accept newcomers, especially those not listed among the Four Hundred. So we just went our way and enjoyed the summer weather and the beach. I particularly loved being around Marguerite's three youngsters, Bob, Betty, and Billy. We didn't give any parties that first year. But through Harriet and Arthur James, we gradually met most of the Newport people and began to receive invitations. Mrs. Cornelius Vanderbilt seemed to like me right from the start, and being accepted by the acknowledged leader of Newport society did a lot to help us get established there.

Newport in its heyday had been the most lavish social center in the country, but I started going there toward the end of that era. The most fabulous party I ever went to was given in 1928 by the Stewart Duncans (of Lea & Perrin's Sauce fame). They had one of the largest homes on Narragansett Bay and their guests' yachts were moored in front of the house. On one of the yachts were several opera stars from the Metropolitan who sang for us as we sat on the lawn overlooking the water. In the house there was dancing, with several famous orchestras playing in different rooms, while outside on the lawn there were at least two more dance floors, each with an orchestra. I think the party, which went on all night, cost something like a hundred thousand dollars. The guests, nearly a thousand, came to Newport from all over the world.

Not all the parties were this lavish, of course. Mrs. Arthur Curtis James's parties were on the conservative side—we once had to listen all evening to Mr. James play Bach on his pipe organ. Mrs. James was adorable but, in a word, her parties were stuffy. They had a large home and connected with it they had a complete Swiss village with cows and goats and ducks and chickens. The people who took care of it wore Swiss costumes. She also had famous gardens, one that had nothing but blue flowers, another with only red flowers, another with yellow. A hundred men worked in the gardens and the Jameses kept forty more employed on their yacht, the *Aloha.*

54

Mrs. Cornelius Vanderbilt was the *grande dame* of Newport. When invited to her home, Beaulieu, the guests would always arrive right on time, but she, the hostess, would be nowhere in sight. Half an hour after all the guests had arrived, she would make a dramatic entrance. She always wore a jeweled headband to match her gown. She had hundreds of headbands and they were her mark of distinction. She was one of the great hostesses of the world, so she could do as she pleased, and everyone accepted it. One time she brought a whole New York stage company to her home to present their hit play for her guests—for just one performance.

During one of my first summers at Newport I met a man whom I shall just call Mr. X. I didn't know much about him other than that he was a bachelor from New York. We dated casually a couple of times and he was good company. All of a sudden one day a lawyer in New York called me saying he had a letter from a woman claiming that I had had a rendezvous with her husband in St. Louis on a certain date. Unless I gave her seventy-five thousand dollars she was going to sue him for divorce, naming me, and then sue me for alienation of her husband's affections. Her husband turned out to be this Mr. X, who had told me he was not married.

I immediately went to New York and stormed into the lawyer's office. He showed me the letter. I glanced at it, then threw it down on his desk.

"That's the biggest lie that was ever told on me," I fumed. "You just determine where I was that night and then tell that woman to tend to her own darn business."

Fortunately, I could prove I was in New York on the date mentioned, and nothing more was heard from the lawyer. Mr. X and his wife were nothing but blackmailers who figured they could collect a good sum from me or perhaps from my father just to keep my name out of the papers.

Like all unattached women with money, I've had my experiences with the professional fortune hunters. They frequented places like Monte Carlo and Newport, and they were gay and debonair and often titled. I got so I could spot one of them a mile off. They would manage an introduction and commence to wine and dine you and send flowers. Then they would stare rapturously at your diamonds and tell you you were the most beautiful creature in the world. Why, those playboys would even look up a woman's financial status before preparing their traps. But thank goodness I've always been wise to them and never have become involved.

During the presidential campaign of 1928, I had my first taste of practical politicking. I went with Father to the Republican convention in Kansas City and saw Herbert Hoover and Senator Charles Curtis nominated. I had known Charley Curtis for many years, and he now asked me to work for him in Oklahoma. I was appointed State Chairman of the Hoover-Curtis Junior League and had charge of a staff of organizers who went out to colleges and towns throughout the state, enlisting voters in our cause. Just before the election I arranged a big Republican rally at the Skirvin Hotel, with Curtis' sister, Dolly Gann, as the principal speaker. Hoover and Curtis carried predominantly Democratic Oklahoma by almost two to one, and I have always liked to think that our Hoover-Curtis Junior League campaign had something to do with the victory.

During the next couple of years, the Vice-President was my escort occasionally at social events. Charley Curtis was warm and outgoing. He was part Kaw Indian and had dark skin and fascinating brown eyes. He never forgot a name or an incident, and on our drives out to the country, he would tell me, in his cornfield voice, about the Indians in Kansas and Oklahoma and about his early career as a race-horse jockey.

Our names were sometimes linked romantically, but Charley and I were really just good friends. In the spring of 1930, I gave a party for him at the Mayflower Hotel. During the evening, Congressman Hamilton Fish, noticing that the Vice-President and I had been together most of the evening, started kidding me.

"Why don't you invite Charley up to your place at Newport?" the New York Republican Congressman asked me.

"Well, I've been thinking about that, and I just might do it," I replied.

"I'll bet you can't get him up there for a weekend without Dolly," challenged Ham Fish, with a twinkle in his eye. Everyone in Washington knew how closely Dolly Gann kept watch over her brother, who was a widower.

"I'll bet you a dinner I can," I answered.

On the morning of July 24, I got a phone call from Ham Fish.

56

All he said was, "Okay, you win." He had just seen this story in the New York *Times:*

CURTIS TO BE GUEST
AT NEWPORT HOME

NEWPORT, R. I., July 23—Vice President Curtis will visit Newport next month. He will arrive on Aug. 15 for a stay of two or three days as the guest of Mrs. George Mesta at the Rocks.

Mrs. Mesta gave a dinner in honor of the Vice President in Washington last Spring, and the invitation was extended at that time.

On the evening of his arrival Mrs. Mesta will give a large dinner with thirty-five or forty guests in honor of the Vice President. This will be Mr. Curtis's first visit to Newport.

And nowhere in the story was there a mention that the Vice-President would be accompanied by his sister. I had not invited her.

Actually, I think Dolly was pleased that her brother came alone, for I heard later from a mutual friend that she had once said of me, "Now there's the woman I'd like Charles to marry—if she'd have him."

The announcement in the *Times* caused no little stir in Newport. Newport was pretty snobbish in those days, and in addition to the fact that Curtis had no social standing, a few of the hostesses pointed out that he was part Indian. Yet he *was* the Vice-President of the United States, and no Vice-President had ever before visited Newport while in office. The town announced a big celebration for him, and I soon had more requests for his presence at parties than could possibly be filled during his stay. Of course, as soon as Charley arrived, he completely won over even the most snobbish of the Newporters, because he was so natural and had such charm.

Before the Vice-President came, I rehearsed my sister's three children on how to bow and curtsy, because I wanted to show them off to our honored guest. Just before dinner on the first day of Mr. Curtis' visit, Marguerite and I took him upstairs to see Bob, Betty, and Billy. When we entered the nursery, there were the youngsters all dressed up in their best clothes—but tied onto their chairs with large linen napkins! They had been so naughty that their French governess, Mamzelle, a tartar for discipline, had tied them up for a few minutes to keep them still. All the children could do was giggle and nod. The Vice-President considered it a great joke.

I think Charley Curtis enjoyed himself that weekend. He romped with the children, walked on the beach, and we had poker games late at night—in those days I was a pretty good poker player. Charley was full of life and had a wonderful sense of humor. And I learned a lot about the workings of government from being with him.

It was through the good offices of the Vice-President that I was honored in the summer of 1931 by being presented at the Court of St. James. Charles Dawes was then Ambassador to England, and Mrs. Dawes gave me a lesson beforehand on how to make a royal curtsy: head down, stoop just as low as you can, but don't lose your balance. Marguerite had come with me to England and brought the children. I was so nervous about my presentation that Marguerite went along in the carriage as far as the palace gate, then got out and took a taxi back to the hotel. But I made my curtsy without disgracing myself. Then I had the special honor of having supper with Queen Mary and King George at a small reception after the presentation.

When Marguerite was divorced in 1931, she and her three children came to live with me in New York. For the next six years we made our home together and those three children became as dear to me as any child of my own could have been. Their governess, Lina Le Favre, whom we invariably called Mamzelle, was very small, about five feet one, had fiery red hair, and was so dominant that at times she seemed six feet tall. She was convinced that she was the only one of us three who knew anything about bringing up children. I remember one night I went in to kiss little Betty good night and the room seemed terribly stuffy. I knew Mamzelle allowed the window in the children's rooms to be opened only a crack, the way they do in France. Of course, Mamzelle caught me in the act of raising the window. She shrieked, threw up her arms, and went to Marguerite.

"Zat Madame Mesta, she has no children! She does not know a ting about children!" she shrilled. And Betty slept with the window open a fraction of an inch.

Billy was as lovable as they come, but was a rascal! We never knew what he'd be up to next. When he was seven years old, he pulled an awful trick on Mamzelle. She always went in a taxi to pick up Betty and Billy at their schools. This particular afternoon, Betty was not along. As Billy climbed into the taxi, he shouted: "Help! I'm being kidnaped!" He kept this up all the way back home, shouting and carrying on until the taxi driver began to think that maybe Mamzelle *was* kidnaping him—the Lindbergh case was fresh in people's minds at the time. When they drove up in front of the hotel, the taxi driver got out and asked the doorman to identify Mamzelle.

Bob, four years older than Billy and three years older than Betty, was a serious-minded boy who liked to think of himself as the man of the family. I will always remember the day he left for summer camp the first time. Marguerite felt that Bob needed to get away from the predominantly feminine atmosphere of our household. I knew it was just breaking Marguerite's heart to think of sending Bob off for six weeks, so I insisted on going to Grand Central Station to see him off and then cheer her up on the way home. Marguerite seemed to be controlling herself beautifully as she gave Bob last-minute instructions at the station. A few moments later when I watched our little Bob mingling with all those other boys and realized he would be on his own for six long weeks, I burst into tears. Marguerite had to comfort Auntie Perle all the way home.

When Marguerite and the children first came to live with me, I had an apartment at the Pierre. Bringing up three children in a New York hotel had its drawbacks, and I am sure the management of the Pierre was as pleased as I was when I bought a house at 44 East Seventy-fourth Street. The kitchen and dining room were on the first floor and there were two lovely drawing rooms on the second. The bedrooms were on the third and fourth floors and the servants' quarters were on the fifth.

Marguerite, of course, immediately launched into a complete remodeling and redecoration program, and when she finished, we had a real showplace. She blended Empire and Regency styles into a setting of pale greens and mauves and beige. It became an ideal place for entertaining.

The big house was a gift from heaven to Marguerite's three youngsters after they had been cooped up in a hotel. For a while, they nearly drove Marguerite and me frantic. Bob and Billy thought our elevator was their private plaything. There was the time when Bob had seen his first Tarzan movie and came running through the house dressed in a loincloth and swinging a baseball bat. The children soon discovered that it was great fun to listen in on telephone conversations. We had extensions all over the house and as soon as the phone would ring, all three children would rush to an extension and eavesdrop. This was rather disconcerting when a beau of Marguerite's or mine would phone and after a while Billy would come out with some comment like, "Oh, mush!" Marguerite and I finally had separate phones installed on each floor, with no extensions.

The children would play Marguerite and me against each other. They knew that when Marguerite was strict on some things, they could get Auntie Perle in just the right mood and make her say yes. One Christmas, Billy wanted a tepee, Betty wanted an electric stove, and Bob wanted a chemistry set. And that is what I got them, much to Marguerite's disapproval. Marguerite was right, for as it turned out, these were not wise gifts. Betty's miniature electric stove nearly burned down the house and Bob's chemistry set filled the place with foul odors. Billy was so enchanted with his tepee that he would not sleep in his bed, but insisted upon sleeping on the floor in his tent—and he caught a bad cold.

And there were other memorable occasions: Billy riding from floor to floor in the dumb waiter, or getting himself stuck between floors in the elevator; Betty getting a big wad of her chewing gum stuck in my silver fox fur. Auntie Perle never had any children of her own, but there is nothing imaginable I haven't been through with Marguerite's.

I went through plenty with Mamzelle as well. Before she came with Marguerite, Mamzelle had been with a Russian family of royal blood, and she was constantly trying to instill in the children a sense of the greatness of nobility. From what Mamzelle said, one might have thought that democracy was a passing fad, and that the United States would soon crown a king. Betty learned the lineage of Russian czars before she could name the first Presidents of the United States. I was often tempted to have Marguerite fire Mamzelle as a bad influence, but she was loyal, intensely protective, and very athletic. She played baseball and tennis with the children and taught them all to speak good French. Because of these redeeming qualities, Marguerite insisted that we overlook Mamzelle's eccentricities.

60

WHENEVER MY LIFE GREW TEDIOUS, no matter where I was, I would head back home to Oklahoma to visit with Father and William. On one of my trips to Oklahoma City, Conrad Hilton visited the Skirvin Hotel and suggested that Father lease it to him. Father had enlarged the hotel so that it now had four hundred rooms. Hilton's proposal sounded good financially, and Father asked William and me to accompany him to Dallas, where he planned to close the deal with Hilton. When we got to Dallas, Connie Hilton made the mistake of bragging too much on Father's expert management of the property. Father became convinced that he could run a hotel better than Hilton could, called the deal off without further ado, and continued to run the Skirvin in his customary arbitrary fashion.

One day my friend Helen McLean, who was visiting me, found a well-known Oklahoman sizzling in the lobby.

"That doggoned Bill Skirvin won't let me in my room!" he complained. "He's put a plug in the lock and I can't even get my hat."

"What did you do to Mr. Skirvin?" asked Helen.

"Not a thing," the man replied.

"Well, there must be some reason," Helen suggested. "Did you say anything to him?"

The man thought for a moment.

"I don't think I said anything *bad*. All I can recall is that as I passed him in the dining room this morning I told him the coffee was terrible. But I was only kidding."

What the man didn't know was that he might just as well have punched Father in the nose: Father had a fixation about his coffee. He felt that having the best coffee in the country was the most important thing in his hotel. He had a special blend made, and was always trying to improve it. And when he would go to another city,

61

one of the first things he would do would be to go to the best hotels and sample their coffee.

Another of Father's peculiarities was that he hated to be awakened at night. One cold winter night the room clerk got him out of bed because Lew Wentz was complaining that gas was escaping in his room. Wentz, who came from Ponca City and was about the wealthiest man in Oklahoma, was a good friend of Father's and the most powerful Republican in the state.

When Father got to Lew's room he sniffed around. There was indeed a leak in the gas pipe in the bathroom, and it was fixed the next day. But Father was in no mood to be considerate, even to a close friend.

"Nobody ever got hurt yet in this hotel by leaking gas, and there's not a thing wrong with this room," he told Lew roughly. "Now, you just get back in that bed and quit calling the clerk and interrupting my sleep." And with that he went over and opened the window wide, slammed the door, and went back to bed. Lew told that story all over Texas and Oklahoma.

Father and I were sitting in the lobby one day when a man came up to him with a check.

"The clerk said for you to okay this, Mr. Skirvin," the man said, and handed him a company check for $100. Father asked the man his name, gave him a penetrating look, then took out his pen and okayed the check.

"Do you know that man?" I asked Father.

"No," Father replied. "But I can tell he's all right. I always can tell intuitively about these things."

Just then there was a commotion over by the desk, and we saw the man in question go sprinting out the door. It turned out that the clerk had sent the man over to Father because he suspected something, and had used the delay to look up a list of checks reported stolen from a large company. Sure enough, the check Father had okayed had been stolen. When the house detective had approached to make the arrest, the thief saw him and broke away. Father was a little sheepish about that at first, but he was soon telling others this joke on himself.

The help in the hotel and a lot of people in town called Father "The Colonel" because he was an honorary colonel on the staff of every Oklahoma governor, starting with Martin E. Trapp in 1924.

62

The Colonel and the colored help had a constant battle about gambling. He had given orders that there would be no gambling, but the waiters and bellboys often had a floating crap game going in the bakeshop or in the basement. Since Father usually whistled when he walked along by himself, it wasn't often he would catch them. But sometimes he would put his mind to catching the offenders in the act. Waiting till the pot was big, he would surprise them. The men would scatter, Father would pocket the pot, save it until December, then pass it out to the men as a Christmas present.

The colored people just loved Father though, since he was usually kind and reasonable, as well as fair. Father had his favorites at the hotel, and one of them was a tall, fine-looking young colored boy by the name of Garner Camper. Garner, who started out as a room-service waiter, would just do anything for the Colonel. And Father always had great fun in trying to catch Garner in the middle of eating one of the hotel's special three-dollar sirloin steaks, then making him pay for it, full price.

One evening I passed Garner in the hall as he was wheeling a service table away from a room. He had a wide grin as he showed me a steak that had come from the room of an elderly lady who had suddenly decided she wasn't hungry. A few minutes later, as Garner was eating the steak, Father walked into the kitchen. Of course Father wouldn't accept Garner's protests that this time he had obtained a steak that had already been paid for. I came to Garner's rescue and explained what had happened. Father was still dubious, because I was always jumping to the defense of the help, but he finally decided we were telling the truth—after he had checked the orders with Room Service. Garner continued to work for Father at the hotel until he went into the Army during World War II. Later he and his wife, Edna, worked for me for a good many years. The Campers are now with Marguerite and George Tyson in Nevada.

Another favorite of Father's was Jack Brooks, who claims he holds the distinction of having been fired by the Colonel more times than anybody else. Father would fly off the handle at the help when they would do some "boneheaded, numskull trick." Brooks would take a guest to the wrong room or be out having a smoke in the alley when he was supposed to be on duty in the lobby. Father would hear the desk clerk banging and banging on his bell. Fuming, he would stomp out to the alley. Any other bellboys who happened to be out there would scatter, but Brooks was a slow mover and Father would always catch him.

"What're you doing out here when you're supposed to be in there bellhopping?" Father would demand. "You're fired."

"Well, Colonel, I was jes—"

"I don't care what you were just doing," Father would storm. "You're no good and I'm through with you. Go get your money and get out of here."

"But, Colonel, them other boys—"

"I don't want to hear any of your excuses, either. You're fired! Go get your money right now."

So off Brooks would go, looking hangdog and pathetic. Two days later he would approach Father in the lobby.

"Colonel, I hear you need a good man here at the Skirvin," Brooks would start out.

Glowering, Father would snap, "Where in hell have you been? You get back here and get on the job!" And thus Brooks would be rehired and all would be well until the next time. Before Brooks left to work as a porter for the Liberty National Bank, he was fired and rehired, according to his own count, twenty-seven times.

The worst mistake Brooks ever made was when Lawrence Tibbett came to Oklahoma City to give a concert. The opera star checked in late in the afternoon and immediately sent his tuxedo to the hotel's valet shop to be pressed. Mr. Tibbett returned to the hotel shortly before performance time, only to find his pants missing. Brooks insisted that he had returned the suit, but under Father's rapid-fire questioning, he admitted he might have taken the pants to another room. While the famous singer waited impatiently in his B.V.D.'s, Father got every employee on duty going through all the hotel rooms with passkeys looking for the missing item. There were several startled guests, especially one spinster who insists to this day that a bellboy opened her door without knocking and asked in an excited voice, "Have you got Lawrence Tibbett's pants in your closet?" Finally, when the trousers still hadn't been found, Father went down to the valet shop and there they were, right on their hanger, where Brooks had overlooked them. The concertgoers that night never did learn why Mr. Tibbett hurried onto the stage a half-hour late.

Father was very particular about how things were done at the hotel. Sometimes one of the help would be sweeping the side alley next to the Rock Island depot in a way Father thought inefficient. "You don't know the first damn thing about using a broom," he would complain. "Now, watch me and learn how." And he would grab the broom and proceed to sweep the entire alley, not stopping until he got out to Broadway. Some of Father's cronies occasionally caught him at this. He would ignore their wisecracks, as they watched from the entrance to the alley, and sweep right on around their feet.

In 1930, Father induced me to go in with him on an oil venture. Ever since he drilled a water well in our back yard in the early 1900s he had always felt Oklahoma City was an oil region. And Father was right. By 1929, the first large well had been discovered in the area, just six miles south of our old home. Father and I leased some land about a mile from where we had formerly lived, and we started drilling. Each well cost us about seventy thousand dollars and there was always the gamble that the well might go out of control and spray oil all over the community or cause a disastrous fire.

Some friends of ours in the Oklahoma City Field had a well coat the state capitol. They not only had a monstrous clean-up job on their hands, but damages to pay. Some other drillers in the same field had a well catch fire. Nearby houses were ruined, and it took days to put out the fire. Father and I could have been wiped out, had such a thing happened to us, but our luck held. We struck oil, and our best well had a potential of 40,000 barrels per day.

With the money we were making on our Oklahoma City leases, Father suggested we go in together to build an extension to the hotel. Although this was during the depression, the oil boom was on in Oklahoma City and the Skirvin Hotel was always crowded. I agreed to help, and at a cost of two million dollars we built a fourteen-story hotel across the street from the Skirvin, calling it the Skirvin Tower. Since Father thought the ballroom in the Skirvin was too small, he designed one in the Tower that covered two entire floors and held twenty-five hundred people. Today it is still the biggest hotel ballroom in Oklahoma.

During the mid-thirties, Father got me to go in with him on another oil prospect: a wildcat venture east of Oklahoma City in virgin territory more than forty miles from where any commercial oil had been found.

Father and I, together with my brother William and veteran oilman Joe Cromwell, spent ninety thousand dollars buying twenty-four thousand acres of oil leases, had the area worked over by seismologists and geologists at a cost of twenty thousand dollars, and finally picked out the best spot for our test well. We called it the Beeler Well No. 1 because it was located on a farm owned by a family named Beeler.

Drilling started in 1937. We were using a large rotary drilling rig. When we got down about a mile, rainbows of oil and a lot of gas began showing up in the slush pit. It really looked good. We ran steel casing into the well and then waited while the cement set. There was great excitement in the nearby towns. People kept coming out to watch, and royalties soared from twenty to two hundred dollars an acre.

On the first of August we were ready to bring the well in by bailing it. The casing went down 5100 feet, so we had a column of mud that deep. We started bailing with a 30-foot-long bailer, lowered by a steel cable over the top of the derrick and into the casing. The idea was that after you bailed out some of the mud, reducing the weight of the remaining column, the gas pressure would bring up the rest of the mud and shoot it over the derrick. With the mud out, the oil follows—in theory. Then you shut the gate valve and open the side valve and let the oil flow into your tanks—and start spending your money.

There were at least two hundred onlookers as we started bailing —bankers, businessmen, and reporters from as far away as Tulsa. It was a hot day, in the high nineties. People had brought box lunches. There was an atmosphere of high expectation. We bailed down to 500 feet but nothing happened. Mr. Cromwell began to look a little glum. "Let's bail down another five hundred," he said.

At a thousand feet some gas began to break through the mud. Everybody got excited, thinking the well was going to clean itself. We waited and watched. And watched and waited.

Father, William, and Joe Cromwell were about ready to call it a day. "Don't give up, it's going to be a well yet," I insisted.

At sunset, when we had bailed almost 3000 feet, the well suddenly cleaned itself, the mud gushing high into the air. Everyone shouted and cheered. After the mud came gas, and more gas . . . and still more gas . . . but no oil. It was nothing but a gas well. And although it could have produced a million feet of gas a day, it was too far from a pipeline to be commercially feasible. If it had been an oil well, with the thousands of acres we had under lease, we could have made fifty million dollars. But it wasn't an oil well. Sadly we capped it and drove back to Oklahoma City.

Even though the Beeler well was a dud, a number of other oil ventures I had gone into with Father were producing steadily and we were collecting money in large amounts. It had been Father's habit to collect all the income from our various oil properties, and to hand over at irregular intervals whatever net amounts might be due me. I didn't mind this arrangement until he began to use my share of the income for investments of which I did not approve. We had some very heated and prolonged arguments. Our affairs got so involved that I finally went to an attorney, a move that made me sick at heart when I saw how much Father resented it. Looking back, I realize that I should have stopped right there—but I have a streak of stubbornness. I started litigation with Father over the money matters and over the operation of the hotels, and the legal bickering went on for several years. Even though Marguerite and William were drawn into it, too, Father remained friendly with all of us, and there was no personal bitterness as there sometimes is in lawsuits for an accounting between members of a family. And I continued to stay with Father at the Skirvin Hotel whenever I was in Oklahoma City. The court eventually appointed an expert hotel man to take charge of the Skirvin Hotels, but Father still had plenty to say about their operation even though he was approaching eighty years of age.

One afternoon while I was in Oklahoma City on my oil undertakings, I received a huge box of yellow chrysanthemums. The card said, "To Mrs. George Mesta whom I greatly admire." It was signed, "Carl Magee," a name that filled me with excitement. Carl Magee was famous in the Southwest as the fearless newspaper editor who had uncovered the Teapot Dome scandal, which sent to prison President Harding's Secretary of the Interior, Albert Fall. I had heard that Carl Magee was a widower. I had never formally met him, although I had seen him many times at Chamber of Commerce meetings and other large gatherings. While editor of the

67

Oklahoma *News,* he had stirred up many civic battles. In some of them he clashed openly with Father, and Father had never forgiven him.

As I was arranging Carl Magee's flowers, Father walked in and saw the florist's box.

"Who are those from?" he asked.

"Carl Magee," I replied.

Father got red in the face. "What are you doing getting flowers from that man?" he demanded.

"I don't know," I replied. "I've never met him. But I think it's sweet he sent me flowers."

"Well, I don't think it's sweet. And I don't want you to have anything to do with him," said Father, and he walked out of the room.

At that moment the telephone rang. It was Carl Magee and he wanted me to dine with him that night. If it hadn't been for Father's opposition, I most likely would have said no, especially on such short notice. But I said I'd be happy to accept and told him to call for me at the suite at six-thirty. I knew Father would be out having a drink with some of his pals at that hour so there would be no danger of the two men meeting.

Carl Magee called for me and we drove to a quiet restaurant. He was a tall, lanky man with piercing, yet kindly, blue eyes. He was rather quiet and reserved, and at first I was a bit in awe of him because of his reputation as a crusading newspaperman. His richness of experience made him wonderful to listen to. Carl had been a schoolteacher and a lawyer before he became an editor. He also had a mechanical bent: not long before I met him he had patented a parking meter.

Our evening together was delightful, and we parted with a date arranged for the following week. This time Carl and I took a long ride in the country. He stopped the car overlooking the Cimarron River and we sat and enjoyed the beauty of the scene. There was a feeling of relaxation and easiness between us.

All of a sudden Carl turned to me.

"I know this may sound forward of me, and you don't have to answer, but I've seen your name linked with several different men back East," he said. "Are you serious about any of them?"

I didn't give him a direct answer.

68

"In our short time together I have realized I could grow very fond of you," he confided. "If you are serious about someone, I would like to know it. And if not, I would like to know if I have a chance with you."

I didn't know what to answer. I knew that I admired Carl greatly and felt that I really could care for him deeply. But I have never liked to be pinned down.

"No, there's no one else," I said at last. "But I don't know how to answer the other part of your question. It's just too soon to know. You'll have to give me time to know you better."

We dated constantly from then on. In a few months he left Oklahoma City to become editor of a string of newspapers in the Rio Grande Valley. He would fly up to Oklahoma City every weekend when I was there, and I found myself spending more and more time away from Washington, New York, and Newport.

When Carl and I were together we often took long drives into the country. Sometimes I would pack a box lunch and we would picnic at Lake Shawnee. Or we would stop at a roadside stand and perch on the high stools and have hot dogs and coffee. Carl never touched liquor, and shunned dancing and party-going. And when I was with Carl, I never even thought about the things by which I had always judged my other beaux—their gaiety and their ability to dance.

Carl was interested in most everything. He often took me to lectures and civic meetings. He discussed world affairs and national questions. He was always giving me books or articles to read—and I would have to find out what was in them so I wouldn't appear ignorant. Between dates it was almost as if I had homework to do. I had always hated to read—and I still don't have the patience to wade through most books. I would get my secretary to read the books Carl gave me and she would give me a review or digest of what was in them. Carl's efforts made me stretch my thinking so that I became aware of things which had never interested me before. I couldn't help but compare Carl Magee with George Mesta. George had pampered me and treated me like an ornament, and I had loved it. Carl was treating me as his mental equal (which I most certainly wasn't), and his respect for my opinions was encouraging me to think things through for the first time in my life. Through Carl's vivid interests and forthright, honest viewpoint, I came to have a

69

more realistic attitude toward politics and national affairs. Carl wouldn't let me get away with just looking on the surface of things; he made me look into the real heart of issues.

As soon as word went around in Oklahoma City that Carl Magee and I were going together, I began to hear disturbing remarks to the effect that he had once killed a man. Six months passed before I heard the details from Carl himself. One day he asked me to marry him. He was intense and positive, a very strong man in every way. When I was with him I could think of no one else. I was in love with him, yet I couldn't bring myself to say yes. In the back of my mind was all the talk about the shooting. I made no reference to it for fear of hurting Carl.

He brought up marriage again a few weeks later and I again evaded answering. Carl held me at arms' length and looked at me a long moment. Then he said, "Is it because of my past that you won't marry me?"

I admitted that his reticence about the matter had made me wonder. Then Carl told me this story:

In 1920, because of his wife's failing health, Carl had moved from Oklahoma to Albuquerque. With some borrowed money, he had purchased the Albuquerque *Journal* from United States Senator Albert Fall. Fall had used the paper for his own political purposes, but Carl immediately made it a voice of truth. And the truth in New Mexico politics quickly flushed out corruption directly concerning Senator Fall. Carl discovered that the big cattlemen in New Mexico were being granted the use of Federal lands at ridiculously low rates. As soon as he started exposing this in the *Journal,* the political powers in the state made moves to silence him. Violence was threatened to him and his family, and a gunman once tried to ambush him on a lonely road. One of Carl's political foes, Judge D. J. Leahy, convicted him of criminal libel and later of contempt of court, and both times sentenced him to prison. Both times Governor Hinkle pardoned Carl. Then the vested interests started applying financial pressure and called in Carl's bank notes ahead of time. Carl lost his paper in 1922. Undaunted, he got together more money and started a weekly in Albuquerque, *Magee's Independent.* By this time Albert Fall had become President Harding's Secretary of the Interior.

Carl dug more deeply into things, and then went to Washington

70

to report to a Congressional committee on his discoveries. His information led to uncovering the conspiracy, in which several oil companies had been illegally given leases on Federal oil reserves, including the Teapot Dome reserve in Wyoming. It turned out that Fall had received more than $200,000 in Liberty bonds as a bribe from an oil company to help get the leases. Fall was convicted of accepting bribes and was sent to prison for a year and heavily fined.

In the wake of these events Carl's newspaper prospered and became a daily, and Carl became a public leader in New Mexico. But his enemies never forgave him. In August, 1925, he was to preside over a meeting of the State Asylum Board in Las Vegas, New Mexico. His wife asked him not to go: Las Vegas was the headquarters of his enemies. But Carl was not one to be cowed by threats, and he insisted on going. At the last minute, his son Ted slipped a pistol into his father's pocket.

In Las Vegas, Carl was sitting in the lobby of the Meadows Hotel talking to a woman newspaper reporter when Judge Leahy walked in, approached Carl from the rear, and struck him without warning. Carl collapsed on the floor with a dislocated neck, and remembered nothing that happened thereafter until he regained full consciousness in a hospital several hours later. But in his semiconscious state, with Judge Leahy kicking him, he tried to protect himself with the gun his son had given him. One bullet struck Leahy in the arm. Another struck and killed a young state highway employee and friend of Carl's, John Lasseter, who had come to the scene trying to help him. While Carl was recovering in the hospital, his tragedy was deepened, for his eldest son, Carl, Jr., was killed in an airplane accident. Later, Carl was tried for the accidental slaying of Lasseter. He was acquitted.

Carl told me all this without any display of emotion, but by the time he had finished his story I was sobbing. I loved him so much and felt his sorrow and torment so deeply that it was some time before I could think calmly again. At last I told him that I did love him, and loved him all the more for what he had been through.

We continued to see each other regularly. Carl wrote to me every day. It sometimes took me hours to decipher his letters. He was one of those old-time newspapermen who had never learned to use a typewriter. His handwriting was small and cramped and there was practically no difference between the o's and a's and e's. But

71

legibility aside, they were the most beautiful letters I've ever read.

Carl expected me to write to him each day, but I could never seem to put down in words the feelings I had in my heart.

Early in 1939, Carl came to see me in New York. "I've been very patient, Perle," he said. "I've been asking you to marry me for nearly two years now. And I think it is time you made a decision about our future."

"Oh, Carl, I do love you," I said, "but let me think about it just a little longer."

"No, Perle, I can't wait any longer," Carl insisted. "If you really loved me, you would marry me. I just can't go on like this."

My heart wanted to say yes, but my mind said no. I still wasn't sure that we had enough in common for an enduring marriage. And I didn't want to remarry unless I was absolutely certain that it would last.

"Be patient a little while longer," I finally told him.

Carl just looked at me. When I saw him off at the station, he kissed me good-by. Then he said calmly, "Will you reconsider, Perle? This is the last time I'll ask you."

I blew him a kiss and said, "Maybe later."

The train pulled away and that was the last time I ever saw Carl Magee. He wrote one last letter, and that was it. I kept waiting for another, but it never came. Finally, I came to accept the fact that I had lost Carl. In the years that followed, I realized that if everybody waited to be absolutely certain before taking the plunge, few people would ever get to the altar.

After Carl went out of my life I sold my New York house and bought one in Boston. I wanted to be near Marguerite and the children. But after a month or two in Boston I became restless again. After a period of traveling, I returned to Washington.

I NOW BEGAN to take an increasing interest in politics and national affairs. Because of the influence of my father and George Mesta, I had always been a Republican. After my brief flurry of working for Hoover and Curtis in 1928, I had pretty much ignored politics except for what rubbed off during my contacts with prominent government officials at parties in Washington. During the early part of 1936, when I was back in Oklahoma City, Father told me that the local Republicans were trying to build up Alf Landon as a presidential candidate. Through friends in Kansas City, I had met the Kansas governor several years before. I knew also that Landon had many good friends among the oilmen in the Southwest, and that they could be counted on for financial backing.

When Teddy Roosevelt's son, Col. Theodore Roosevelt, Jr., came to Oklahoma that January for a Young Republican convention, I gave a reception for him at the Skirvin Hotel. I invited a number of the convention delegates: Governor Landon's secretary, Willard Mayberry; oil multimillionaire Lew Wentz; and Frank Harper, an Oklahoman who had been secretary to Colonel Roosevelt's father when Teddy was in the White House. Whenever I got an opportunity during the party, I put in a good word for Landon as the best possibility the Republicans had to beat Franklin Roosevelt.

A few months later, Mr. and Mrs. Frank Phillips invited me to spend the weekend at their home in Bartlesville, Oklahoma. Frank Phillips (of Phillips Petroleum Company) was one of the powers in the Republican party, and that weekend several prominent Republican politicians, including Alf Landon, were also his guests. I wasn't in on any of their serious discussions, although I did get into a poker game with them and won eighty dollars. After the game broke up, the men retired to another room. I could sense that something was brewing—that these men hadn't congregated just for poker and small talk. Jane Phillips and I were still up when the men reappeared in a body just before midnight. Frank was all smiles. "Alf has decided to run for President," he said, placing his hand on Landon's shoulder. "Let's toast the next President of the United States." And we did.

I helped organize the campaign activities of the Oklahoma State Council of Republican Women, and we held a big Republican Women's rally early in May. I arranged for one of Governor Landon's chief advisors, Justice William A. Smith of the Kansas Supreme Court, to be the principal speaker.

That summer, I attended the Republican convention in Cleveland, taking along a good friend of mine from Newport. She turned out to be an unfortunate choice as a companion. I wanted her to go with me to the convention hall every day, but she was interested only in the social events. When I suggested taking her to meet Landon, which I thought would be a great honor, she merely said, "Why should I? I'll never see him again." So I went around alone. And before I knew it, even though I couldn't stand the smell of those smoke-filled rooms, I found myself suddenly filled with the political fever.

After the convention, I went to Oklahoma City to campaign. The Landon-for-President headquarters was, of course, in the Skirvin Hotel. Perhaps because I was scared to death of getting up and making a speech, I developed a theory that the best way to influence voters was through their children. I had the hotel chef bake hundreds of cookies, day after day, and I distributed them at every little town that had so much as a drugstore or gas station. Marguerite and the children were in Oklahoma at the time and I took ten-year-old Betty along on my trips. While she repeated a carefully rehearsed vote-for-Landon slogan and passed out the cookies, I handed out campaign buttons. I figured that if we gave cookies to the children, they would tell their parents that Alf Landon had nice friends and was a good man and should be President. From the favorable reactions we got I had no doubt in my mind about the outcome of the election.

On election night I was in New York watching a play. I assured everybody around me—even tapping strangers on the shoulder—that Landon was about to win easily. During intermission, we went

74

outside and found the newsboys selling papers with headlines that Landon was losing. I refused to believe it, and went back into the theater telling those around me not to pay any attention to the papers.

There are times when a trait of stubbornness makes one look extra foolish, and this was one such time. In his landslide, Roosevelt carried forty-six states. He even took Oklahoma by more than two to one, despite my ardent efforts for Mr. Landon.

The defeat didn't discourage me, however. I liked what little I had learned about campaigning, and I still kept my interest in Republican politics. The following year I was appointed a representative from Oklahoma to the meeting of the Republican National Policy Committee, headed by Dr. Glenn Frank. Working on this committee enabled me to meet such other active Republicans as Cecil B. DeMille, Mrs. Ogden M. Reid of the New York *Herald Tribune,* and Sewell Avery, head of Montgomery Ward.

In the summer of 1937, Marguerite announced to us that she was going to be married to George Tyson of Boston. I decided to give them the wedding at Beachmound, the home I had purchased in Newport several years earlier. I don't think George Tyson, a very proper, conservative investment broker from Boston, knew when he proposed to Marguerite that he was about to get mixed up with the whole Skirvin clan.

How the wedding ever came off as well as it did, I will never know, for Marguerite, Father, and I all thought we were running things singlehanded. And with three Skirvins giving orders at the same time, anything can happen. We all got into an argument right at the start over the use of the word *obey* in the ceremony. Father and William thought it was safer for George's sake to have the word right there in black and white. Marguerite and I insisted it be left out, and we won the argument. George was so bewildered, all he could do was nod his agreement. Bob, by that time a young man of fourteen, was an usher. Betty, eleven, was the flower girl, and ten-year-old Billy was the ring bearer. Billy was so full of the dickens we weren't certain what would happen. And sure enough, he went up the wrong aisle with the ring cushion and then, in the scramble to get back to the center, dropped the ring.

Bob was not entirely happy about his mother's getting married again. He was very subdued before and during the wedding. After-

75

ward, when Betty and Billy were very much in evidence eating enormous pieces of cake, we didn't see Bob anyplace. The bride excused herself and went looking for her eldest. She found him in the garden, being walked back and forth by Mamzelle. He had tried to drown his sorrow in champagne.

The next event was Father's doing a frisky schottische with the groom's elderly and dignified Aunt Annie from Boston. I am sure George breathed a sigh of relief when he drove off for the honeymoon, although Billy's jumping on the running board to yell "Good-by, Pop!" as they started off down fashionable Bellevue Avenue, could not have been too settling.

I spent part of 1938 in New York City. One of the most interesting parties I gave that year was a dinner for former President Hoover, just after he had returned from a trip to Europe. Alec Templeton, the brilliant blind pianist, was very popular at that time, and I arranged for him to play for us. I was looking forward to a wonderful evening. Among the guests I invited were J. M. Davies, president of the Lackawanna Railroad; Will Hays, who had been Postmaster General under Harding; Count and Countess Villa of Italy; Rosa Ponselle; Julia Berwind, from Newport; Mr. and Mrs. Stephen Pell of Fort Ticonderoga; Frank Houston, a New York banker; Bill Chadborn, a New York attorney; and Lawrence Richey, Mr. Hoover's secretary.

As soon as dinner was finished, most of us gathered around Mr. Hoover in the large drawing room to hear his impressions of Germany. This was the period when Hitler was making himself master in Europe, and we were all anxious to get Mr. Hoover's interpretation of recent events there. Alec Templeton's father, who was also his manager, arrived with his famous son, showed him to the piano in my small drawing room, and without asking if we were ready, had him start playing. When only a few guests came in to listen to the music, Alec's father became very indignant. He told me if we did not give his son our undivided attention, he would not allow him to play.

I asked Alec's father to be patient, assuring him we would be glad to listen to his son when Mr. Hoover had finished talking. The elder Templeton considered this an insult, and walked out, taking his son with him. We didn't lack for entertainment, however, because Rosa Ponselle later on sat down at the piano and for more than an hour sang arias and ballads to her own accompaniment.

76

During the party, Sarah Pell got me off to one side and asked me why I wasn't working with the National Woman's Party. "What's that?" I asked, and then had a hard time stopping Sarah as she tried to explain everything about the Equal Rights for Women campaign. Little did I realize, when I offhandedly told Sarah I would be glad to help out, that I would soon become an ardent feminist.

She came over the next day to tell me in more detail about the National Woman's Party. I had always assumed that the Nineteenth Amendment gave us women all the rights we needed. Sarah explained that the amendment provided only the right for women to vote, and that there were hundreds, maybe thousands of laws still existing which restricted us. I became an immediate and active convert to the cause, and it has occupied much of my time and energy for the past twenty years.

I took part in the organization of the World Woman's Party, which was started in 1938 to protect the existing rights of women in all nations and to extend these rights, and was promptly named International Publicity Chairman for the new organization. My first big job was to promote the opening of our world headquarters at the first international meeting of our party, in Geneva, Switzerland, in August, 1939.

I arranged with the National Broadcasting Company to provide a transatlantic radio broadcast of our opening ceremonies, and then set out for Europe. On the way to Geneva, I stopped off in Paris to ask Grace Moore to sing at our opening. I knew we needed a big name to attract attention. I had known Grace in New York and she had been to several of my parties, although we were not close friends.

The World Woman's Party had no money to pay for entertainment, so I personally offered to pay Grace two thousand dollars and expenses if she would come for the opening day. She agreed.

Our organization had taken a beautiful villa overlooking Lake Geneva. It had a large balcony, so we decided that Grace would sing there and forthwith invited townspeople of Geneva to come hear her. But when Grace arrived a few hours before the opening and discovered that we wanted her to sing outdoors, she refused to perform. I tried to persuade her tactfully.

"We have invited the public of Geneva. There will be more than six thousand people outside, including visitors from all over

Europe," I argued. "We couldn't possibly get them indoors." But Grace was adamant. Finally, I took her husband aside.

"Grace told me she wanted this money to give to your family as a present," I said, reminding him of a conversation we all had had in Paris. "Well, either Grace sings outside, or the deal is off."

He went back and talked to Grace, and a few minutes later she agreed to sing.

It was a balmy moonlit evening and the crowd of listeners extended over the lawn and all the way down to the lake. Grace never sang better in her life. Our transatlantic broadcast went over without a hitch, and we had some inspiring speeches. Later, Grace apologized to me for her obstinacy.

Although our opening ceremonies were tremendously impressive, I am sorry to say we did not fare so well in our attempt to unite the world's women to fight for their rights. Prominent feminists from almost every country in the world were present as observers, but very few as official delegates. We lit a torch and handed it to a representative from England, who handed it to a woman from France, and so on. While this was very stirring as a ceremony, that's all it really was. The nations of the world were still far from united in the cause of equal rights for women.

I recall a talk I had with a German feminist.

"You don't need to talk to us about women's rights," she said arrogantly. "We already have a larger percentage of women in public office than you do—we have eighteen in our legislature."

"You may have them in your legislature," I countered, "but you don't allow them to do anything. You have a dictator running things."

"Hitler is the savior of Germany and will be the savior of the world," she answered. The discussion ended right there.

One of the reasons for starting a world-wide woman's party was so we could do more effective work at the League of Nations. The National Woman's Party of the United States had made little progress at Geneva because the League delegates would say, "Your country doesn't belong to the League, so why should we listen to your National Woman's Party?" However, with the help of women all over the world, we were able to get a permanent League of Nations committee on the status of women. And although the World Woman's Party office at Geneva had to close in 1941 because of the war, the committee that had been formed became the forerunner of the present-day Status of Women committee of the United Nations.

I returned to the United States in September, 1939, a few days after the start of World War II. Continuing my work for the National Woman's Party, I went to the 1940 Republican convention at Philadelphia to help lobby for a plank supporting an equal-rights Constitutional amendment. Neither the Democrats nor the Republicans had ever backed such an amendment in their party platforms. The National Woman's Party had sent a delegation to make the official presentation to the Resolutions Committee. I was not on this delegation, but had been asked to do what I could as a lone wolf.

After all the arguments pro and con had been formally presented, and while the Resolutions Committee was working on the platform planks, I sent in a message asking if Herbert Hyde, the committee chairman, would see me for a moment. A United States attorney in Oklahoma, Hyde was an old friend of mine. When he came out, I asked if he had anything in the platform on equal rights for women. He showed me the plank the committee was considering. It had been watered down until it was pointless.

"Oh, that won't do at all," I told Mr. Hyde. "The National Woman's Party speaks in the interests of millions of women. *This* is what women want"—and I handed him our resolution backing adoption of our proposed Constitutional amendment. He thanked me and went back to the committee session, where three other of my good Republican friends—Alf Landon, Glenn Frank, and Senator George Pepper of Pennsylvania—were working.

The next day, the Resolutions Committee's proposed platform was read and adopted by the convention, and for the first time in history, a major political party went on record as supporting a Constitutional amendment to provide equal rights for women!

When not busy lobbying, I was in the galleries hollering for Wendell L. Willkie. For me he was the man of the hour. Willkie knew the pulse of the people and seemed to reach the heart of every American. He wanted the Republican party to become more liberal, which was exactly the way I felt. I had never met Willkie. My enthusiasm for Curtis and Landon had been partly due to personal friendship, but I was for Willkie because of what he stood for. I

79

shouted myself hoarse for him. On the way out of the hall after his nomination, I ran into Pennsylvania's Senator James Davis, Secretary of Labor under Harding, Coolidge, and Hoover, and an old friend from Pittsburgh.

"Isn't it wonderful!" I whispered through my hoarseness. "We'll surely beat Roosevelt with Wendell Willkie."

Senator Davis harumphed and looked at me with disdain.

"You have rooted for Willkie and got him," he said. "But I'll tell you right now that *we* don't want him and are not going to support him." Of course, he was counting himself as one of the old machine Republicans.

I was so stunned I almost forgot to lose my temper. Rallying, I managed to tell off Senator Davis. I then determined to work to my limit for Willkie. I spent a few days in the East soliciting contributions for the campaign. I remember going out on Long Island to see Will Coe, a New York financier and one of the richest men in America. Before I left, after a weekend of talking Willkie, I had Coe's check for twelve thousand dollars.

Then I headed for Oklahoma City, persuading Marguerite and George Tyson to come along and bring the children to help in a town-by-town tour of Oklahoma, Kansas, and eastern Colorado. I had overcome my stage fright enough to be able to give one carefully rehearsed short speech at women's clubs or wherever I could get together an audience. I would pass off Betty, Billy, and Bob as "my family." Still believing that a sound way to the voters' minds is through their children, I would have Betty and Billy and Bob pass out literature and buttons to every child we saw.

We started out with our car full of buttons and folders. George, always the thrifty Bostonian, would caution, "Now just one button to each person," but I would say to the child, "You must have some brothers and sisters and friends. Here—" And I would fill the child's hands with buttons. We had to wire headquarters to send more campaign fodder before we had been on the road three days.

As we got into the flat country of eastern Colorado the weather turned warm, nearing a hundred every day. Neither Marguerite nor I can take intense heat, but we were too imbued with the Willkie spirit to quit. I had heard somewhere that it was cooling to hold on your lap a block of ice wrapped in newspapers. We tried it. I started out with the block on my lap. As the sun got higher, the ice started melting pretty fast. The wrapping began to soak through. I shifted the block to Marguerite. She soon gave it to George. It went on down through the children, then back to me. George got madder each time he had to hold the ice. He finally blew up.

"I'll be damned if I'll hold this one more minute, even for Wendell L. Willkie!" he shouted. That evening he and the children took the train to Denver where they sat in a cool hotel room and waited for Marguerite and me to finish what he called our foolishness.

As we went through those small Western towns in late August, I began to notice a waning of enthusiasm in the responses we received. From the speeches we were hearing on the radio, it seemed to me that Willkie was changing some of his ideals and becoming more conservative. I felt he was losing the common touch that had made him so popular at the convention only two months earlier. When we reached Denver I phoned Joe Martin, who was running Willkie's New York headquarters, and told him I wanted to see him. I got on a plane that afternoon, landed in New York at six the next morning, and arrived at Joe's apartment at the Roosevelt Hotel an hour later.

"Something has happened, Joe," I said. "Willkie has changed and the people can feel it." The Republican House leader told me that Willkie was so busy he couldn't write his own speeches.

"I can tell that," I said. "It looks to me as if the Old Guard is trying to make him over in their image."

After we had talked a while, Joe said he would telephone Willkie on the campaign train and give him my report. It was only a little after eight o'clock when I left Joe.

"If anyone sees me coming out of your apartment at this hour of the morning, what will they say?" I joshed.

"And to think we wasted our time talking politics!" Joe kidded back as he showed me to the elevator.

I went back to Oklahoma and continued working for Willkie to the bitter end, although I had lost much of my enthusiasm. I felt he was neither being true to his principles nor convincing to the conservative Republicans. I was disappointed, of course, when he was defeated. But this time I had seen it coming.

After my disillusionment over Willkie, I took one of the most important steps of my life. Until the late nineteen-thirties, my in-

81

terest in politics was mostly connected with my friendship for the people I knew, and most of these had been Republicans: my father, my husband, and his friends and the people I went around with in Washington, New York, and Newport. But through my friendship with Carl Magee, I had begun to do some thinking about what the two parties stood for. I found myself more and more impatient with the actions of the Republican party. It seemed to me that the Democrats were doing a lot more to meet the needs of the people. I didn't approve of everything in the New Deal program by any means, but I had gone through the slums right behind the Capitol, house by house, and I had become an advocate of Federal housing programs, both for slum clearance and for helping people with low incomes to buy homes of their own. I had also seen conditions in the steel mills in Pittsburgh that made me feel that the workingman should be helped. Although I was never a deep student of political philosophy, I was fed up with Republican conservatism. The status quo, so much admired by most of the Republicans I knew, did not seem worth conserving.

I debated a long time, but finally decided to change my political affiliation. It was especially difficult because I didn't want to lose the many good friends I had in the Republican camp. But by the time the 1944 campaign got under way, I had taken the big step and registered as a Democrat.

Right here I'm going to make a little confession. My name was originally spelled P-e-a-r-l. I was born Pearl Reid Skirvin. But when I had started going to Europe in the twenties, I found that my French friends always spelled my name their way, P-e-r-l-e. In view of the French ancestry on my mother's side, I decided it would be quite natural for me to spell my name the French way. It was just a feminine whim, I guess, but I started signing *Perle* when writing to my family and to close friends, and they soon adopted that spelling too. So for the past thirty years I have been Perle, and Marguerite's children have never known me any other way than as Auntie Perle. When I made the big decision to change my political affiliation, I also decided to change the spelling of my name officially. So it was off with the old Republican Pearl and on with the new Democratic Perle!

EIGHT: *Auntie Perle Goes West*

A FEW EYEBROWS were raised early in 1941 when I announced to my Washington and Newport friends that I was going out to Arizona to live. No one could picture Perle Mesta at home on the range, and I must admit that I wasn't particularly interested in roughing it. But in 1939 Marguerite and George had bought a ranch near Prescott, and now they were spending much of their time out there. I missed seeing the children. Life in Washington and Newport seemed a little dull without them. When William asked if I wanted to go in with him to buy a ranch adjoining Marguerite's, I readily agreed. We purchased an eighteen-thousand-acre ranch eighty miles north of Phoenix. There were eighteen hundred head of white-faced Herefords on the property and some buildings where the foreman and cowhands bunked and kept the equipment—but no suitable domicile for me. Therefore I stayed with Marguerite and George. They had a rambling old house on their ranch and Marguerite was getting ready to remodel it.

At first the ranch meant only an investment to me, and I let William see to the running of it. In 1942, however, we were in the war, and our cattle were suddenly a crucial food source. William's oil interests took up much of his time, so I decided I would run the ranch.

The first thing I did upon assuming command was call in my foreman, Jenks Ruth.

"The cattle are too skinny," I complained. "And it's no wonder, the way you and your men run those poor things up and down the hills and rope them."

Now, if there is anything cowboys don't like, it is to have someone who doesn't know a fetlock from a forelock tell them how to

83

run a ranch. But in those days, I wouldn't admit I didn't know everything. To prove I was no bluffer, I picked up a halter and went to the corral to select and saddle my own horse. I had told the cowhands I would help them round up a couple of strays that day.

It didn't work out quite the way I expected. I forgot to fasten the latch on the corral gate and just as I reached the horse I wanted, the gate swung open and the whole herd stampeded out. It took the boys most of the morning to bring them all in again.

I was also rather unpopular in my efforts to reform the cowhands' characters. I would talk to them about not drinking so much and about going to church on Sunday. But they would pull those big hats down over their eyes, look at the ground, and say, "Yes ma'am," and then go right on leading the same type of life. Those men surely must have dreaded to see me coming. After a while, though, when I slowed up enough to learn a little about ranching, I became less dogmatic, and we all got along somewhat better.

I even got Jenks to try to teach me how to rope a calf. He started out showing me how to get my rope into a small loop. That I could do. Then he showed me how to make bigger loops and finally how to swing the rope and throw it. I wasn't much good at throwing it, but after I had practiced several days, Jenks finally decided to test me out. He drove a small calf past me and I tossed the rope at its neck. But I threw too soon and too low. The rope caught the calf's hoof and almost broke the poor thing's leg. I gave up roping, then and there.

Undaunted, Jenks offered to teach me to drive a car. I had never been behind a wheel, much preferring to do all my driving from the back seat. Marguerite said, "Now, Sister," (she always calls me Sister unless she's mad at me) "this is the ideal time and place for you to learn. You can drive on the wrong side of the road or anywhere you want to out here on the ranch."

I said I'd try. Jenks had a Model-A Ford and he was very patient with me. I was getting along fairly well, weaving from one side of the road to the other only part of the time. Then we came to a dry wash with some very deep ruts.

"Now, not too fast," warned Jenks.

So of course I stepped on the gas instead of the brakes. We bounced into the ruts, the bottom of the car hit the high spot on the road, there was a grating of metal against dirt, and we came to a jarring halt with the rear wheels off the ground. When Jenks looked under the car he mumbled something about being "hung up" with a crankcase or something being knocked off. I probably have the mechanical details wrong, but I recall that a neighbor had to pull us out with his truck and tow us the twenty miles back to the ranch house. It cost me a hundred dollars to fix Jenks's car. I haven't been behind the wheel of another one since.

Trying hard to get into the Western spirit, I wore a fringed skirt and blouse and a lady's Western hat with a little strap under the chin. Billy used to give me a look, shake his head slowly, and say, "All Auntie Perle needs is a six-shooter." I could never completely go Western, however, because I found it impossible to leave the ranch house without taking my gloves and handbag. I just didn't feel right without them.

And I never quite came to terms with the snakes and lizards and bugs. The day I encountered a rattlesnake coiled right at the door of my bedroom, I decided that measures had to be taken. I made Billy the Chief Snake and Bug Catcher and paid him fifty cents a week to keep all wild life out of my room. And when Billy declined to get on the job until noon I cut his salary to twenty-five cents.

Ranch life was a wonderful experience for the children. Betty and Billy were away at school and came home to the ranch only on vacations. Bob, who was in his late teens, had a small herd of his own on part of his parents' ranch. He was a serious young man and did a good job with his ranching. Billy's vacation days were spent in working around the place and hobnobbing with the hands. When he was about fourteen I discovered he had been smoking secretly. I told Marguerite. We decided it would do no good to lay down the law: Billy already knew smoking was forbidden. I cooked up a plan with one of the cowboys to play a trick on Billy. When they were out together one day, the cowboy rolled a cigarette and handed it to my nephew.

"Gee, Harvey, thanks!" Billy said. He had trouble getting it lit. Harvey helped him. Billy took two deep breaths and gasped and choked. We had arranged for Harvey to mix the tobacco with a little dry cow dung. Billy didn't try to smoke again for several years.

In the summer of 1943, Betty invited one of her Boston girl friends, Helen Byrd, Admiral Byrd's daughter, to come out and visit her. The morning after Helen arrived, I was sitting in bed

85

reading a newspaper when she came into my room. At first I didn't look up.

"Look at what I've got, Mrs. Mesta," said Helen. She held up a king snake. It looked at least five yards long. And it was writhing.

I shrieked my way under the covers and did not reappear until Helen had removed herself and her specimen. That was my introduction to Helen's hobby of collecting and preserving snakes, bugs, and spiders. I was further unnerved a few days later when I unscrewed the top of a large cold cream jar and found within it, floating in alcohol, a huge, furry tarantula. As though one such hobby were not enough, Helen also was fascinated by old bones. Every time she and Betty would go out riding, Helen would come back dragging bleached cattle skulls and bones. When the dear child finally left us, she mailed home most of her clothes because her suitcase was crammed with her more interesting material. I confess to a feeling of relief when we kissed Helen good-by at the airport and she took off with her bag of bones and her pickled tarantula.

With Betty reaching the age where boys were no longer just a nuisance, Auntie Perle, always the romanticist, decided that her darling niece needed a little assist. Betty was a pretty teen-ager, with lovely blond hair. She had only one serious handicap—Mamzelle. The governess had been with the family since Betty was two, and as Betty started maturing, Mamzelle did everything in her power to keep her a child.

On Betty's twelfth birthday, I bought her some dress shoes—her first with heels. Actually they were only Louis heels, about an inch high. Betty proudly showed the shoes to Mamzelle. "Humph!" said the governess, and she flounced right off to Marguerite.

"I do not approve of zee high, high heels," she said. "Mees Tyson, I do not like to interfere, but if Bettee ees going to wear heels like zat at her age, I will have to leave." But she didn't.

Mamzelle chaperoned Betty every place. Until she was fifteen, Betty never had a date and her only association with boys was with the friends of her brothers. And they usually ignored her except when they all played tennis or went swimming. There she kept up with them, and they treated her like another boy. Betty was mortified to have Mamzelle always with her, and sometimes worked off her feelings by introducing her to strangers as "My third cousin from Brittany with red hair who is visiting us."

In 1941, when Betty was fifteen, I started plotting to help her escape from the clutches of Mamzelle. Betty was going to school in Boston, and Billy, then fourteen, was attending Culver Military Academy in Indiana. When I found out that Culver had a big dance scheduled during Betty's Easter vacation, I suggested to Marguerite that it might be nice for me to take Betty there for the weekend—without Mamzelle. Marguerite agreed, and I phoned Billy and told him to get Betty a date. I specified that he be the most handsome upperclassman in the school. Billy's principal delight at that time was eating, so I bribed him a little by promising to bring him a huge homemade chocolate cake.

On the way from Boston to Culver, I personally carried the cake aboard the train and guarded it like a box of jewels. Betty and I spent most of our time on the train looking through the Culver yearbook, picking out the best-looking boys and wondering which one Billy had secured. With hundreds of boys to choose from, we had high expectations.

Billy was at the station to meet us, and a grin spread from ear to ear when I gave him the cake.

"Now, tell us about the date you have for Betty," I said. Billy tried to change the subject, but I persisted. He admitted it had been very difficult to get a blind date, but that he finally had gotten a nice young man for Betty, and the date would pick her up at the inn just before the dance. That was all we could get out of him. Billy was still at the age where dances were a bore, as were girls. The only important things were football and chocolate cakes.

Betty and I ate dinner alone at the inn, and she felt a little left out because the other girls all had their dates with them. After dinner, I decided that Betty should wear something unusual—something to catch the eyes of all the boys. I considered having her hold flowers, but discarded that because then her dancing partners couldn't get close to her. Suddenly I had an idea. Her formal was of a lovely soft blue and black velvet, and I saw that the hem had a lot of extra material. I got out my sewing kit and made her two thin velvet wristbands with little bows on them, with snaps to hold them on her wrists. She really looked lovely.

Just before eight, we went down to the lobby. Billy soon showed up with a scrawny, shy, fourteen-year-old freshman who probably had never before had a date and who was so scared he could hardly say hello. Betty's face dropped and she had a hard time not crying. Billy of course dashed off just as soon as the introductions were made.

Betty managed to hide her feelings, and we started off for the gymnasium where the dance was to be held. Betty's date was much too young to drive, so we had to walk the three blocks. It was a cold windy night. Betty and I started walking faster and faster. The date kept dropping back farther and farther. When we arrived at the gym, the boy was nowhere in sight. A few minutes later we received a message that he had suddenly gotten sick to his stomach. Later, I felt sorry for the poor little boy, he was just so scared. At the moment I had no time for sympathy—I was too mad at Billy.

In the gym I got out my opera glasses (I had brought them because I didn't want to miss any of the action) and spotted Billy dancing in the distance.

"Billy Tyson—come here at once!" I hollered in my best cattle-woman's voice. Everyone heard it, of course, and Billy turned several shades of red. But I was mad clean through. I told the rapscallion it was now up to him to take care of his sister. If he failed to, I said I would tell his commanding officer a thing or two about his behavior. The threat worked. Billy started dancing with his sister, although holding her at arms' length and looking quite pained. When the music stopped, he made some excuse and dashed off, leaving Betty alone on the floor, near the end of the stag line.

Betty proved equal to the occasion. She noticed a nice-looking upperclassman nearby and started talking to him about how wonderful Culver was. When the music started up, he asked her to dance. And in a few minutes, boys were cutting in and the young man she had picked up began cutting back in to establish "his" date. Betty had a wonderful time. And to make things better, the snaps holding the wristbands kept coming undone, and the boys would gallantly help Betty snap them back on. She had turned a youthful moment of despair into triumph.

The next day I went over to see Billy's room just before he was to have a "G.I." inspection. I decided to make my own inspection first, and found several things dusty, including the radiator and the top of his dresser. Before Billy had a chance to clean them, the inspecting officer entered the room. I didn't want to see Billy get any more demerits (he already was close to the limit), so I started asking questions of the officer to divert his attention. At first I stood in front of the dresser, then I moved over to hide the radiator, all the while making the officer answer so many questions he could hardly catch his breath. The strategy worked: he left without noticing the dust.

I need not have worried about Billy, however. When he graduated from Culver, it was with honors. He was captain of his football team, second in command of the entire school, captain of his squadron, and he won the Chicago *Tribune* medal for best infantry candidate.

At the ranch during the summer of 1941, I had another opportunity to help Betty escape from the perpetual childhood in which Mamzelle would have kept her. Betty had a violent crush on nineteen-year-old Angier Newcomb, one of Bob's Boston friends who had come out for the summer to help on the ranch. Of course Angier hardly knew Betty was alive. He had been around her for years and to him she was just Bob Tyson's kid sister. I persuaded Marguerite—over Mamzelle's violent objections—to let Betty wear lipstick for the first time, but even a heavy application of "Purple Passion," with matching fingernails, failed to arouse Angier's attention.

One day George Tyson decided that all the children should see the Grand Canyon. At Betty's insistence, I went along. Mamzelle also went. When we got to the canyon, George was disgusted because Betty was reading movie magazines, Billy was buried in paperback Westerns, and Bob and Angier were gawking at girls. None of the children seemed to notice the magnificent scenery. Just before dinner, Betty came to me to ask my help in getting Angier to pay her some attention. I began to dream up a plan.

At dinner, when George started grumbling about no one caring for the Grand Canyon, Betty suddenly became interested, hung on his every word, and started asking questions about what was at the bottom. Then she said to Angier, "Doesn't it sound wonderful? And the only way to see it is to take the burro ride down. Wouldn't that be fun?" Betty said this loud enough for George to hear, but Mamzelle, sitting beside him, also heard and immediately divined that something was in the wind.

"Monsieur Tyson," she said, "Bettee has nevaire been interested for anything like zees. I am suspeechous."

George was astounded. "Why, I think it is perfectly natural for a young girl to want to go down into the canyon to see at close hand one of the seven natural wonders of the world," he replied.

Betty and I had carefully rehearsed our table conversation, and it worked like a charm. I chimed in that I would also like to make the burro trip. George remarked that maybe the visit was going to be worth while because at least two of us were interested in seeing the canyon. Mamzelle got madder and madder.

"Donkee treep, nozzing. Bettee just wants to be alone weez zee boy," she muttered to George.

I ignored Mamzelle and turned to Angier. "If you would like to come along too, I will pay for it. I hear it is the most exciting trip in the West."

After dinner Mamzelle came to me. "I am een charge of Bettee," she said, her eyes blazing. "What do you know about raising children? You have nevaire had any."

"Well, you never did either!" I retorted.

I knew that Marguerite would not want Betty going down into the canyon without one of us grownups along, which was the reason I volunteered. I thought there wouldn't be much to a burro ride, even if it did last all day. After all, if I could encourage a romance, a little discomfort would not matter. I phoned Marguerite that evening and readily got her approval for the trip, omitting reference to Betty's crush on Angier, and Mamzelle's opposition.

When Mamzelle found out about this, she exploded. She had never left Betty, even on a vacation. "I know wot you are tryeeng to do. But if Bettee goes on zee treep, I weel quit."

"Betty is going on zee trip," I said grimly.

Mamzelle turned on her heel and an hour later disappeared on the bus for Prescott.

Betty and Angier and I got up early in the morning and went to rendezvous with our burros. I had spent a small fortune the night before on riding pants, shoes, and a big wide hat, so I could ride in comfort. In my mind it was all arranged. Angier would ride just behind Betty so he could watch her all the way down and all the way back. I had coached Betty to play helpless, assuring her this would bring out the protective instinct in Angier. For myself, I had decided to ride far back in the line, leaving Angier as much as possible alone with Betty.

Well, just as I was saying to Angier, "You ride behind Betty and keep a careful eye on her," the guide, a leathery, cantankerous old mule skinner from Arkansas, came along and upset everything. He singled out Betty and placed her on the second burro, right behind a twelve-year-old boy, and then directed me to take the next one. He wanted the two children directly behind him, he said, so they would be perfectly safe. He assigned Angier a burro at the end of the line, right behind a beautiful blonde of college age.

I almost got into a fight with the guide trying to trade places with Angier, but to no avail. As it was, the guide probably would have thrown me off the trip if Betty hadn't intervened. She realized that if I didn't go, she couldn't go either.

George was at the rim to see us leave, and he, at least, was happy. I was so mad that I almost forgot to be scared when my burro leaned over the side of the trail to munch some flowers and I looked out over his head at endless space. I could see Betty, just ahead of me. She was in tears. When we got to the first stop and dismounted, we looked back. Angier and the blonde were laughing and talking, so we didn't even bother to go back to see him. At the bottom of the canyon, where we dismounted in a group to eat our box lunches, neither Angier nor the blonde were to be seen. Our guide was not concerned about their absence. "Courtin', I reckon," was his only comment.

On the way back, I began to pay the price. It had been a long time since I had done any serious riding, and the wear and tear on my *derrière* was severe. By the end of the day my interest in nature, burros, and even in matchmaking had worn thin.

Angier and the blonde disappeared again after supper. Betty took solace in her movie magazines and I went to bed. George was somewhat bewildered by the sudden cooling of our ardor for the wonders of the Grand Canyon.

When we got back to the ranch, Marguerite was out for my scalp: Mamzelle had been through to pick up her things and had given a scurrilous report about my evil influence on her daughter. But even though one battle plan had failed, I wasn't ready to quit trying to help Betty.

We made our first breakthrough with Angier a few weeks later. I went on a shopping trip to Phoenix and took Betty and Angier with me. When we arrived, I had what seemed to be, but definitely was not, a sudden inspiration. "Let's have a swim at the Biltmore," I said. Of course, this meant I had to buy Betty a swimming suit. Betty had a marvelous figure and though her mother would not have approved, I saw to it that she selected a two-piece suit.

This time Auntie Perle's scheme worked—even though Marguerite never allowed Betty to wear that suit again. Suddenly Angier began to notice Betty, and by the end of the summer a romance was in full swing. When Mamzelle got over her pique and returned to work, it was too late. I had achieved my aim of cutting Betty loose and getting her out of the dependent child stage.

NINE: *Of Parties and Politics*

ALTHOUGH ARIZONA BECAME my legal residence, I never learned to enjoy ranch life in uninterrupted stretches. I knew that raising cattle was helping the war effort, but I wanted to be doing more. My opportunity came in 1942. I was in New York on a visit when Milton Shubert telephoned to ask if I had some free time I could devote to a worthy cause. It appeared that some good workers were needed for the Washington Stage Door Canteen; Mrs. Roosevelt had suggested that I might be able to help. I went to Washington the next day and introduced myself to Mrs. Lawrence Langner, who was in charge of the project. The old Belasco Theater on Lafayette Square had just been converted into a canteen, but there was already a shortage of operating capital. Armina Langner didn't want to ask for help from the New York headquarters. She thought the Washington Canteen should be supported by the people of Washington.

"Of course it should," I told Armina. "We can raise our own money here." I enlisted several of my friends and we started soliciting everybody we knew. We went around selling what we called Angel Tables. For a hundred dollars anyone could sponsor a table at the canteen, and practically everyone we asked was anxious to help. I stayed in Washington for several months and I was at the canteen almost every day. I helped organize the volunteer workers. I rolled up my sleeves and made salads and sandwiches to serve the boys. We took care of as many as twenty-five hundred G.I.'s a day. This was a different kind of party-giving for me, because I was part of a team of hostesses whose problem was to keep a party atmosphere going continuously.

Many of the boys I met were lonely and scared. During the first World War the soldiers I met had seemed quite dashing and glamorous. But now I was struck deeply with the youth of the soldiers.

93

I went down to the Canteen on Christmas Day in 1942 and found a youngster sitting off by himself and looking lost. I sat down with him and we talked. He told me that his two older brothers had already gone overseas and one of them had not been heard from for many months. Now he was going. The boy started to cry as he talked about his home and his folks and Christmas. I tried to comfort him as best I could. But there are times when words are empty.

Evalyn Walsh McLean was one of our "angels" and one evening in 1943 she went down to the Canteen with me, wearing her famous Hope diamond. The G.I.'s gathered around her and she slipped the fabulous jewel off her neck and gave it to the boys to hold and pass around. She seemed almost to regard it as a trinket.

I had never known Evalyn McLean very well until the war years. Instead of giving the lavish parties for which she was famous, Evalyn entertained almost exclusively for wounded veterans. To these parties at her beautiful Georgetown home, Friendship, she invited just a few outside guests—only the people she knew would be kind and understanding with the service men, some of them returned from the fighting with amputated legs or disfigured faces. I felt it a privilege to be included at some of these parties.

The experiences I had talking with the G.I.'s at the Stage Door Canteen and helping entertain them at Evalyn McLean's parties turned out to be invaluable to me. Somehow during my sheltered marriage to George Mesta and in the social whirl that followed at Newport, in Europe, and in New York, I had lost touch with the real people of our country. I had been wandering for most of my life without much purpose. Now I was inspired to do something more than just have a good time and give parties for fun.

The Equal Rights for Women movement gave me one constructive outlet for this new-found desire to accomplish something in life. One of the men I met in 1942 while lobbying for the National Woman's Party was soon to play an important part in my life—Harry S. Truman. Senator Truman was sympathetic to our cause and in 1943, by means of a letter, he helped us get the support of the National Federation of Women's Clubs. I began attending sessions of Congress to learn more about our government, and I closely followed the work of Senator Truman's War Investigating Committee.

In June, 1943, I was visiting in Oklahoma City when Senator

Truman came to town for a big Democratic rally at the Skirvin Tower. I gave a reception for him at the Skirvin Hotel. Gladys Tillet, then Chairman of the Women's Division of the Democratic National Committee, was in town for the rally, and I asked her to stand in the receiving line with me and Senator Truman, Oklahoma's senior senator, Elmer Thomas, and Robert Kerr, then Governor of Oklahoma. I invited all the prominent local Democrats plus about twenty-five of the city's Republican leaders, and several newspaper people, including my good friend Margaret Harrison. Most of the prominent Republicans failed to show up. They told me later they were so mad at Roosevelt they wouldn't have anything to do with a party for any Democrat.

The dinner given during the Democratic rally drew the largest number of people that had ever gathered in Oklahoma for a hotel banquet. Nearly twenty-five hundred people sat at the tables in the Silver Glade Room of the Skirvin Tower. The manager of the hotel, Henry Dickson, performed like a magician in producing an excellent meal despite the severe food rationing. He had saved ration stamps for more than a month for the event, but was able to produce the whole dinner using only five hundred ration points. Of course we had to have fowl instead of beef: we consumed fifteen hundred chickens.

Senator Truman gave the principal speech. As I sat there listening to him, I was impressed by his ability to be at one with the average man. He didn't use a lot of high-sounding words but just spoke frankly and earnestly about how the Democratic party should devote its thoughts and actions to the speedy winning of the war and the consummation of a lasting peace. Those of us at the head table also had an opportunity to see just how natural Harry Truman was in his manner when he went and got his own plate of chicken after the waitress somehow had skipped him.

In March, 1944, Father was critically injured in an automobile accident in Oklahoma City. Marguerite and I joined William at Father's bedside as quickly as we could. Although the doctors were quite worried about his chances for survival—he was then eighty-four—Father was confident he would recover. About the third day after the accident we were all in the room when Father announced, "When I get out of this damn-fool place, I'm going to head straight for Arizona and get into the cattle business." Marguerite told him there was a beautiful ranch for sale adjoining hers on the Hassa-yampa River, and Father's face brightened as he asked William about the geology of the ranch country. Father was always on the lookout for oil. Every place he went, he would pick up a rock, scratch it with his knife, and then sniff, hoping for some indication of another Spindletop.

Father's condition did not improve, despite his own optimistic outlook. He would rally one day and then take a turn for the worse. About a week after the accident, William and Marguerite and I were all in his room. Father's usual vigor had almost entirely vanished. I took his hand in mine.

"Father," I began, "I'm more sorry that I can ever tell you that I have given you so many heartaches and caused you all that trouble with—" I never got to finish.

Father perked right up. "Why, I've forgiven you. There's nothing but love in my heart for all three of you children; you're all I have."

Marguerite was crying and so was I. She stooped over and kissed him and William patted his cheek. Father looked up at William. "Son," he said, "always look after your sisters; they need someone like you."

"Of course I will," said William, "but, Dad, you'll be here with us and I'll look after you, too."

We remained with him almost constantly. Three days later he just slept away peacefully and quietly and that was the end of a great father.

Father had always said he wanted his favorite minister, William H. Alexander, to officiate at his funeral. Father had never taken an active interest in organized religion, but he sometimes went to the First Christian Church to hear "Reverend Bill" preach. The Reverend had been in show business years before and Father enjoyed the dramatic way in which he presented religion. Also, the minister would drop in to Father's office occasionally and say a little prayer for the hotels and for good business, which stimulated Father's donations to his church. William Alexander was—and still is—one of the most popular preachers in Oklahoma City.

When we went to see him about conducting the services for Father, we discovered that he, too, had been in an accident. Though he was propped up in bed with an injured leg, he insisted that he wouldn't miss Bill Skirvin's funeral for anything in the world. And sure enough, on the day of the funeral, Reverend Bill was helped out of his car. Painfully he made his way on crutches to the platform of the chapel. More than three hundred of Father's good friends, including almost a hundred colored people, had come to pay him last respects, and Reverend Bill gave a wonderful eulogy. He said that Oklahoma had lost one of her most beloved citizens. "There isn't a man in Oklahoma who can walk past the Skirvin Hotels without recalling the great-hearted man who built them," said William Alexander. "His humor and indomitable spirit were with him to the end." And then the minister told a story about Father that he had heard from a nurse at the hospital. It seems that a few days after the accident, Father had asked a nurse to give him a shave.

"We'll have to see about that, Mr. Skirvin," she had answered. "You're a very sick man."

"I'm never too sick to get slicked up when there's a pretty young lady like you around," countered Father, and then added, "By the way, what are you doing tonight?"

As Reverend Bill told the story, many of the people in the chapel nodded their heads. Yes, indeed, this was their old friend Bill Skirvin speaking—himself to the end.

With the 1944 party conventions coming up, I became active in Arizona politics and was named an alternate delegate to the Democratic convention in Chicago. I still had a good many Republican friends, so I decided to go to Chicago early and watch the Republican convention just for fun. I went with another interested Democrat, Bess Farley. (Jim, her husband, was on a trip to Mexico.) We had dinner one evening with a woman newspaper columnist and Bess happened to mention in passing that she would like to see Dewey get the nomination. As it appeared in the paper, Bess Farley seemed to be backing Dewey for President. This was embarrassing to Jim, who, while he had split with Roosevelt over the third-term issue, was still a very prominent Democrat. Jim has always blamed me for getting his wife into this situation. But then, some of my Republican friends blamed Bess and Jim Farley for my switch to the Democrats. You can't hope to please everyone.

In 1944, I did not actively work for Roosevelt because I was not in favor of a fourth term—or even a third term for that matter.

Of course, he really didn't need my help. I was also opposed to Henry Wallace succeeding himself as Vice-President, and I was delighted when my man for the job, Harry Truman, was selected by the President and nominated.

Most of my time at the Democratic convention was spent working for the National Woman's Party. I was appointed Arizona representative to the Platform and Resolutions Committee and tried to get the committee to endorse our proposed Constitutional amendment. There was heavy opposition to this plank, however. Eleanor Roosevelt had written a letter opposing it, several leaders of organized labor fought it, and Secretary of Labor Frances Perkins flew to Chicago to speak against it. Mrs. Roosevelt and Miss Perkins were against our amendment because they were afraid it would nullify some of the protective legislation already enacted for women.

Emma Guffey Miller, Democratic Committeewoman for Pennsylvania, led the Equal Rights for Women forces through several rough and tumble Platform Committee sessions. Despite the opposition, we stood firm. When it came time to vote, two-thirds of the committee stood up to approve our amendment plank, and the next day it became an official part of the 1944 Democratic platform. The National Woman's Party considered this a great victory and I was pleased to have had a part in pushing it through. Both parties had now endorsed the amendment in their platforms; they have continued to do so at every subsequent convention.

Soon after returning to Washington early in 1945 I called Mrs. Truman and asked her if I could give a party in honor of the Vice-President. She checked with Harry and called back to say they would be delighted.

I decided to hold the party at the Sulgrave Club, where I was then living. The club manager, Miss Jane Anderson, said she could seat only seventy-five comfortably, but I talked her into finding a way to take care of ninety. Since this still didn't include all the friends I wanted to invite, I asked the rest to come in after dinner. I was helped in getting ready for this party by Ethel Tyson, the lovely girl from Prescott, Arizona, whom my nephew Bob had married in 1943. Bob was then in the Army and Ethel was staying with me.

The party was held on March 8 and the Sulgrave Club was beautifully decorated with bright spring flowers. Tulips bordered the staircase to the second floor. The Vice-President and Mrs. Truman stood beside me at the top of the staircase to welcome the guests. One of the first to arrive was Speaker of the House Sam Rayburn. And as though to prove this wasn't to be exclusively a Democratic affair, House Minority Leader Joe Martin came up the stairs right behind Sam. Mr. Truman chatted and joked with all of the guests as they arrived. I had invited quite a few of his Senate colleagues and their wives: the Owen Brewsters, the Claude Peppers, the Homer Fergusons, the Pat McCarrans, the Chapman Revercombs, the Alexander Wileys, and the bachelor Senators Arthur Capper and Theodore Green. Senator Joseph Guffey was there with his sister Pauletta; Senator Albert "Happy" Chandler came alone. Supreme Court Justice and Mrs. William O. Douglas were there, as was Secretary of Agriculture Claude Wickard and Mrs. Wickard, Assistant Secretary of State William Clayton and Mrs. Clayton, Ambassador and Mrs. Patrick J. Hurley (just back from China), Netherlands Ambassador and Madame Loudon, Mrs. Woodrow Wilson, Rosa Ponselle, airplane builder Glenn Martin, Representative and Mrs. Mike Monroney and Representative and Mrs. Christian Herter.

Margaret Truman, then attending George Washington University, was greeted by her parents with mock formality as she went through the receiving line. I also had invited several of Margaret's young friends. And from the Armed Services there were Rear Admiral and Mrs. Clark Woodward, Admiral and Mrs. Edward Kalbfus, Admiral William Standley, Major General and Mrs. Leroy Lutes, Major General James Ulio, and White House Senior Aide Colonel Don Lowry.

Among my other guests were former Senator Henry Ashurst, former Senator James J. Davis with his daughter Jane, Ethel Tyson, Dr. Anthony Sindoni of Philadelphia, Mr. and Mrs. Leslie Biffle, Mrs. Robert Low Bacon, Mrs. Raymond Clapper, Mrs. Igor Cassini, Mrs. George Holmes, Ford Frick, Fred Roy, Roger Firestone, Miss Carolyn Nash, Misses Emily and Nannie Chase, Cornelius Moore, George Williams, Mr. and Mrs. Frederick H. Brooke, and Mrs. Gurnee Dyer.

I held my breath a little when Mr. and Mrs. Louis Bromfield arrived with columnist George Dixon. The Bromfields and I had been long-time friends, but he had recently become rabidly con-

99

servative and anti-Democrat, and I wasn't quite sure what he might say to Mr. Truman. And as for George Dixon, you never can be sure what he will say or write. I greeted the three with enthusiasm —"Oh, so nice to see you"—and then while still smiling, I added under my breath to the men, "One false move out of either of you and you'll be thrown out."

Everyone seemed to be in a gay mood at dinner. I remember someone mentioning to Margaret Truman that Senator Ashurst could name the entire roster of Vice-Presidents. And Margaret, who was sitting next to the former senator, said impishly, "I didn't think there was any man in the United States silly enough to fill his head with such useless information."

Among the toasts offered after dinner was one by Admiral Standley to the Marines—then fighting so valiantly in the South Pacific. And as the toast was drunk, Pat Hurley voiced his approval with one of his famous Oklahoma Indian war whoops.

Louis Bromfield poked a little fun by saying, "You know, the Vice-President doesn't *have* to come to parties like this. The Constitution says he only has to preside over the Senate and cast a vote in case of a tie." And then writer-farmer Bromfield complained that there were too many city slickers in Washington.

"I am an honest farmer," said Louis. "Or, anyway, a farmer. I just told a fellow I met here that he ought to quit this life and get back to the land. But he says he can't because he is Secretary of Agriculture."

After dinner, the gay atmosphere continued. While the tables were being cleared, we went into the hall and small rooms and Sidney and his orchestra played for us. Then we went back into the large room for talk and entertainment. I had hired New York ventriloquist Al Robinson, whose dummy, Alkali Ike, now proceeded to make mild fun of the V.I.P.'s. But the best entertainment came from two of the guests. Rosa Ponselle sang a few arias and then persuaded the Vice-President to accompany her as she perched on top of the piano and did an impersonation of torch singer Helen Morgan. Egged on by the guests, Mr. Truman followed with a solo performance of Paderewski's "Minuet."

While the Vice-President was playing, one of my government guests who knew of President Roosevelt's deteriorating physical condition, whispered to me: "Harry had better have his fun now.

He may be President before long." A little more than a month later, Mr. Roosevelt was dead and Harry S. Truman was President.

Shortly after Mr. Roosevelt's death, while the new President was still in Blair House, I was invited to have lunch with the Trumans. Margaret was present, as was Lewis Schwellenbach, who was soon to be named Secretary of Labor. As I sat there, it didn't seem possible that I was the luncheon guest of the President of the United States. Mr. Truman was just as natural and at ease as he had been a few weeks before at my party. But sitting there listening to him discuss labor problems with Mr. Schwellenbach, I couldn't help but think back twenty years to the last time I had dined informally with a President of the United States, Calvin Coolidge. I had been to the White House then as Mrs. George Mesta, the wife of a heavy contributor to President Coolidge's successful campaign. But this time I had gotten here on my own as just plain Perle Mesta, who had happened to strike up a friendship with a senator from Missouri and his wife.

In April, I went out to San Francisco for the organizational meetings of the United Nations, where I did some lobbying for the National Woman's Party. It was a great thrill to be sitting in the galleries on June 26, when the newly adopted charter was read aloud with its preamble statement of the intention of all the nations ". . . to reaffirm faith in fundamental human rights, in the dignity and worth of the human person, in the equal rights of men and women and of nations large and small." My organization, together with other women's groups, had succeeded in getting into the charter of the world organization a fundamental declaration that we still have not been able to get into the Constitution of the United States.

When I returned to Washington from San Francisco, I recalled how the parties of Mrs. Henderson and of Evalyn McLean had been useful politically, and I decided that the way I was best equipped to serve the Democratic Administration was by bringing important people together. The Democrats I knew in Washington were by and large a high-spirited group who enjoyed parties. By the end of the summer the war was over and Washington society was beginning to perk up, so I started looking for a house large enough for entertaining. One of the possibilities was the former home of the Herbert Hoovers at 2300 S Street. I had visited in it several times while Mr. Hoover was Secretary of Commerce.

It was a Georgian Colonial brick house and sat on a hill quite near the street, with spacious grounds to the rear. There was a large entrance hall, music room, a library, a good-sized drawing room, and a spacious dining room. When I inspected it, the house was nicely furnished with antique pieces, including lovely old rugs and Meissen ware. The house was the nearest thing I had seen to what I needed, and it was centrally located: I took a lease, moved in, and immediately prepared to step up my entertaining.

"You were one of the few Democrats who had a big house and enough money to give parties," Mr. Truman told me recently when we were reminiscing about those days. "Democrats who have that much money usually become Republicans," he added with a grin.

The fall social season had not quite started when our family had a tragic blow. Our beloved Bob Tyson became suddenly ill and passed away in the Army hospital in Louisville, Kentucky.

I had gone up to Newport after opening the S Street house, and was there when the sad news came. All the joy and anticipation of the coming season was gone, and instead of returning to Washington, I stayed on in Newport with Marguerite and George. I had bought a new home there, Midcliff, and the activity of decorating it helped Marguerite to take her mind off her sorrow. After a few weeks, Marguerite insisted that I return to Washington, promising me that she and George would join me there for Christmas.

When I started to feel like entertaining again, Garner and Edna Camper came down from Newport to take charge of the house. The Campers are practically members of our family. Edna provides those little touches like arranging flowers throughout the house and keeping things in perfect order. And she is a wizard with scissors and a needle. If it came to an emergency, Edna could take a bolt of satin and turn out a beautiful ball gown in a few hours. Garner comes in like a steam roller, hires the extra help, buys the supplies, and organizes the household down to the smallest details. And although he has sometimes been called bossy, he has such a likable manner that nobody takes offense.

Garner has a marvelous faculty of never forgetting a name. He also remembers exactly the kind of drink each guest prefers. And nothing pleases guests more than the kind of attention Garner gives them. When he talks to Democrats, Garner is a Democrat; when he talks to Republicans, he is a Republican. What a born diplomat!

I missed having young people around my house, so early in 1946 I asked Mrs. Truman if I could give a dance for Margaret. A number of small affairs had been given for Margaret since her father had become President, but I wanted to give her a real bang-up party. Given the go-ahead sign, I invited the most eligible and handsome young men in Washington, Philadelphia, New York, and Boston, plus all the White House military aides and a dozen eligible bachelor officers from the nearby Marine base. As it turned out, there were three men to every girl. No wallflower problem that night! I engaged Emil Coleman's dance band even though I had to fly them in from California because of their crowded schedule. I also hired the Hit Parade radio star, Joan Edwards, to sing. And I called Dean's in New York and ordered a beautiful pink and green cake with Margaret's name inscribed on the top. Betty was flying down from New York for the party and I entrusted her with the mission of convoying the cake. Poor Betty! The cake was about two feet in diameter and a foot high. In its box, it was quite a bundle. Betty had to turn on all her abundant charm just to be allowed to take the thing into the passenger compartment. And when she finally got settled in her seat with the box on her lap, she couldn't budge for the whole trip. My cake and my niece both arrived in good condition, however.

Before the dance I had a dinner party at the Sulgrave Club for some of Margaret's young friends. I also invited Rosa Ponselle because I knew how much Margaret admired her, singer to singer. I shall never forget Rosa's performance at the dinner table. Rosa, who is always very dramatic about everything, announced as we began our soup that she was on a very strict diet and couldn't touch a thing. As the meat and vegetables were served, Rosa looked longingly, but declined to accept any, all the while munching mournfully on a piece of melba toast. When the salad was served, we all said that surely couldn't hurt her.

"No, no!" said Rosa, and gave us all a lecture on the caloric content of French dressing.

Then the dessert was served—a luscious chocolate mousse, piled with whipped cream and topped with grated bittersweet chocolate.

"Ohhhh," she sighed, "that looks so good!"

"Go on and have a bite, Rosa," I teased. "A little old *bite* isn't going to hurt you."

"Well. . . ." She deliberated a suspenseful moment. "All right, just a little." The butler offered the serving dish and Rosa's "just a little" filled her plate. After she had eaten that with great gusto, she said, "Maybe I'll have a little of that salad," and proceeded to do so. And before we left the table, she had worked her way backward through the entire meal!

The dance was the first big party in my new home. Margaret and Betty and I were in a receiving line when the party started at ten-thirty, but before very long, the two girls had been whisked away by the young men. Margaret was a real belle of the ball and danced every dance. There were a few surprised looks when she showed us she could do a mean samba. But that night I don't believe Margaret thought of herself as the President's daughter. She was just a lovely young girl having a good time. And she whirled around the dance floor until the party ended at 2:30 A.M. When she left she threw her arms around me and kissed me, saying, "Oh, Perle, it was the most wonderful evening I've had in my life."

This was about the only one of my Washington parties at which there was no political discussion. At all the rest, during the Truman Administration, the senators, Cabinet members, government officials, White House staff members, or ambassadors would gather in little groups to discuss issues of the day. Or sometimes a few of them would go off into a side room to hold more lengthy private conversations. I would make up my guest lists with an eye to the national or international topics most important at the time of each party. Occasionally I would be given suggestions by Administration staff members as to guests they would like to see invited.

One day in 1946 I had a call from Democratic National Committee chairman Bob Hannegan asking if I could do a small favor for the Administration. It seemed that an important delegation of Chinese industrialists was to be in town for another forty-eight hours on a delicate mission, and Hannegan thought that relations might be improved if a reception could be given for them. It was short notice but I did all I could, arranging a tea for the next afternoon, inviting some Washington socialites, some Administration wives, and various government officials. I overheard one of the society women whispering, "Why is Perle giving this party for these Chinese?" And I just let her and her friends wonder. I think the visitors from the Far East left my house with more of a feeling of being accepted by Washington. Some years later, when one of the members of that delegation was back in the United States, he told me that my party had been the turning point in their negotiations. He said that the next day they had worked out details for some U.S. Government credits for Chinese industry which they had been unsuccessfully trying to arrange for several weeks.

It is impossible to determine precisely how much is actually accomplished at Washington social gatherings. Much of the benefit may be indirect. Sometimes friendships made at parties turn out to be helpful years later. And sometimes people attribute more weight to party conversations than is deserved.

At one of my luncheons during the Truman administration, Roberta Vinson, whose husband Fred was then Chief Justice, sat between Bess Truman and Nell Donaldson, the wife of the Post-master General. Roberta told me that Mrs. Donaldson whispered to her, "Who would you like to see become the new postmaster of the District of Columbia?" Roberta said, "Oh, I'd like Roy North to get it; he's a neighbor of mine." Mrs. Donaldson said, "I'd like that too," and then added jokingly, "Tell Bess Truman and maybe she'll tell the President."

About that time Bess asked, "What are you girls whispering about?" So Roberta told her and added, "Tell your husband we think Roy would make the best postmaster he could get for Washington." A few days later North was appointed to the job. I'm sure this was strictly a coincidence, but if that conversation had been overheard, it might have been considered skulduggery in high places.

Roberta Vinson is of great help to a hostess. She is gay and bubbly and witty and I don't think any party can ever sag as long as Roberta is around. Like I am, she is always outspoken and frank —and we sometimes have fierce disagreements. One of the best stories about Roberta's frankness concerns a trip she and her husband made to Chicago with the President soon after he had taken office. I think it was for an Army Day celebration. Roberta, who rarely drinks, saw the others aboard the train having old fashioneds and decided to try one. She was sitting beside the President, and after a few sips, she proceeded to tell him what she thought was wrong about the Administration's program.

A few weeks later the Vinsons were invited by the Trumans to

105

attend a Washington concert. Afterward they went along to the White House. The President and Mr. Vinson were having a drink. Mr. Truman asked Mrs. Vinson what she would have.

"Nothing, thank you," replied Roberta.

"Oh, have just one small one," suggested the President.

"I'd better not," said Roberta meekly. "Remember what happened the last time I had a drink with you. I told you what was wrong with your program."

The President laughed. "Well then, have two this time, and maybe you can tell me what we can do about it."

I sometimes used my parties to try to forward a project or issue in which I was interested. During 1946 and 1947 I was a great advocate of universal military training, and I knew that General Eisenhower, then Army Chief of Staff, favored it too. At a party I gave for Ike and Mamie in 1947 I purposely brought up the subject at the dinner table. I had an admiral there, the Secretary of the Army, and several senators, and saw this as an ideal opportunity for a fruitful discussion among top authorities. And so it proved to be. It was also at this party that Ike delighted us all with his memorable singing of "Abdul Abulbul Amir."

Early in 1947, I screwed up my courage and decided to ask Mrs. Truman if she and the President would like to come to a party. I knew that since the days of Evalyn McLean's parties for Warren Harding, no President had attended a social gathering at a private home, except one belonging to a Cabinet member, the Vice-President, or a member of his own family. But I also knew that Mr. Truman liked fun as much as anyone, and I saw no reason why he should be left out of parties just because of the precedent set by his predecessors. So I called Mrs. Truman and asked if she and the President could come to dinner. She said, "I'll check and let you know." In a few minutes she called back and said the President would be most pleased to accept, and she gave me a date in April.

Several days before the party, I had a visit from the Secret Service. They interviewed each of the servants, inspected every nook and cranny of the house for places where people might hide, charted all the doors and windows, and even looked over the surrounding neighborhood for areas from which someone might be able to take a shot at the President.

106

The day before the party, Mrs. Truman called to say that Harry wanted to know if he had to wear his white tie and tails. I knew he would rather not, but I had advised the other guests it was "white tie." I debated for a moment whether to change this and notify the men, torn between the President's desire for comfort and the custom that male guests wear full dress suits at a social event attended by the President. We finally decided that out of respect for the office of the President, the men, including Harry S. Truman, would just have to wear white tie and tails.

George and Marguerite and their son's widow, Ethel, were all staying with me then. I wish Betty could have been there to help too, but she had been married the previous summer to John M. R. Lyeth, Jr., of Grosse Point, and was home in Michigan expecting a baby. Long before the day of the dinner, I had sworn my family and all the help to secrecy because I didn't want it to leak out to the press that the President was coming to a private home. My invitations had not specified a guest of honor but had indicated "dinner at seven forty-five"—fifteen minutes ahead of the usual time. It is the custom when entertaining heads of states to have the other guests assembled before the honor guest arrives. By seven forty-five, all my guests had duly arrived and were chatting expectantly in the drawing room. Marguerite and George and I took up a position by the front door. The Secret Service had set up a two-way radio right by the entry hall, and I could hear the men talking from their vantage points along the route. "Just passed Connecticut and K . . . in one minute should be at Massachusetts and Florida." It was so exciting! And right on the nose of eight, the White House limousine pulled up at 2300 S Street.

Garner opened the door, grinning broadly. He was just bursting with pride, and it had been one of the hardest things he had ever faced, not to be able to tell everyone he knew in Washington that "we" (he always included Marguerite and me, of course) were going to entertain for the President of the United States. Garner was so excited about the occasion that he had gotten into a row with the butler in charge of serving the drinks: he wanted to be both on the door and also serve the President his cocktail. Although Garner should have done only one or the other, he felt so strongly about it that I decided to overrule the other butler and let Garner have his heart's desire.

Marguerite and George and I met the President and Mrs. Truman at the door. George tells a story on me that when the President complimented me on my dress, I replied, "Thank you very much—it's only the best I have." Then we escorted the President and Mrs. Truman into the drawing room where all the others were assembled in a semicircle. Drinks were served before we went in to dinner. Garner found out what the President wanted, and went to the service pantry to fix it. A Secret Service man watched his every move, and then kept an eye on him until he reached the President, I suppose to make sure he did not add anything to the drink. (Another Secret Service man watched my cook, Augusta France, and her assistants all during preparation and serving of the meal.)

Despite my repeated warnings to Garner not to bother the President, when he handed him the drink he said, "I've never met a real live President and I'm happy to meet one tonight."

"Oh, so you think I am alive, do you?" the President joked.

"In every way, in every way," said Garner, beaming.

My dining room, big as it was, was not large enough for all my guests, so we had set up an extra table in the library. Each man, as he came into the house had been given a little card showing his table location and the name of the lady he was to escort to dinner.

I gave everyone a few minutes to mingle and talk, and then we went in to dinner. At my right was the President, of course, and the table in the dining room was seated like this:

Perle Mesta

President Truman	Sec. of Treasury Snyder
Mrs. Vinson	Mrs. Clark
Sec. of Interior Krug	Charley Ross
Mrs. Tydings	Mrs. Bradley
Nicholas Brown	Governor Vardaman
Miss Evelyn Burden	Mrs. Lucius Boomer
Earl Stewart	General Vaughan
Mrs. Ross	Mrs. Brown
Leslie Biffle	Senator Maybank
Mrs. Maybank	Mrs. Krug
Senator Tydings	Atty. General Clark
Mrs. Snyder	Mrs. Truman

Chief Justice Vinson (my host)

The table was set with my Meissen dishes. I also had long-stemmed red roses and white carnations in large bowls on the table and some large dishes of fruit with luscious grapes hanging over the sides.

Marguerite was hostess to the table in the library, which was seated like this:

Marguerite Tyson

Clark Clifford	General Bradley
Mrs. Vardaman	Mrs. Clifford
Admiral Foskett	Lucius Boomer
Ethel Tyson	Mrs. Earl Stewart
Colonel Lowry	Beverly Bogart, Jr.
Mrs. Richard McClary	Mrs. Foskett
Cornelius Moore	Percy Blair
Mrs. Vaughan	Mrs. Biffle

George Tyson

While we were at dinner, the telephone rang in the library. Garner answered it and immediately called Marguerite to the phone. It was a reporter calling from Chicago. He wanted confirmation that the President was at our house as well as information for a story. Marguerite sent Garner to me with the message. I was very disturbed, and turned to the President to tell him that despite all my precautions, the news had somehow leaked out.

"Oh, don't worry about that, Perle," the President said, unconcerned. "When we left the White House, I told the reporters we were coming here for dinner."

After dinner, we women gathered in the music room while the men went into the drawing room for their customary smoke and liqueur. When we all got back together, I noticed the President deep in conversation with Senators Maybank and Tydings. I thought to myself: Even at a party, he can't escape from being President. He seemed to be having a good time, though, and appeared relaxed. But I could catch an aura of responsibility and seriousness that was unlike his usual easygoing nature. And I think the rest of us were all a little in awe that the President of the United States was with us. Certainly we were not as carefree as we might have been. Not that President Truman didn't join in the fun. Far from it. About ten o'clock he hiked up the tails of his

109

pesky full dress coat and sat down at the piano. The guests started calling out their requests.

"There's one piece I'm *not* going to play tonight," he announced. And we all knew he meant the "Missouri Waltz." I think he got awfully tired of hearing that every place he went. Then Mrs. Tydings sang a few numbers. Not to be outdone, Senator Tydings said he had a new song to sing us. The Senate and the President had been feuding, and the President had just vetoed one of Senator Tydings' favorite bills. When the Senator started to sing, "Why do you do me like you do, do, do . . ." he was drowned out by gales of laughter. After that, we all gathered around the piano and had a songfest.

Late that night, after all the guests had gone, Marguerite, George, Ethel, and I were sitting in the drawing room having some coffee and comparing notes about the party. Ethel made a remark that neatly summed up all our reactions:

"He was so dear and sweet that I almost forgot he was the President. He just seemed like Margaret's daddy."

TEN : *Truman's Triumph*

IN THE SUMMER of 1947 I decided to try a little experiment. I knew from experience that the staid Newporters did not approve of those who invited summer guests not listed in the *Social Register*. The aristocratic shell of Newport had been cracked during World War II when the Navy took over many of the old homes to house its men in training. There had been a concerted move after the war to restore the pomp and ceremony to some of the hallowed halls and to Bailey's Beach. But I felt that it would do some of the society people good to meet representatives of the Truman administration. They might possibly wake up to what was going on in their country politically, even if the visitors were not of the Four Hundred but were just plain folks and *Democrats*. In Newport, I had been looked upon with some disapproval since shifting my political allegiance, for of course it was taken for granted along Bellevue Avenue that everyone just had to be a Republican.

Marguerite, aided by New York decorator Ailsa Shaw-Thomson, had worked a transformation on my Newport home, Midcliff, which was right on the beach and had a magnificent view of the rugged coastline and the blue Atlantic. The reception room was in yellow, the drawing room in my favorite soft beiges with an eighteenth-century English atmosphere. The dining room, which seated twenty-four, was eighteenth-century Italian with the walls in off white with brilliant Italian yellow. One of the most delightful rooms was a good-sized loggia with slate floor laid in a pattern like an English garden maze; it was furnished in modified Chippendale off-white bamboo. The loggia opened right onto a lovely lawn, so that entertaining could be done indoors or out. Midcliff was bordered on the north by a house owned by Robert Young, the railroad man and financier. And thereby hangs a story.

111

Mr. Young's house did not have a beach, and when I bought my house, I had been informed it was customary for the owner of Midcliff to allow the Youngs and their servants to use my beach. About six-thirty one morning, soon after I had moved in, Garner went down to the beach to talk to one of Mr. Young's servants he saw in swimming (no one except servants ever got up that early at Newport). When he got to the beach, the fellow was swimming about fifty feet out, and Garner struck up a conversation.

"How is the old boy to work for?" Garner shouted. "I hear he's pretty tough on the help."

"That's just one man's opinion. He's really all right," the swimmer told Garner as he came out of the water and started drying off. Garner offered him a cigarette and they chatted for a while.

"Sometime when you're not busy, come on over and I'll show you around Mrs. Mesta's house and give you a drink," Garner said.

"Thanks," replied Garner's new friend. "I've got to go now for breakfast."

Three nights later, I gave a party and Garner was at the front door announcing people. One of the incoming guests puzzled Garner. As I have mentioned before, Garner has a perfect memory for names. He knew he had seen this man somewhere but couldn't place his name.

"Pardon me," asked Garner. "I seem to have forgotten your name."

"Robert Young," said the guest, and at that instant Garner realized this was the man he had been talking with on the beach. Mr. Young laughed. Garner, of course, wanted to fall through the floor, and he felt little better when he met Mr. Young's butler next day and heard how Mr. Young was telling everybody the joke.

The first beachhead in our Democratic "invasion" of Newport was established by the Vinsons. I had some difficulty in convincing the Chief Justice to come, and Roberta told me later it took a lot of persuasion on her part to get him to accept. The year before, when he had been Secretary of the Treasury, he had refused my invitation because he felt that with Newport's accumulation of wealth, to go there and hobnob with the Vanderbilts and the Astors would embarrass President Truman, whose entire program was for a different class.

The Vinsons arrived in July and stayed a week. Their visit was one of the most refreshing things that had happened to Newport in years. They were entertained by Mrs. Hamilton McKay Twombley; by Freddy Prince at his home, Marble Palace; we went to tea at Mrs. Vanderbilt's; and I gave a large party for them. The Chief Justice captivated everyone with his warm personality. Of course the Vinson visit worked two ways, because the Chief Justice discovered that many of the Newport men were really clear thinkers about government matters despite their inbred Republicanism. And he also found out that he could get into a good poker game, even in Newport.

Two unusual incidents occurred during their visit. When I saw Bob Young at Bailey's Beach a few days before the Vinsons arrived, he said he would like to meet my guests if they had time. And when they arrived and Fred said he also would like to meet Bob Young, I took them over to my neighbor's for a call. But during the conversation, Bob Young suddenly started talking about a railroad case that was then in the courts and might get to the Supreme Court. I immediately rose and informed our host that we had another appointment. I didn't want to have anything to do with putting the Chief Justice in a compromising position.

The other incident occurred when we were at the Marble Palace, one of the truly great showplaces of Newport. After showing the Vinsons all through the house and gardens, Freddy Prince told the Chief Justice that he wanted to give the whole place to the Supreme Court for a vacation spot. Mr. Vinson thanked him for the offer and said he would discuss it with the President and the other justices. Actually, they never even considered it. Fred Vinson told me later that if the Supreme Court accepted it, it would look as though they were being influenced to protect the rich. And besides, he said, the Court would never be willing to pay the tremendous cost of maintaining such a place.

After the Vinsons left Newport, there was a veritable parade of Administration people to my house: Secretary of the Army and Mrs. Kenneth Royall, Attorney General and Mrs. Tom Clark, Secretary of the Treasury and Mrs. John Snyder and their daughter Drucie, General and Mrs. Omar Bradley (he was then head of the Veterans' Administration). I also managed to work in a big dinner

113

party for Republican House Leader Joe Martin. And Mrs. Woodrow Wilson spent a week with me.

My relations with *some* of the Newporters were somewhat disturbed that summer, I am afraid. I first got into hot water at a public auction of the crystal and porcelain from the Prescott Lawrence villa. The auction was staged on the lawn outside the house, and a number of antique dealers from New York were there, as well as some of the leading local socialites, all hoping to get a bargain. I had my eye on a Sèvres service of the period 1830. It had belonged to King Louis Philippe of France.

When the auctioneer put up the first plate from the service, the bidding was opened at ten dollars. I bid twenty-five. Miss Ruth Twombley said thirty.

"Forty!" I piped up.

"Fifty," said Miss Twombley.

"Sixty!" said I.

"Seventy," replied Miss Twombley.

"I bid a hundred," I said determinedly. For a moment there was silence. One hundred dollars was too much for one plate.

"Going . . . going . . . gone!" said the auctioneer. "Sold to Mrs. George Mesta."

When I got the next plate for the same price I could feel the burning glances from my Newport friends. They were probably saying to each other, "That stubborn Oklahoman doesn't know any better and she's going to outbid us, no matter what, so let's let her have them."

After that my only competition was from the antique dealers. When the next few pieces all went to me, I suggested that the auctioneer offer the rest of the service as a package. He did, and I got it for $2250. I also purchased for $1075 a rare collection of crystal glass bearing the seal of Louis Philippe. Although the antique dealers and Newporters thought I was crazy to pay so much, I think I got the last laugh. The things I bought that day for less than four thousand dollars are now valued at more than twice that much.

My relations with some of the Bellevue Avenue crowd were further clouded a few days later when the New York *Daily News* ran the following article:

MRS. MESTA, CAPITOL HOSTESS,
TAKES NEWPORT SOCIETY REINS

By Nancy Randolph

NEWPORT, R.I., Aug. 9—Social leadership here has definitely changed hands. No longer does New York's venerable Mrs. Cornelius Vanderbilt appear as the reigning sovereign of this super-exclusive spa. The crown now adorns the sagacious head of Mrs. George Mesta of Washington, D.C., who week after week brings the nation's leaders here to Midcliff.

This weekend, the Secretary of War and Mrs. Kenneth Royall will be Perle Mesta's house guests, along with Col. Don Lowry, chief aide at the White House, just back from a trip to Rio. Previously, Chief Justice and Mrs. Vinson and Gen. and Mrs. Omar N. Bradley have visited Midcliff. What other capitol celebrities, there's no law against guessing.

Of course that newspaper story hit far from the truth, despite the generosity of the writer toward me. I was nowhere near being the leader of Newport society, nor did I desire to be. Mrs. Twombley and Mrs. Vanderbilt were still the leaders in my book, as in everyone else's, and I was quite content to let them lead. The repercussions from this newspaper story were not too loud, mostly because few social people at Newport ever looked at the New York *Daily News*. I continued to go to Mrs. Twombley's and Mrs. Vanderbilt's social events, and late that summer Mrs. Vanderbilt even took one of her rare nights out to come to a party of mine. Not only did she come to the party, she took part in the spontaneous entertainment by doing a whistling duet with Washington society columnist Betty Beale. And they were very good!

During that summer I also found time to further my career as a matchmaker. Madame Henri Bonnet, wife of the French ambassador, had been having her niece from Switzerland, Sophie Mayer, visit her in Washington. I took a liking to Sophie, who was shy, quite pretty, and very naïve. She was nineteen, but in maturity only about fifteen, as she had been sheltered in her upbringing (perhaps she had a governess like Mamzelle). At one of my parties during the winter, she had met a White House aide and developed quite a crush on him. With my perennial matrimonial interest in

115

other people, I invited both Sophie and the White House aide, along with some other young people, up to Newport for a weekend. I thought that with sailing, the beach, and the lovely evenings, one thing would lead to another.

When Sophie arrived, I took her aside and gave her some advice. "Now, dear, you must tease the fellow just a little," I counseled. "A man as nice and gentlemanly as he is needs a little encouragement."

All the young people spent the afternoon on the beach, but by evening I saw that my romantic plot had not thickened a bit. I had another chat with Sophie. I told her that American girls are more forward than European girls and that if she was ever going to catch her man, she would have to be a little aggressive.

"Now, he will have on his dress uniform at dinner tonight," I said. "You know, the one the White House Army aides wear with the little whistle attached to gold braid."

Sophie nodded obediently.

"After dinner, I want you to say how lovely the sea looks in the moonlight. Then, of course, he will take you out on the terrace to look at it. At that point tell him how handsome he looks in his uniform. You could even pick up the little whistle and blow it," I suggested. "You will be very close to him then and he will perhaps kiss you."

"Oh, Mrs. Mesta," giggled Sophie. "Do you think so?"

Sure enough, after dinner I saw the two of them disappear through the French doors. After a suspenseful interval I heard a blast on that whistle that made me jump. The couple quickly reappeared, the young man looking thunderstruck and Sophie looking brokenhearted. Obviously I had given her the wrong advice. Perhaps I should have known better, but when it comes to trying to match up some of the nice people around me, I'm afraid I'm an irrepressible optimist. My disappointments only seem to whet my desire to try again.

During the Christmas season of 1947, I had a small, informal Sunday-afternoon dinner for the President and Mrs. Truman and some of her family who were visiting in Washington. My brother, who had come east from Oklahoma City, played the piano while we all gathered around and sang Christmas carols. And Margaret

Truman even sang one number alone—the only time I can recall her ever singing at a social gathering. My niece, who had just been divorced, was staying with me at the time. After dinner, she brought down her four-month-old baby, Marguerite, to show her off to the President. He took the little bundle in his arms and rocked her a minute. "Just like my Margaret used to be," he said. Then he gently handed her back to Betty and sat down at the piano and played Brahms's "Lullaby" softly while the baby dropped off to sleep in her mother's arms.

Another enjoyable party I gave was for General and Mrs. Bradley just after he had taken over for General Eisenhower as Army Chief of Staff in February, 1948. During the evening, I happened to see presidential assistant Clark Clifford whisper something to Senator Alexander Wiley, after which the two stepped out of the room together and didn't return for half an hour. Years later, Clark Clifford told me how really valuable my party had been that night. It seemed that the President had been wanting to discuss an important piece of legislation with Senator Wiley, who was then Chairman of the Senate Judiciary Committee, but because of the resentment many Republican senators felt toward the Administration, the President had not felt free to ask Wiley to come to the White House—nor could he have sent anyone to see Wiley on Capitol Hill without it arousing undue comment. At my party, Clark Clifford had been able to take Wiley aside and explain the President's position, which helped greatly toward working out a solution.

Another less important problem of the day was solved in an unusual way at this same party. Several months earlier there had been a formal White House dinner attended by several foreign military attachés, all of them resplendent in their formal dress uniforms. The President had remarked to his personal military aide, Major General Harry Vaughan, that the American military men looked pretty shabby in comparison with the foreigners. General Vaughan explained that because formal dress had been suspended during the war, most of the high-ranking officers either did not have dress uniforms or else could no longer get their old ones buttoned. Thus they had been wearing field uniforms.

"Well, I'm tired of seeing you fellows at formal events looking like a bunch of bus drivers," said the President. "Why don't you get a uniform you all can wear, and that looks good? Go see Forrestal about it."

When Vaughan approached Secretary of Defense James Forrestal, he was told that the problem of uniforms was one that had to be worked out by the heads of the military services, and he suggested Vaughan see the Secretaries of the Army, Navy, and Air Force. Vaughan did, but nothing happened. Several weeks later, Mr. Truman, who has a phenomenal mind for detail, wanted to know what progress had been made. General Vaughan related how the services couldn't agree, and added, "I think I may have a new uniform made anyway." He told the President what he had in mind. Mr. Truman said, "Go ahead." So the General went to a tailor and ordered an ordinary full dress suit, directing that it be embellished with brass buttons on the front, gold braid shoulder knots, and gold stripes sewn onto the sleeves and trousers. He reasoned that a uniform like this would be especially good for reserve officers, who could take off the trappings and continue to use the dress suit for formal civilian wear.

General Vaughan was wearing his new uniform for the first time the night of my party for General Bradley. As soon as he saw Vaughan, Omar Bradley was complimentary: "Harry, where did you get it? It looks fine." General Vaughan gave him the name of his tailor. "I'm going down there and get one of those made for me," said the Chief of Staff. He did, and of course when the Chief of Staff wore the new uniform, that made it official for the Army, and the other services soon adopted it.

In 1948, as the presidential election approached, my work for the Democratic party grew in importance when I was named an assistant to the Finance Chairman of the Democratic National Committee and also co-chairman of the 1948 Jefferson-Jackson Day celebrations for Washington. These were both essentially fund-raising jobs, and at that time the coffers of the Democratic party needed all the help they could get. Tickets for the annual Democratic celebration sold for a hundred dollars each. Our staff really worked hard and I sold tickets to whomever I could—even to some Republicans.

My eagerness to sell tickets got me into an argument with James Forrestal. I was at the White House at a small reception the

Trumans had to unveil a portrait of Margaret that had just been completed. While we were standing around talking, I went over to Forrestal and asked him to buy a ticket for the dinner. He said he was not planning to attend because he felt that, as Secretary of Defense, he should be nonpolitical.

"How can you say you are nonpolitical when you're in the Cabinet?" I demanded. I thought he was being disloyal to the President at a time when Mr. Truman needed all the support he could get.

Despite Forrestal's absence and that of several of the Southern Democrats who were angry with the President over his Civil Rights message to Congress, our dinner had a record turnout of twenty-nine hundred. In fact we had so many people that for the first time in history it was necessary to hold the celebration simultaneously at two hotels. Mr. Truman ate dinner at the Statler and gave a short extemporaneous talk, then hurried over to the Mayflower to make his formal speech, which was radiocast throughout the nation.

Both the Democratic and Republican conventions were held in Philadelphia that year, and again, as I had done in 1944, I showed up three weeks ahead of time so I could watch the Republican antics. The press made quite an issue of my early arrival, and one reporter asked if I was wavering in my politics. I assured him I wasn't. "I'm here as the leader of the Truman underground," I said.

I took part in the Democratic convention as a delegate from Rhode Island, which had become my legal residence after I sold my interest in the Arizona ranch in 1945. One of the most touching things I remember about that convention was Alben Barkley, hoping for the one chance in a million that there might be a deadlock and he would get the presidential nomination. Of course he couldn't oppose President Truman openly, and as he was then seventy years old, people held his age against him. But Senator Barkley would say, "Why, Churchill is in his prime, and he is four years older than I am; Blackstone was Prime Minister of England at eighty-four and Oliver Wendell Holmes didn't retire until he was ninety-one."

Although Senator Barkley was an old and dear friend of mine, I was solidly for President Truman. But I was very pleased when the President picked Barkley as his running mate. I was with the

Trumans in a private room at the convention hall when Barkley came in to greet the President just after the vice-presidential nominating ballot was concluded. Barkley was a mighty good actor. Even though what he really wanted was to be President, I heard him tell Truman, "This is the surprise of my life, to be nominated for Vice-President."

The Democratic women leaders put on quite a splash. India Edwards, Chairman of the National Democratic Women's Division, was tremendous in her speech during which she talked about the high cost of living under the Republicans and dangled a steak in front of the television cameras. And Emma Guffey Miller also brought women into the headlines with a speech on peace, dramatized by releasing hundreds of "doves of peace"—which had everybody ducking.

India Edwards had asked me to give a speech at one of the workshop meetings she had set up to indoctrinate Democratic women in how to campaign in their home precincts. I had labored for two weeks on this speech, and had gotten several people to help me with it. The day before I was to give it, I had lunch with my good friend Louis Bromfield. Of course I told him about the speech I was going to give and also about my nervousness.

Louis was very sweet and said, "Would you like me to read the speech and see if I can improve it any?"

I jumped at the chance of getting such a famous writer to work over the material.

The next morning I phoned him bright and early. "How is my speech, Louis?" I asked expectantly.

"Well, Perle, I don't know just what to say." Louis sounded mournful. "I'm afraid I've mislaid your speech. I can't find it anywhere."

"Louis, you couldn't have!" I cried in horror. "I'll come right down to your room and help you look for it."

"No, Perle," Bromfield answered. "I know for a fact it isn't here."

I was frantic. I hadn't memorized a word of the speech because I planned to read it. I called India Edwards and told her what had happened and she came right over. We worked furiously during the three hours we had left, pulling the speech and ourselves together just in time. It wasn't until several months later that the ultraconservative Republican Bromfield confessed what he had done. As he had started reading my speech, which was designed to incite the Democratic ladies to work hard to beat the Republicans, he got madder and madder. Finally, he tore it up and flushed it down the toilet.

On the first night of the convention I gave a big party. I had it at the Barclay Hotel and it was crowded, as such parties most always are, because I never can shut off the guest list where I should. The summer night was hot, and the huge television lights made it even worse. Some of the press, who at that time didn't give Truman a ghost of a chance against Dewey, chided me for calling it a victory party. They referred to it as a wake.

I received even more ridicule when I started to campaign among my friends at Newport. George Tyson took every opportunity to try to squelch my enthusiasm.

"Your old pal Truman hasn't a chance in the world against a fine conservative like Tom Dewey," he maintained. And my brother-in-law wouldn't even be seen with me when I showed up at a lavish Newport party wearing a king-size "Truman for President" button on the front of my formal gown.

One night in September while I was attending a dinner party in Newport, I received a long distance call from Washington. Louis Johnson, then in charge of fund raising for the Democratic party, told me that the National Committee was broke. There wasn't even enough money to keep the campaign train going, and the President had asked if I could help out. When I hung up, I told my hostess I would have to leave, and made my farewells. Some remarks were made about the nature of my assignment. One wealthy businessman said, "So you're going to join Trembling Truman's train." He later was to rue that remark.

That night I got a plane out of New York and joined the campaign train in Gainesville, Texas. I was given a compartment at one end of the Trumans' private car. A fund-raising plan was soon worked out. I would telegraph ahead to wealthy friends of mine along the route and say I was on the Truman train and that the President would like to see them. When these oil millionaires and others boarded the train, I would see them first and tell them how much the country needed Truman and how awful it would be if Governor Dewey were elected. If I saw I was getting no response,

I wouldn't call President Truman in, but would just introduce the man to the President as we passed his compartment on the way out. However, if I thought my prospect worth while, I would have the porter ask the President if he had time to join us.

Sometimes, if I felt an added push was necessary, I would start to cry a little as I explained how hard up my party was. When the President appeared, I would ask him to answer whatever questions my prospect had asked me. Truman was terrific. He knew just what to say and when to say it.

I kept insisting to everyone I met that Truman was going to be elected. My confidence wasn't based just on hopefulness, as it had been in the Landon campaign. I could tell we were winning from the reactions of the crowds whenever the train stopped. I would get off and go around to the platform where the President was speaking. By this time he had thrown away his prepared speeches and was "giving 'em hell" with wonderful, spontaneous talks that matched the mood of each crowd he met. When we got to Oklahoma City, people lined the streets six deep along the way to the State Fair Grounds, where the President delivered a nationwide radio speech.

After the broadcast, the President went to the Skirvin Hotel for a reception. How I wished Father could have been there that night, for it had always been his desire to have a President of the United States come to his hotel. He had had the "Presidential Suite" all ready and the hotel decorated for a visit from President Wilson in 1919, when Wilson was touring the country seeking support for our participation in the League of Nations. But Wilson suffered a stroke the day before he was to arrive in Oklahoma City, and had to cancel the rest of his tour. I think Father, Republican though he was, would have been proud to see his daughter standing in the receiving line with the President, Mrs. Truman, and Margaret, and introducing them to the good people of Oklahoma City.

After the train trip, I continued with my fund raising, pulling in quite a sum for my party. About half of the contributions came from Republicans. Of course, I realized that a lot of them were giving me a thousand dollars and giving their own party five thousand. They believed Dewey was going to get in, but they wanted to cover themselves—just in case.

On election night I stayed home in Newport while Marguerite

and George attended a Republican victory party at a club. I had told George that he might as well be prepared for Dewey's defeat, citing the evidence I had seen while traveling with Truman. "You don't know what you're talking about," George insisted. "You're just saying that because you like the Trumans so much."

The "victory" party broke up early in the morning when it became evident that Dewey had lost. When George tried to sneak into his room, I heard him. I poked my head out into the hall just long enough to crow, "Now will you believe me?"

"Yes, dammit," muttered George, and slammed his door.

With the excitement of the 1948 campaign over, I was enjoying a few days of rest at Malabar, the Ohio farm of the Louis Bromfields, when I received a call from the White House asking me to come to Washington as soon as possible. It seemed that arrangements for the Inaugural Ball were all snarled up, and the President wanted me to see if I could help straighten them out. There also was the problem of funds: the Democratic party was in debt, and Louis Johnson thought maybe we could make enough money to pay off some of our obligations by selling box seats for the ball.

I had a meeting with the Inaugural Ball committee, and before I knew it, I was appointed co-chairman of the ball. The day this was announced in the newspapers, a friend telephoned me—the same Newporter who had referred to the President as "Trembling Truman." Now he was singing a different tune.

"I'd like to buy a good box for the Inaugural Ball," he said.

"You don't mean you're coming to Trembling Truman's inauguration!" I exclaimed in mock surprise.

"Yes, I am," he replied curtly. He still hadn't recovered from the election results. But he was a big businessman and wanted to be seen at the ball.

"It will cost you three thousand dollars," I told him.

"All right, I'll take it," he said.

Several others who had ridiculed the President now wanted to buy boxes and I really made them pay. The least I got from any of them was a thousand dollars. With my purse bulging, I went triumphantly to the White House.

"I'm just collecting money right and left for these boxes," I told the President. And I dumped the checks on his desk.

President Truman looked at several of the checks and then shook his head. "I'm afraid we can't take these, Perle," he said. "This ball is for the people of the United States. We don't want to gouge anyone—not even Republicans."

My heart sank. I tried to argue that at least we ought to accept more from the ones who had said such terrible things about us, but the President was firm. He said two hundred and fifty dollars was the price set for the boxes, and there would be no exceptions. He told me to return the checks.

I went back to see my Newport friend. "I've changed my mind about the price of the box," I said, handing back his check. "Or rather, the President changed it for me. We can take only two hundred and fifty dollars."

Looking pleased, my friend wrote out and handed me a new check for the smaller amount.

"Thank you," I said. "Now I want a donation for the Democratic party of twenty-seven hundred and fifty." And I got it. And I got similar donations from my other high payers. My mother always used to say that if I didn't get a thing one way, I'd get it another.

I don't believe I ever worked as hard in my life as I did during preparations for the Inaugural Ball. It was held at the National Guard Armory, an old barn of a place, and there were thousands of details to be worked out. I left my house early each morning with a lunch box under my arm and did not return until late at night. The armory had been used by the F.B.I. during the war for personnel training, and had been turned back to the District without being fixed up. With the help of a decorator, we figured out how to mask the bare walls by using sixty thousand yards of fireproof fabric. We ordered pink celluloid coverings to soften the glaring lights in the ceiling. This gave a party atmosphere and was flattering to the ladies. We also figured out how to get in additional tiers of boxes (and hence more revenue). And although the legal capacity of the armory was six thousand, we worked out certain safety measures with the Fire Department so that we were able to increase the capacity. We wound up packing in twelve thousand people.

With the help of co-chairman Edgar Morris and Wilson Wyatt, we gradually cleared up all the problems—except that of the tickets. We had received more than twenty-five thousand requests for tickets and the pressure for box seats was tremendous. The faithful workers for the Democratic party naturally received the preference for choice boxes, but otherwise every effort was made to keep the distribution of tickets as bipartisan as possible.

The day of the inauguration, I thought all the problems had been solved—until I arrived at the armory. A track meet had been held the night before, and I was greeted by the sight of six track lanes marked in whitewash right across our dance floor. Washing the lines off only made matters worse. The floor had not been thoroughly cleaned for years and the partial washing only called attention to the dirtiness of the rest. I insisted that the whole floor —it covered two and a half acres—had to be scrubbed.

One of the committee members, Jack Logan, shanghaied fifty scrubwomen from various government buildings. We lined them up across one end of the armory and they scrubbed their way to the other. But it still wasn't clean enough to suit me, so Jack hired sixty men to spread and sweep seven hundred pounds of cornmeal across the floor. They were sweeping up the last crumbs when our first guests began arriving.

The Inaugural Ball turned out to be a great success. A military aide met each party of arriving guests and escorted it to its box through an arch of sabers formed by a color guard. There was wonderful music from six bands: those of Guy Lombardo, Benny Goodman, Xavier Cugat, the United States Marines, and the local orchestras of Barnèe Breeskin and Sidney. And that night I had one of the greatest thrills of my life. As ball co-chairman, it was my honor to be on the President's arm when he made his grand entrance. What a moment that was—with the bands playing "Hail to the Chief" and spotlights dancing around us as we walked down the steps to the Presidential Box! We were closely followed by Mrs. Truman on the arm of another co-chairman, Edgar Morris. Soon after the President and Mrs. Truman were seated I had to go back to my chores of unscrambling ticket mix-ups and trying to line up the Grand March. But I didn't mind: I had had my big moment.

ELEVEN: *Call Me Perle*

WHEN I RETURNED to Washington in the fall of 1948 after the election, I decided not to renew the lease on the S Street house. Instead I took a place on Foxhall Road called Uplands. It had been built by Mrs. J. Borden Harriman, although she had long since sold it. The dining room was rather small but it had beautiful parquet floors and wood paneling; the entire room had been brought over from a French château. There were lovely wooded grounds all around the house, and it was far enough from the road to be quiet and much more restful than the S Street area had been with all its bustle.

Marguerite and George spent much of their time with me at Uplands. One of our first parties was for the new president of Columbia University and his wife, better known as Ike and Mamie. This was a more modest party than the one I had given for the Eisenhowers the year before. I had only twenty-three guests, among them: Senator and Mrs. Stuart Symington, Mr. and Mrs. William Randolph Hearst, Jr., Mr. and Mrs. George Allen, General and Mrs. Wade Haislip, Mr. and Mrs. James Van Alen (from Newport), Secretary of the Army and Mrs. Kenneth Royall, Bill McAvoy, Herb May, Mr. and Mrs. Ed Foley, Mr. and Mrs. Ray Henle, Peggy Palmer, Fred Roy, and George Williams.

After dinner, while the rest talked in the living room or listened to the music of Sidney and His Strings, Ike, George Allen, my sister, and Peggy Palmer played bridge in the upstairs library. When I went to look in on the bridge players, Ike was dummy, and he turned to chat with me.

"Well, Perlie," he asked, using his own favorite version of my name, "have you been to the Stork Club lately?"

He was still ribbing me about the time a few months earlier

when I had gone to New York for his installation as president of Columbia. After the ceremony, Ike's brother Ed had taken me to the Stork Club and we had danced practically all night long. It was about 4:00 A.M. when he took me home. Ed was staying with Ike and Mamie, and when he tried to sneak in, the door squeaked and everyone in the house knew what time he got home. And if they didn't kid us about it the next day!

Toward the end of February, 1949, we held another big Jefferson-Jackson Day dinner in Washington. Our Democratic party bank account was still showing a deficit because of the heavy expenses of the campaign, so again I pitched in to help sell tickets and obtain contributions. We did even better than the year before, selling thirty-five hundred tickets at a hundred a plate, and jamming both the Statler and Mayflower banquet halls. Just before the dinner, Les Biffle, Secretary of the Senate and a prominent behind-the-scenes Democrat, announced to me that he was putting me on the program as a speaker.

"Les, that's the meanest trick I ever heard of!" I exclaimed. "I don't have time to prepare a speech. And anyway, with all those important people there, why do you want me to speak? I'd just make a fool of myself."

But Les is a very persuasive gentleman and before I knew it, I had agreed. It was only a little two-minute speech but I was scared stiff. Afterward, the President stood up and said, "If I'd known you could do that well, Perle, I'd have put you to work giving speeches during the campaign."

Mrs. Truman had a cold that night and couldn't come to the dinner, so as co-chairman I was moved up to the seat next to the President. Several strangers who came up to the head table to greet the President smiled at me and said, "Hello, Mrs. Truman." The President winked when this happened and motioned for me not to say anything. But I was so embarrassed I kept blurting out, "Oh, no—I'm Perle Mesta! Mrs. Truman is at home ill this evening."

A luncheon date with India Edwards a few days after the Jefferson-Jackson Day dinner set in motion a chain of events that was to change my life radically. India was doing a wonderful job as head of the Democratic women and was also Vice-Chairman of the Democratic National Committee. But she was troubled because women weren't getting to do more things in government.

127

"It could do a lot for the women of our country if the President would appoint a woman to some high diplomatic post," India said—and I agreed. We then discussed several people, but none of them seemed right.

"You know," India said thoughtfully, "my daughter suggested to me the other night that Perle Mesta ought to be an ambassador, and I think maybe she is right."

"Oh, no!" I protested. "That's ridiculous, Why, I don't know the first thing about diplomacy. There are a lot of women who are better qualified than I am for a diplomatic post."

"I'm not so sure," replied India. "And I know you are one person President Truman would like to appoint to some position."

What India said seemed so farfetched I didn't give it another thought.

That spring, I made the most of the beautiful setting I had at Uplands and did a lot of entertaining. I had parties for Chief Justice and Mrs. Vinson, Speaker Sam Rayburn, Secretary of the Treasury Snyder, Secretary of Defense Johnson, and for the Egyptian and the Brazilian ambassadors.

The highlight of the season came when the President and Mrs. Truman accepted my invitation to a dinner party in their honor late in April. Since my dining room was not big enough for the large party, we enclosed the porch for the occasion. There was a protocol question at that time around Washington as to whether Vice-President Alben Barkley's daughter, Mrs. Max Truitt, who was his official hostess, should be given the position at parties equivalent to that of the wife of a Vice-President. The State Department's Protocol Division had not made a ruling by the time I gave my party, so I avoided the problem by seating my guests around nine small tables, with a host or hostess at each:

Table 1:	Table 2:
Mrs. Mesta	George Tyson
Pres. Truman	Mrs. Truman
Mrs. Vinson	Chief Jus. Vinson
Speaker Rayburn	Mrs. Clark
Mrs. Tydings	Hon. Joe Davies
Sec. Snyder	Mrs. Truitt
Mrs. Langner	Sec. Johnson
Vice-Pres. Barkley	Mrs. Snyder

Table 3:	Table 4:
Margaret Truman	Marguerite Tyson
Rep. Kennedy	Ambassador Silvercruys
Sophie Mayer	Mrs. Davies
Marvin Braverman	Gen. Vaughan
Jane Lingo	Mrs. Miller
Midshipman Carr	Sen. Tydings
Drucie Snyder	Mrs. Johnson
William Tyson	Atty. Gen. Clark

Table 5:	Table 6:
Mrs. Boomer	Mrs. Clifford
Sen. Green	Lawrence Langner
Mrs. Dawson	Mrs. Bradley
Charley Ross	Leslie Biffle
Mrs. Willis Kimball	Mrs. Connelly
Carol Miller	Cornelius Moore
Mrs. Biffle	Mrs. Vaughan
Gen. Haislip	Judge Jones

Table 7:	Table 8:
Sen. Kerr	Mrs. Ross
Mrs. Haislip	Gen. Bradley
Matt Connelly	Mrs. Rufus Patterson
Mrs. Mitchell Palmer	Donald Dawson
William Boyle	Mrs. Steelman
Mrs. Alexander Surles	Max Truitt
Clark Clifford	Mrs. Boyle
	Richard Newton

Table 9:

Betty Tyson
Sen. Magnuson
Mrs. Kerr
John Steelman
Mrs. Reece
John B. Reece

This time I didn't insist that the President wear white tie and tails, but still I wasn't quite prepared for Jack Kennedy to be wearing brown loafers with his tuxedo! I seated Jack, then a congressman from Massachusetts, next to Margaret Truman (I was always trying to make a match for Margaret).

We had the Three Suns for music and entertainment. Also Vice-President Barkley treated us to a pretty fancy buck and wing, and before the evening was over, a few tunes were played by the President. In fact, the President was enjoying himself so much that instead of going home at his usual hour, he stayed on. At eleven-thirty Senator Bob Kerr came to me.

"I know it isn't proper to leave before the President," he apologized, "but I have to take a plane at midnight and it looks as if Mr. Truman hasn't even thought of going home." So he excused himself and left. The party finally broke up at 1:00 A.M.

Early in May, India Edwards phoned me saying she had something very important to discuss, and could I come right down to her office? India always comes right to the point. As soon as I sat down in her office, she said, "I've just been to see the President, and he wants to appoint you as the first Minister to Luxembourg. He isn't sure you'll take the job. I told him I thought you would. Will you?"

For a moment I was too flabbergasted to answer. Finally I told India I needed some time to think it over. Naturally I had been flattered at her suggestion a few months earlier about my becoming a diplomat, but I had not taken it seriously. It had seemed to me there wasn't a chance in the world for one who had absolutely no Foreign Service training to be named to the diplomatic corps.

In the next few days I sought the advice of my family and friends. My brother advised me not to go. He underscored my own reservations about lack of training and made the point that I was too outspoken to be a diplomat. Fred Vinson also told me not to take the job. He said that I was of more value to the Democrats right where I was, both as a fund raiser and as a party giver. Fred said that bringing Republicans and Democrats, senators and White House staff, civilians and military people together at social gatherings was one of the most important things that could be done for the country, whereas Luxembourg didn't really need a minister.

My sister, on the other hand, was enthusiastic about the possible appointment. She thought it was a great opportunity for me, and that I shouldn't decline it. Erwin Canham, the editor of *The Christian Science Monitor,* and a friend whose judgment I valued

130

greatly, advised me that I could do a great deal of good for the United States in the assignment. Even though a tiny country, Luxembourg was a listening post for all Europe, Mr. Canham said. Another friend of long standing, Hope Ridings Miller, insisted that my experience in getting people together at parties was the best possible qualification for a diplomatic position where the chief requirement was to further friendly relations between two countries. India Edwards, always the practical politician, wanted me to accept the appointment because it would help to raise the standing of women in politics. If I were rewarded like this for my services to my party, it might inspire other women to work hard in politics. And it could also demonstrate that women could do these jobs just as well as men. India made me feel I would be practically disloyal to my country if I declined the appointment.

Rumors about the proposed appointment began to leak out— Washington is the District of Rumor. I heard from friends that a top State Department official felt that the President would be degrading the Foreign Service with such a purely political appointment. And after the rumors started, the jokes began. In Washington, jokes are rumors' cousins. I was at a luncheon given by the Women's Press Club for Tallulah Bankhead, when one of the newspaperwomen asked Tallulah if she would like to be an ambassador. And Tallulah replied, in a voice that could be heard all over the room, "Yes, dahling, I'd love to be an ambassador. But I haven't enough money."

I didn't discuss my decision with President Truman, because he let it be known that he didn't want to talk to me until *after* I made up my mind. I was silently grateful to him for this. Of course the President knew that if he asked me personally to take the post, I would not refuse. Late in May, I drove out to a luncheon at Edith Benham Helm's country home with Mrs. Truman. During the ride not a word was mentioned about my appointment, but I could feel that Bess was consciously steering clear of the subject. I realized I could not put off my decision much longer.

That night I did some soul searching. There were so many arguments in my mind against accepting. I would have to be away from my country for a long time and I didn't know the language. I might fail somehow, and a failure in this undertaking would not be just my own, but would hurt the President, the country, and the chances of other women for similar appointments. But offsetting these and other points was the challenge of the appointment. We Skirvins have always loved a challenge. I thought about my long-departed husband and wondered what his advice would have been. Even though George had believed the place for women was in the home, I felt that he would have said, "You do what you think is right, honey." So I prayed earnestly to be guided to make the right decision. Then I went to sleep. And when I awakened the next morning, I had my answer.

The President's announcement of my appointment set Washington's tongues to wagging. I had luncheon at the Sulgrave Club one day with columnist Elise Morrow. This is the way she described the scene in her column:

> Mrs. Mesta's entrance into the fashionable, light turquoise dining room was the signal for a cats' field day. It was an historic entrance, like a scene from 'The Women,' or some similar comedy of feminine manners—or lack of manners. The bright eyes all turned as we came in.
>
> Mrs. Robert Taft . . . had the good grace to say, "Congratulations.' Another woman at Mrs. Taft's table then purred to Perle, 'Do you know anything about Luxembourg dear? Have you ever been there?' Perle thrust out her jaw, in a characteristic Mesta expression, and said, 'Don't worry . . . I'm quite prepared.' It was as if she had said, 'Sister, stop right there . . . don't fool with Aunt Perle.'

There were howls from the Republican newspapers, and a few stories were "leaked" from the State Department, conveying the displeasure of some officials there. The Senate Foreign Relations Committee approved the appointment unanimously without even calling me before them, but when my nomination went before the Senate for approval, Forrest Donnell of Missouri, an enemy of the President, tried to block the appointment. He kept the floor for more than an hour, reading from authorities on the duties of diplomats. He claimed that diplomatic appointments should not be made for political reasons, on the basis of friendship, or on the basis of being able to extend hospitality. He alleged that my appointment was made only because of my heavy campaign contributions, my friendship with the President, and my party-giving. He chastised

132

the Foreign Relations Committee for not even calling me to testify. He ended by stating flatly that my background did not justify the nomination and that the appointment marked "a step backward to the spoils system."

Influential senators rallied to my defense.

"She may not have come before the committee," said New Hampshire's Charles Tobey, "but we've all been before her."

After the laughter subsided, Senator Tom Connally, Chairman of the Foreign Relations Committee, arose to defend his committee's position.

"Luxembourg is what is called a Grand Duchy, and its ruler is a Grand Duchess, a female—a woman, if you please," said Connally. "Would it be so out of harmony with the concept of women in government if we should find a minister to the Grand Duchy who was a woman? The Senator from Missouri wants a man with striped breeches and a silk hat perhaps," continued the white-haired Texan. "Career men are all right in their place, but they are apt to get in a rut by going to tea at four o'clock and wearing the same kind of clothes. Their minds have got little grooves in them. I favor some fresh air from outside, some fresh strength. It is said that Mrs. Mesta entertains. That is what career men do, so she has at least that qualification. She will have contacts with diplomats of other nations and with the Grand Duchess. It is no discredit to her that she meets people without offending them, that she can get along with them and that she can extend hospitality."

Senator Donnell immediately stormed back. "I have no objection to a woman holding high office, if she be qualified, but merely being a woman does not qualify her."

"She is an outstanding hostess," countered Senator Russell Long from Louisiana. "Doesn't that require ability?"

"I've no doubt about that," replied Donnell. "But I've seen many hostesses not qualified to be ministers."

"Would the Senator care to name some?" asked Long.

"We're not here to examine into the qualifications of all the hostesses in town," was Donnell's reply. "The Senator could do that himself better than I can."

Senator Donnell tried to keep the debate alive by questioning Senator J. Howard McGrath about my campaign contributions and asking if I had contributed money in 1946 to purge Roger C.

Slaughter. Slaughter, a Democrat, but a political enemy of Truman, had been defeated in the Missouri primary for re-election to the House of Representatives.

Senator McGrath, who was also Chairman of the Democratic National Committee, said he knew of no such purge fund but that my contributions had indeed been extraordinary. "Mrs. Mesta worked magnificently toward the success of the last two Jackson Day dinners and she is entitled to a great deal of the credit for the one just this year which added three hundred thousand dollars to the party's treasury," Senator McGrath added.

Senator Donnell demanded to know how much the nominee had donated to Democratic party funds.

"I couldn't say precisely," Senator McGrath shot back. Then he grinned and added, "But it is more than a thousand dollars."

And with that, Vice-President Barkley ended the debate and put the question: "The question is will the Senate advise and consent to the nomination of Mrs. Mesta as Envoy Extraordinary and Minister Plenipotentiary of the United States of America to Luxembourg? Those in favor say aye."

There was a resounding chorus of ayes.

"Opposed?" The one loud and vigorous no was emitted by Missouri's Republican Senator Donnell.

I was far from the scene of this debate, hiding out at the Drake Hotel in New York, scared to death that the Senate would not confirm me. I wanted to be out of reach in case the verdict was unfavorable.

My dear friend Senator Theodore Green phoned Marguerite in Newport, told her the good news, and learned where I could be reached by phone. Thus it was Senator Green who broke the news to me. I almost wept with relief.

On July 7, 1949, I was sworn in by Undersecretary Stanley Woodward at a ceremony in the State Department auditorium. Ordinarily, this ceremony is performed in a small room on the fifth floor, but so many of my friends were there that the auditorium had to be used. Vice-President Barkley was at my side during the ceremony, and several Cabinet members were there, as well as a group of senators and Supreme Court justices. Secretary of State Acheson gave me my official commission.

The next six weeks were hectic. I closed Uplands, put things in order at my Newport house, and had an intense series of briefings at the State Department. I tried to get Hope Miller, an experienced newspaperwoman, to go with me as press attaché, but Hope reluctantly had to say no because of her father's illness. However, I was able to get Dorothy Williams of the United Press to go along instead. I made arrangements to leave New York on the *America* on August 16.

Major General John Franklin, president of the United States Line, gave me a farewell luncheon in the ship's dining room a few hours before I sailed. It was a wonderful send-off. Present were about sixty of my good friends from Washington and New York. Mrs. Truman and Margaret were there, the Vinsons, India Edwards, and the new Treasurer of the United States, Georgia Neese Clark. Helen McLean came on from Fort Smith, my brother was there, and George Tyson came down from Boston (Marguerite was then visiting in England).

Just before the ship sailed newsmen came aboard and I held a brief press conference.

"What is the first thing you will do when you reach Luxembourg?" I was asked.

I sensed the reporter's critical attitude. "Meet the people," I replied.

That about finished that line of questioning.

"How does one address you now?" another reporter asked. "Your Excellency? Madam Minister? Or what?"

"Oh, just call me Perle," I said.

Always before when I had left on voyages to Europe, I had felt an exhilaration and a keen desire to reach my destination. This time these sensations were missing. I was all alone as I faced a strange new experience, leaving behind all the people who had been so kind to me and who had helped me so much. Faces on the dock became a blur and I wept like a baby.

I was grateful for the few days of rest on the ship after the hectic days that had followed my appointment and confirmation. One evening at dinner, the ship's captain told me that the chef was a Luxembourger. I had a meeting with him as soon thereafter as possible. Our chat about his country gave me a warm, friendly feeling and helped calm my fears somewhat.

When the ship put in at Cóbh, Ireland, I had a wonderful surprise. Opening my stateroom door in response to a knock, I found Marguerite and Billy standing there with big smiles. They accompanied me the rest of the way to Luxembourg.

Just before we debarked at Le Havre, chef William Seiter presented me with a magnificent layer cake. It had sugar roses all over the top, and Seiter had packed it in a big box so I could carry it safely. Marguerite had arranged for a car to meet us at the ship and we had a leisurely drive to Paris.

Without advising me, the State Department had scheduled a press conference for me in Paris at one o'clock. I knew nothing of the appointment, however, and did not arrive until 4:00 P.M. By then the press representatives were hopping mad (even as I would have been), so without even going first to my room, I held the conference in the garden of the Ritz Hotel. For almost an hour I answered questions, some of them rather unkind. For example, "Does Madam Minister think that giving parties can ease the cold war?"

"If giving parties would do it," I said confidently, "I would certainly like to give all the parties I could."

The next morning we took off for Luxembourg. My personal chauffeur was now ready with my own Packard limousine, which I had brought with me on the ship. The American Embassy provided a car and French chauffeur to lead us to Luxembourg. We were quite a caravan as we drove out of Paris: the American Embassy car leading the way, packed to the roof with some of my fifteen pieces of luggage, plus Marguerite's and Billy's baggage; then my limousine with Marguerite, Billy, and me, more luggage, and my cake, and then strung out behind us five carloads of reporters. It is about two hundred miles from Paris to Luxembourg, and we should have been there about two o'clock. At two-thirty we still were driving. I had been informed in Paris that the Luxembourgers planned to have a big celebration for me when I crossed the border, the first American minister ever appointed to their country.

When we finally reached the border, there was not a dignitary in sight and the guards wouldn't even let us pass. The French chauffeur jumped out and started arguing with the border guard, waving his arms excitedly. I went over, but couldn't understand a word of what they were saying. The reporters immediately gathered around. One of them explained to me that we couldn't get in because my chauffeur had no international permit for my car. I would have to pay import duty of a thousand dollars before taking the car in. The arguing and gesturing continued until one of the newspaper men solved the mystery. We had made a wrong turn a few miles back, at Longwy, and instead of being at the France-Luxembourg border, we were at the France-Belgium border.

We backtracked to Longwy and found the right road. By the time we found our way to the proper place of entry, all the dignitaries with their flowers and speeches had hurried off to the entry gate at the Luxembourg-Belgium border, having heard that I was by mistake entering there. It was getting a little like something by Gilbert and Sullivan. We drove into Luxembourg City unescorted—and then no one knew where the American Legation was. Finally, a little boy hopped onto the fender of the leading car and guided us. Of course it made a marvelous story for the press to have Madam Minister get lost en route to her job. When I read a magazine article a short time later implying I was a nitwit for losing my way, I remembered that the car which had misled us was driven by a French chauffeur who was supposed to have driven the correct route many times before. I will never be able to prove it, but I firmly believe that a certain American magazine reporter had a hand in misdirecting us.

Whatever the reason for the mixup, I felt that I had made a pretty undignified start on my diplomatic career.

TWELVE: *The Striped-pants Boys*

IT TOOK ME only a few days in Luxembourg to discover that for the first time in my life, the cards were all stacked against me. The members of the legation staff strongly resented the fact that they had been sent a minister who had no training whatsoever in the arts and duties of diplomacy. I heard reports that Luxembourg officials, while feeling honored that their country had at last been recognized by the appointment of a United States minister, were nevertheless disappointed that President Truman had not seen fit to send someone of recognized diplomatic status (let alone sending a woman!). The small but characteristically vocal Communist element in the country immediately berated me as a "decadent representative of American wealth and capitalism." The one Communist newspaper printed a completely false story about a wild champagne party it said I threw at the legation the night I arrived. Some of the representatives of the American press, ordinarily friendly to me, were standing by like vultures, looking for mistakes that could be written up in order to bear out the contention that my appointment had been a foolish whim of the President.

Even before I could present my credentials and officially take office, William sent me a discouraging clipping from the *Daily Oklahoman*. The story had been written by a correspondent for the Chicago Daily News Service who had visited me the day after I had arrived in Luxembourg. Here are some of the highlights:

> Perle Mesta as a news story is a bust. As an example of ineptness in conduct of foreign affairs, her appointment as Minister of Luxembourg is a DANDY.
>
> I'll give anybody who wants it the fact that she has charm, that she probably knows which fork to use on the oysters, and that she has a bucket of dough which she is prepared to spend.

138

But the time has long since passed when the interrelations of governments can be conducted on that level. And the United States, with the biggest and broadest and most tremendous stake of all, is the very last among the nations of the world to recognize this. . . .

Technically, she is the representative of the government of the U.S. to the government of Luxembourg, and Truman is the head of the U.S. Government. But if foreign service ever is to develop a useful and consistent pattern, then it must be administered and channeled through the man who is responsible to the President for it, Secretary of State Acheson.

I asked Perle if she had had any meetings with Acheson before she embarked on this brave, new assignment and got the look which is reserved, I imagine, for people who spill sticky liqueurs on the stuffed velour. She admitted to knowing him to the extent of paying a brief "formal" call. Otherwise she seems to have had no contact with the State Department whatsoever. . . .

The social contacts within Luxembourg itself will be limited. The entire Congress includes only 21 members. She could run through it at a single dinner. In the diplomatic corps there are only four other resident ministers. . . .

Whatever happens, however much she may charm and enchant the locals, Mrs. M. can never be anything better than No. 2 lady and there is nothing in her background to suggest that she finds this tolerable. Any intimation that she was trying to outdo the royal family would lose her more friends overnight than her fortune could buy in a lifetime. . . . It seems almost symbolic that her party should take the wrong road and hit the uninformed border of Belgium where Mrs. M. wasn't even a name, instead of Luxembourg where preparations had been made to receive her and speed her through.

There are no resident American correspondents in the country. The nearest are stationed in Brussels, Paris and Frankfurt, and Mrs. Mesta's arrival was the first time there has been much call for their presence. On the basis of her performance this week, it will be about the last until Mrs. Mesta resigns.

Practically the only encouragement I received during those first days was the welcome given me by the people of Luxembourg. On the night of my arrival, I was unpacking when I heard band music in the distance. As I listened, it came closer. Soon it was right outside the legation. I opened the front door and watched dozens of people with torches, followed by the Limpertsberg district band, march up the drive. After they played "The Star-Spangled Banner," and marched round and round the legation garden, the leader came to the door to present me with some roses and make me an honorary member of the band. The next day when I went downtown to get my first real look around and do some shopping, people stopped me on the street to shake my hand and welcome me.

My very first social function was held two days after my arrival. I invited Mrs. Seiter, the wife of the chef of the *America,* to the legation to share the cake her husband had baked for me, and which I had hardly let out of my sight since leaving the ship. I told Mrs. Seiter to bring her family, expecting, of course, six or eight people. When the butler opened the door, there was Mrs. Seiter, her sisters, her brothers, her aunts, her uncles, her cousins, and assorted children from the ages of two to twenty—some forty people in all. I made a dash for the kitchen and told the chef to get busy making extra sandwiches. Chef Seiter's cake had come through its long journey in perfect condition, and Mrs. Seiter helped me cut it and serve it to the guests. We had a real family-style party, with the children passing the plates and some of the women helping to pour the tea. Nearly all of them spoke understandable English and they answered my numerous questions about their country and customs, while I did my best to tell them a little about America. That evening I felt much more optimistic about my Luxembourg venture. Despite the problems that confronted me, I knew that the people were warm and sympathetic, and that seemed to make everything a lot better. I was thankful, too, that Marguerite was with me. While one of us might sometimes get discouraged, it would be hard to beat two Skirvins working together.

Luxembourg's ruler, the Grand Duchess Charlotte, happened to be away in Scotland on a hunting trip when I arrived. Until she returned and I could present·my credentials, I was not technically in charge of the legation. It continued to function under the jurisdiction of our ambassador to Belgium, as it had for several years, while its actual running was in the hands of chargé d'affaires George West, who had been doing an excellent job. When I officially assumed my post, West's title would change to First Secretary, because the office of chargé d'affaires is only for legations without a minister.

There were two other State Department officers in the legation, but no attachés. However, the agricultural, economic, military, and other attachés of our embassy in Belgium were accredited to Luxembourg and available for assistance when needed.

The day before the Grand Duchess was to return, I went over to the Grand Ducal Palace to call on the Grand Marshal of the Court and learn about the rigid protocol involved in my formal presentation. I was instructed to address Her Royal Highness always in the third person. And because it is the custom never to turn one's back on the Grand Duchess, I was reminded it would be necessary for me to back out of the room after my audience.

Right after dinner that night, my sister motioned for me to follow her upstairs. Marguerite knew I was anxious about the ceremony and she now insisted that I go through a dress rehearsal. A few minutes later, dressed in my new burgundy velvet gown—I had had it made in Paris especially for the ceremony—I stepped over the threshold of my bedroom and made a deep curtsy.

Seated atop two pillows on one of the Louis XVI armchairs and wearing several bracelets on her head to simulate the crown of the Grand Duchess, my sister regally motioned for me to rise and take a seat near her. For a moment I had a memory of acting this very scene many years before when we used to dress up in Mother's long gowns and play that we were princesses.

I recited the little speech I had memorized and Marguerite nodded approvingly. Then I turned to leave the room.

"Madam Minister!" cried Marguerite. "You must never turn your back on the Grand Duchess!"

Starting over, I backed—and promptly landed a heel in the hem of my long gown. For the next fifteen minutes, Marguerite made me practice backing. When she was finally satisfied that I would not make a fool of myself, I sank into a chair and we had a good laugh at ourselves. If the legation chargé d'affaires had walked in during that rehearsal, he surely would have had a choice morsel to report to the home office.

The presentation of my credentials the following day turned out to be considerably easier than my rehearsal. I had asked all our attachés in Brussels, as well as the three State Department officers at the legation and my press attaché to accompany me to the palace. The chargé d'affaires thought it was a little ostentatious to have so many people attend, but I wanted to put on as good a show as possible and rationalized it by telling myself that this was the first time there had been a United States Minister to Luxembourg.

At the palace I was met by the Court Chamberlain and promptly at 11:30 A.M. a door was flung open and I heard a court page call out: "Her Excellency the Envoy Extraordinary and Minister Plenipotentiary from the United States." He was announcing *me!* It was almost like a dream. Holding my head high, I walked slowly through the doorway.

Her Royal Highness the Grand Duchess Charlotte was standing with her consort, Prince Felix, in the center of a large and beautiful drawing room. After I made my deep curtsy and presented my credentials, I introduced my staff. The Grand Duchess then seated herself on a small settee and, in beautifully accented English, graciously invited me to sit beside her, while the members of my staff talked with members of her court. She is a tall, regal-looking woman and that morning her eyes expressed reassuring warmth and kindliness. And before we had talked a minute, we found we had many mutual friends and all at once, I seemed never to have left home: Her Royal Highness wanted me to tell her all the latest news about her friends Generals Eisenhower and Bradley, Eleanor Roosevelt, and Mrs. Joseph Davies.

After we had visited for perhaps a quarter of an hour, the Grand Duchess arose and told me her country was most honored to have a United States Minister. I thanked her, made another curtsy, and backed out without a hitch, mentally blessing my farsighted sister for her solid part in my success.

An hour later, I gave a big luncheon at the Cravat Hotel for the legation staff, members of the Brussels embassy, and Senator and Mrs. Owen Brewster and Undersecretary of State and Mrs. Cornelius Vanderbilt Whitney.

The next morning when I went to the legation offices, which are in a separate building just-across the driveway from the residence, I faced problems of a different kind. One of the striped-pants boys came in and asked if he and the two other State Department officers could have a conference with me. Something in his tone warned me the velvet gloves were going to come off. I agreed to the conference and waited for the men to appear. "All right," I said pleasantly. "What can I do for you?"

"First, what are we to call you?" one of them asked. "You would like us to call you Mrs. Mesta, wouldn't you?"

"No," I said, "I really wouldn't. You can call me Madam Minister as long as I am representing the United States Government."

Then they started. They had lined up a woman who was an excellent housekeeper and who spoke several languages, and they wanted me to hire her.

"Now just what is this idea?" I asked, beginning to get a little bit peeved.

One of the men said, "This woman knows all about protocol and how to run a household, and she can help you look after the residence and take care of the tourists. Of course we will take care of things in the office."

Shades of George Mesta's dear old Mrs. Shultz! I shuddered but didn't say anything for a moment. I could see that the three of them thought I was just a rich society woman who was interested only in giving parties.

"What do you mean by take care of things?" I asked.

"Well, Madam Minister, we will handle the routine business and prepare and sign the reports for you," the spokesman for the staff replied.

"I believe the President sent me over here to be the minister," I said at last. "There were many women who could have filled this post just as well as I can. But as long as the President picked me, I feel it is my duty to represent the American people and take charge of this office and not just be the official hostess."

The spokesman scuffed his shoes impatiently.

"We didn't mean it exactly that way," he said. "But somebody's got to take care of your residence and the guests."

By this time I was getting pretty irritated.

"Well, I don't need that woman for a housekeeper. And if you think I'm just going to pour tea while I'm in Luxembourg you've got another think coming. I can sign my own name and will sign it. If you think you have a report I can't understand, you explain it to me, and then *I'll* sign it."

I was really getting wound up. I hadn't felt like this since the day I took charge of things at my first board meeting at Mesta Machine Company.

"Now, what time do you men get here in the morning?" I asked.

143

"About nine," one of them said.

"And what time do you go to lunch?"

"About twelve-thirty."

"What time do you get back?"

"About three."

"And I suppose you leave at about five o'clock?"

They nodded.

"Well," I said, "let's get things straight right now. *I* will be in this office at nine o'clock and will stay until one. *I* will take one hour for lunch. *I* will be here at night as late as necessary. And as far as luncheon is concerned, many days I can go without it because I'm so fat it would be a good idea if I missed a few meals."

They couldn't help laughing at that and the tension eased a little.

"You realize we do have a pattern set up for running the office?" the first secretary said.

"I'm sure you do," I replied. "But I may very possibly change things. I have some ideas of my own. I intend to visit the farms and the industries of this country and I want to get to know the people. And, with your help, I hope to learn how to run this office." Although the conference ended on a friendly note, I knew very well that none of our basic differences had been settled.

In addition to the three Foreign Service officers, I had an excellent group of young Luxembourg women as office help, plus my American press attaché, Dorothy Williams, and a very efficient American secretary, Pat Ventura. Pat was really more than a secretary, because she could take care of many tasks by herself without having to question me about them. And she was wonderful to the Luxembourg people and to our many visitors.

My second day in the office I had another run-in with my staff.

"I understand you have been invited to go down into the A.R.B.E.D. iron mine," the first secretary said. I answered that the Minister of Labor had given me such an invitation even before I had presented my credentials.

"We received a formal invitation this morning from the Court Chamberlain," the secretary said. "He wants you to go through the A.R.B.E.D. steel plant and have luncheon with the directors."

"Before I visit the mine?" I asked.

The secretary nodded.

"But I've already told the miners I would go down with them tomorrow," I said.

"The Chamberlain is also vice-president of the steel plant," the secretary said. "It is protocol for you to go there first. And inasmuch as none of the ministers from other countries have ever been down in a mine, nor has any woman official done this, we think it would be most undignified for you to do so."

I let him go on and give me his arguments.

"Thank you for your advice," I said when he had finished, "but the miners asked me first and I accepted, and I always go where I am first invited. Tomorrow I will go down in the mine."

I kept my word. That visit underground was one of the most frightening experiences I ever had. When we were deep in the shaft, the foreman said, "Now we've arranged something for you that we've never before done for a visitor—we're going to dynamite a wall." I turned to the American labor attaché who had accompanied me.

"That's awfully nice of them," I said. "But it really isn't necessary. Don't you think we could skip it?" The attaché was worried, too, but said he thought we should let them go through with it since the miners were obviously proud of having set up the demonstration. So I said a little prayer and then shut my eyes and put my hands over my ears. There was a terrific explosion, the ground shook like an earthquake, and dirt came showering down on us. I opened my eyes and was relieved to find myself still all in one piece and little the worse for the experience. I guess you could say my diplomatic activities in Luxembourg started off with a bang.

A few days later I accepted the invitation to tour the A.R.B.E.D. steel plant. The president of the company was surprised to find how much I knew about the steel business. He and his fellow directors were not only cordial to me, but contrary to the legation secretary's predictions, they were delighted that I had already visited their mine.

During my entire stay in Luxembourg I was never able to reach complete agreement with the Foreign Service officers on my staff. I spent many a sleepless night worrying over the situation. I think I can appreciate their concern that in my ignorance about Foreign Service protocol I would do something to embarrass our country or the State Department. And I would not dispute that they had much more experience than I did in formal diplomacy. But the State Department wants its employees to perform according to a strict pattern—and I'm just not a pattern girl.

In the few weeks before coming to Luxembourg I had done a lot of thinking about what a representative of the United States should do overseas. I knew a good many State Department officers and most of them were men of high caliber and were doing good work. But I also knew of too many young men in the Foreign Service who had no vision and no understanding of what they were sent out to do. In going up through the echelons they lost sight of the fact that they were representing the United States of America and the American way of life. Some of them seemed to think that diplomacy consisted entirely of donning striped trousers and having tea at four o'clock and being very high-hat.

It seemed to me that maintaining and bettering relations between countries was the chief job of diplomacy. Somehow, I wondered why our Foreign Service always insisted that the job of diplomacy be done only at the top levels where tradition and protocol turn it into coldly formal and uninspired negotiations. It seems to me this is the opposite of everything America stands for as a nation. Diplomacy based on simple dignity, on informality, on warm and neighborly greeting would appear to be not only more desirable but more effective.

I had decided, and had told the President as much when I saw him just before leaving for Luxembourg, that I was going to try to express the essence of our American way of life as I saw it. I might make a few mistakes in protocol and I might not perform all the required formal duties in the proper fashion, but I was going to go out and meet the people of Luxembourg and try to do in my own natural way whatever seemed the right thing to do at the time. I also told the President that what I expected to do would be what any American woman might do with a similar opportunity.

As minister, then, I adopted no set policy other than to ask myself each day, "What can I do today that will help my country and will help Luxembourg?"

THIRTEEN: *Doing What Comes Naturally*

ONE OF THE FIRST jobs that confronted me on taking over the legation was to make it livable. The legation residence was a heavy German mid-Victorian graystone structure with fourteen rooms, none of them very large. The gardens were lovely, though, with a fine view over a valley. The house had been owned by the German government prior to World War II and had been used as the German minister's residence. During the war, the Nazis had made it their headquarters when Gustav Simon became gauleiter after the Grand Duchess Charlotte and her government went into exile. I was told the house had included a Gestapo torture chamber, and this might have been true because there were several cell-like rooms in the basement with padded walls. The building had been given a quick paint job when the United States bought it, and some odds and ends of furniture had been obtained. Some of the chairs were so rickety I was afraid they might collapse, and there was one long stiff-looking couch in the drawing room that was strictly early Union Station.

Of course, the house immediately became a challenge to Marguerite. She had been planning to stay with me only a few weeks but she took one look at my quarters and said, "Oh, you can't stand this, Sister, I'll do it over for you." And once she got started, she couldn't leave. Poor George finally got tired of waiting for his wife to return home and came over to take her back. But he liked Luxembourg so much that he stayed on and on. And before long Betty and her little Marguerite joined us, much to my delight, and they rented a house nearby.

I had a little difficulty in getting permission from the State Department to redecorate the residence. I finally won out, after letting them know it didn't represent the good taste that we wanted the rest of the world to know as American.

Marguerite went to Paris and started going through antique shops and visiting dealers, looking for bargains. She found some superb crystal chandeliers, a copy of an Aubusson rug to put into the entrance hall, and a lovely antique rug for the drawing room. I had several of my own things brought over from Newport: some china and silver, a tapestry for the walls going upstairs, a rose taffeta bed, draperies and a spread for the guest room, and all the furniture for my own room.

By early November, 1949, the house looked lovely and we were ready to start entertaining. I used the occasion of a visit by a Senate appropriations subcommittee to give my first big Luxembourg party. The subcommittee was headed by my old Oklahoma friend, Senator Elmer Thomas. I invited the whole group to stay in Luxembourg for two days. I took them over the land where the Battle of the Ardennes had been fought, and also to the American military cemetery at Hamm, where they laid a wreath on the grave of General George S. Patton.

For my party, I invited the Luxembourg Prime Minister, Pierre Dupong; the Luxembourg Foreign Minister, Joseph Bech, and Madame Bech; members of the foreign diplomatic corps in Luxembourg; the Court Chamberlain; the burgomaster (mayor) of Luxembourg City; a few labor leaders and their wives and some other Luxembourg people I had met and liked. In addition to Elmer Thomas, we also had Senator and Mrs. Dennis Chavez; Senator and Mrs. Burnet Maybank and their daughter, Elizabeth; Senator and Mrs. John McClellan; and Senator Willis Robertson. The American violinist Isaac Stern, who had come to Luxembourg to give a concert, was also with us.

After an American dinner featuring filet steaks, we started to dance. I had hired a local orchestra, and had rehearsed them myself to make sure they knew enough American dance music. As the party got going, we taught the Luxembourgers how to square dance, and the burgomaster learned how to call "Yippee" as he sashayed across the floor. We even got the Court Chamberlain, a tall, austere-looking man, to do a rumba. There was one touchy moment when the orchestra started to play "Marching Through Georgia" to honor the senators, most of whom were from the Deep South. I quickly went to the leader and had him switch to "Dixie."

148

Several members of the American press came to cover the party, despite the prediction of that Chicago correspondent two months earlier that they wouldn't be paying attention to me again until I resigned. The attitude of some of the press had begun to improve, as evidenced by an article published in the *New York Times Magazine* shortly after the party, which read in part:

> One excited Luxembourg lady, breathless from her first square dance, couldn't contain her enthusiasm. She rushed up to Mrs. Mesta's sister and said, "Your President couldn't have sent us a nicer present. We do love her." "And she loves you, too," was the perfectly honest reply. Mrs. Mesta thus was launched in Luxembourg and the United States was assured that at least one of its foreign policies, keeping relations friendly with a friendly country, was in safe hands.

Two weeks later I gave another party. This one was in honor of Matthew Woll, a vice-president of the American Federation of Labor. Matt Woll had been born in Luxembourg and was visiting his native country en route to a London conference of trade unions. I thought it might be a good idea if some of the labor leaders in Luxembourg, where unions were not highly organized, could meet a high-ranking American union official. Inviting several union chiefs to my party, I also included Luxembourg's Minister of Labor, some other government officials, and some of the executives from the steel plants. For my efforts, I was rewarded with a scathing attack in the Communist newspaper, *Wochen Zeitung*.

"Luxembourg workers know what they have to think of labor leaders who are being rendered homage by capitalists and reactionary exploiters," the paper said in the course of its long diatribe against Mr. Woll and me.

There were only five Communists in the Chamber of Deputies, but they made their presence unmistakable. A few weeks after I arrived, one of them sent word that he and his colleagues wanted to see me on the following Saturday, assuming, I am sure, that my office would then be closed, as was the custom with all the legations. I replied that I would be happy to receive them at whatever hour they chose, and I made it a point to be in my office all that Saturday. The men did not show up, and during my entire stay in Luxembourg they never made any formal recognition of my presence. Once when I was at a reception for the president of Luxembourg's Chamber of Deputies, the five Communists pointedly walked out of the room as soon as I appeared.

On December 6, the children of Luxembourg have St. Nicholas Day—the day of gift-giving. Their Christmas is entirely a religious holiday, as it is in many European countries. Recalling the joy of that Christmas many years before when I had given a big party for the children of the workers in my husband's steel plant, I extended invitations to the orphanages of Luxembourg, and on St. Nicholas Day, four hundred orphans filed into the large hall I rented for the occasion. We had a wonderful party. The children were quite shy at first, but as they watched the puppet show I had imported from Paris, they filled the room with their laughter. There was ice cream and cake and then, speaking in Luxembourgeois, I gave a thirty-three-word speech of welcome. The children giggled delightedly as I stumbled over the strange words, and then they expressed their thanks in the perfect English phrases they had learned for the occasion. Before they left, each child received a piece of clothing and a toy "from St. Nicholas."

One rainy day shortly after I arrived in Luxembourg, I returned from an outing and found three young men standing at the door of the legation. I had stepped out of a station wagon, and with my raincoat on and a hat pulled over my face I guess I didn't look very much like Madam Minister. I said, "You are Americans, aren't you?" and they nodded.

"We want to see Perle Mesta," said one of the boys.

When I said I was Mrs. Mesta, they didn't believe me. You should have seen their faces when I rang the bell and the butler ceremoniously let us in.

Learning that my callers were G.I.'s on a weekend pass from their base in West Germany, I had an idea. "Do you drink?" I asked. They admitted that they sometimes did.

"Would you promise not to drink too much if I invited you to a party?" I was giving a party that night to get the Luxembourg and American employees of the legation better acquainted.

"We won't touch a drop if you don't want us to," they answered. So I told the boys to come back at seven o'clock.

Those three G.I.'s were the life of the party. One of them played the piano and another sang. And their spontaneity was so catching that everybody had a good time. At midnight as they left, one of the boys told me why they had come to my door in the first place.

"My buddies bet me five bucks apiece I couldn't get in to meet Perle Mesta," he said. "So I've not only had a swell time but made ten bucks on the deal."

While Betty and Pat Ventura and Marguerite and I were cleaning up and comparing notes about the evening, Marguerite told us that one of the soldiers had come to her and said the party had meant a great deal to him because he had been feeling homesick. What Marguerite said brought back to me the memory of those youngsters at the Stage Door Canteen in Washington, some of them fuzzy-cheeked and so young and so sad about having to leave their families for the first time.

I thought for a moment, and a plan began forming. I knew there were thousands of United States troops stationed within a short distance of Luxembourg: in Western Germany, eastern France, and the southern section of Belgium. Maybe we could do something to help entertain them. I turned to Marguerite. "Why don't we give some parties especially for G.I.'s?" I suggested. "Maybe we should make it a regular event and have open house once a month."

And thus my G.I. parties were born. From then on, the first Saturday of every month was open house at the American Legation in Luxembourg for all G.I.'s who could get there. The parties were small at first, but as word got around they grew so big I had to hire a hall. By 1953 I had entertained some twenty-five thousand servicemen and servicewomen. If any taxpayers who read this begin worrying about who paid for all these parties—I did, out of my own pocket. And after every G.I. party I would write letters to the parents of many of the young people I had met, and would mention how Johnny or Jane was looking fine and enjoying Europe.

One beautiful, crisp Sunday morning soon after I became minister, Marguerite and I started another custom—a weekly ride into the countryside to see the sights and talk to the people. Luxembourg is really a story-book country, and Marguerite and I soon fell in love with it. Although it is one of the smallest countries in Europe —only about one-seventieth the size of Oklahoma—Luxembourg has some of the most beautiful scenery in the world. It is nestled between Belgium and Germany, with France holding the border on the south. In the southern part there are lovely valleys and fruit

151

orchards, and around the Moselle Valley they produce some of Europe's best wines. The northern section is more wooded and has small mountains and jagged peaks covered with forests. This is the Ardennes Forest that held the attention of the world for a few weeks in the winter of 1944, when the final German offensive went right through it before being driven back when General Patton's forces came to the rescue. There are many small farms all through Luxembourg. The biggest industry, aside from agriculture, is steel, and Luxembourg has fine iron mines, as well as several big plants and rolling mills.

The capital, Luxembourg City, has a beauty of its own. It is set on mighty rocks and has remnants of medieval walls, as well as buildings and towers dating from the seventeenth and eighteenth centuries. All through the country there are wonderful old castles, and it is sometimes called the Land of the Haunted Castles.

Luxembourg may be only sixty-two miles long and thirty-seven miles across at the widest part, but the country has a rich tradition. Its history dates back to the tenth century, and it was once four times its present size and one of the most influential countries in Europe. In the fifteenth century, Luxembourg lost its sovereignty, but the people never lost their spirit of independence. They refused to be assimilated into the countries that conquered them. Many wars were fought over Luxembourg City, a nearly impregnable fortress with fourteen miles of underground tunnels. At various times, Spain, Austria, France, and Prussia all fought to control the little country. In 1815 Luxembourg finally regained her autonomy, and in 1839 she won her complete independence as a Grand Duchy.

During World War II, when invaded by Germany, Luxembourg fought back through an underground organization led by her government in exile in England. Thousands of Luxembourgers were killed or deported to concentration camps by the Nazis. In 1942 a general strike was called. Although this revolt was violently put down, the Free World gained faith from this first open defiance of the Nazis by an occupied country.

On September 10, 1944, Luxembourg was liberated by the American Army. Three months later the northern half of the country was once again overrun by the counterattacking Germans in the Battle of the Ardennes. Thousands of Allied soldiers lost their lives in this attack, and sixty thousand Luxembourgers saw their homes destroyed. In early January, 1945, the invader was driven back, once and for all.

Today, Luxembourg is a constitutional monarchy. The executive power is in the hands of the Grand Duchess and her cabinet, comprised of six ministers. Legislative power rests with an elected fifty-two-man Chamber of Deputies. All men and women over twenty-one are eligible to vote, and 92 per cent of them take part in elections (which of course is far better than we do in the United States). Luxembourg is a member of the United Nations and NATO and helped establish the European Coal and Steel Community.

I saw for myself that Luxembourg is neither a rich country nor a poor one. I saw no unemployment, I met no millionaires. Most of the people have plenty to eat and comfortable homes. They are just good, substantial, friendly workingmen and middle-class people. Their homes are neat as a pin, and they keep their streets and cities clean.

During our drives into the country, Marguerite and I made it a point to take in community celebrations and the many small fairs. We met the burgomaster of each town. We stopped off at coffee shops and talked with the villagers over cakes and coffee. We visited farms: we saw all the historic places. I have never cared much for sports events, but as minister I would present trophies at a bicycle race or watch a soccer game almost every week. And frequently I would go down to Namur's teashop in Luxembourg City to mingle with the townswomen who congregated there late every afternoon for tea and pastries. We regularly took flowers to the American cemetery where so many heroes of the Battle of the Ardennes are buried. Sometimes we would put flowers on a grave and take a picture of it to send back home to a mother who had written asking that someone from the legation visit her son's grave. Five thousand Americans are buried in the cemetery at Hamm, just outside Luxembourg City.

One Sunday I met the burgomaster of a small village who told me of a water supply problem his people were having. In talking with him, I discovered that he had never even met the burgomasters of the neighboring towns, who might have been of help to him. I decided to hold a party to bring together the burgomasters from all over the country and give them a chance to meet each other.

I ran into opposition right away from my staff. They said that even the Luxembourg government had never called all the burgo-masters together. My doing it could easily be interpreted as inter-fering with national affairs. I went ahead with my plans nonetheless, convinced that what I was doing was right. I found out what kind of food the burgomasters liked and what kind of music they would enjoy. I almost made a *faux pas* when I started to invite their wives. Before the invitations went out, one of the Luxembourg girls on the staff came to me.

"Madam Minister, there is something I must tell you," she said rather hesitantly. "I think you should know that these men would not want their wives to come." And then she explained that in Luxembourg wives are content to stay home and leave affairs of state to the men. And she also suggested I have the party on a Sat-urday, when most Luxembourgers take the afternoon off. The bur-gomasters were farmers, blacksmiths, miners—just ordinary citi-zens—and they had to earn their livings. The job of burgomaster was a nonpaying sideline.

When the controversial Saturday came, my butler informed me that my guests were too shy to enter the legation. Sure enough, some hundred burgomasters, all dressed in their Sunday best, were milling uncertainly about in the garden. I went outside and greeted them there. It took a while for them to get used to the situation. After a bit, when we led them to the garden tables heaped with smoked pork and broad beans and plenty of wines and beer, they started to relax.

It was a very informal party. I had some accordion players mov-ing among the small tables and a few violinists hidden behind some plants. Gradually, the men began talking to each other about mutual problems. After they had eaten, drunk, and talked for an hour or so, I had the musicians get together and play some dance tunes. I asked the burgomaster of Esch for a dance, and Marguerite, Betty, and three of the legation secretaries also chose partners. We danced until we were exhausted, and the party broke up after dark. When the men left they had lost all their shyness and were calling me Perle instead of Madam Minister. After that, every time I went to a town, the burgomaster would say, "Perle, when are we going to have another good party like that?" For me, that was reason enough to make my burgomasters' party an annual event.

Early in 1950, in Paris for a conference, I had lunch at the Ritz with Doris and Jules Stein, who were visiting from New York. Jules, the president of Music Corporation of America, really gave me a start when he said, "Well, Perle, how does it feel to find yourself the subject of a Broadway musical?"

"What in the world are you talking about?" I said in bewilderment.

Then Jules told me that Howard Lindsay and Russel Crouse were writing a musical comedy about a Washington hostess who became an ambassador. "That *couldn't* be anybody but you," Jules concluded.

"I'll bet that's nothing but gossip," I said. "What would they want to do a play about me for?"

"Gossip, nothing," answered Jules. "I got it straight from Irving Berlin, who told me he's writing the songs."

I was so upset by this news I could hardly go on with my lunch. And the more I thought about it, the more worried I got, wondering what they were going to put in the play. And my apprehension mounted a week or so later when I read a newspaper interview with Irving Berlin. The reporter had asked Berlin if Perle Mesta knew a play was being written about her, and Berlin was quoted as replying, "Well, if she doesn't know now, she will before we get through with it."

The next word I heard was from the Steins, who were then back in New York: Howard Lindsay and his actress-wife, Dorothy Stickney, were planning a trip to Luxembourg to get some firsthand information and some "atmosphere." My first impulse was to find an excuse to be out of the country when they arrived. On second thought I realized I had nothing to hide. It occurred to me that if I was very nice to the Lindsays, I might convince them I wasn't as bad as they might have pictured me. Acting on this thought, I wired an invitation for them to be my guests at the legation. I received this reply from Mrs. Lindsay: MY PECULIAR HUSBAND FEELS HE WOULD BE MORE COMFORTABLE IN THE NEUTRALITY OF A HOTEL.

When they arrived in Luxembourg, Dorothy Lindsay told me that her cowardly husband had written the cable and signed her name. "I didn't want to stay at the legation and be charmed out of some of my jokes," Howard Lindsay told me later. They did come to the legation for luncheon, however, and I took them on a motor tour of the country, showed them one of the old castles, and

155

introduced them to some government officials. As we were driving along, Mr. Lindsay told me that his writing partner had gotten the idea for their play when he saw my picture on the cover of *Time* magazine the year before. Since my guest had brought up the subject, I, with my usual forthrightness, asked him to tell me his plot. Stammering, Lindsay told me a very dull story that was nothing like the play Broadway finally saw.

I had been in Luxembourg nine months when I returned to Washington for a consultation with the State Department, a customary procedure with ambassadors and ministers. After my sessions at the State Department, I had an appointment with the President. Instead of going in the side door, as I had always done before to see the Trumans in their family quarters, I marched into the White House through the front door and had a formal appointment in the President's office, just like a V.I.P.

I started to tell the President what I had been doing in Luxembourg, but he seemed to know everything before I told him.

"You must be reading my reports," I said.

"I certainly do read them," the President replied with a grin.

I didn't know whether that was a good sign or whether he had been checking up on me. Then I told him that the State Department people did not approve of some of the things I was doing. I mentioned particularly my going into the mines and bringing the burgomasters together. The President told me to go right ahead, and that if it came to a showdown, I would have his backing.

While in Washington, I made a call on an Oklahoma friend, Josh Lee, who was then chairman of the Civil Aeronautics Board. I wanted to get permission for a nonscheduled airline that was then flying freight to Luxembourg to fly passengers on special nonscheduled flights. My request was on behalf of Youth Argosy, an organization set up to provide low-cost transportation and lodging for students touring Europe. I was trying to make it possible for them to start and end their 1950 summer trips in Luxembourg.

Josh Lee was sympathetic to my request, but said he could not do anything himself; I would have to present my case to the entire Civil Aeronautics Board. This I did, and a short time later the airline was given permission to fly the youngsters to and from Luxembourg at very favorable student rates.

After my Washington consultations, I went up to New York for a few days and was given a luncheon there that I consider one of the greatest honors of my life. Matthew Woll, the A. F. of L. vice-president whom I had entertained in Luxembourg the previous fall, got together with his friend, and mine, Thomas Watson, president of International Business Machines, to co-host the affair. I don't think a party was ever given anyplace by hosts as far apart as those two in their economic viewpoints. As we looked around the luncheon room at the Hotel Pierre from the head table, Matt Woll commented that only in America could such an affair as this take place, with labor and management getting together socially. Among the two hundred guests were William Green, the A. F. of L. president, department store heads Bernard Gimbel and Dorothy Shaver, novelist Fannie Hurst, ex-Ambassador Spruille Braden, decorator Dorothy Draper, Mrs. William Randolph Hearst, Jr., Mrs. Wendell Willkie, and poet Dylan Thomas, as well as such old friends as Ike and Mamie Eisenhower, Bess Farley, Margaret Truman, Cornelius Vanderbilt, Jr., and Sylvia and Leonard Lyons.

A few days after this luncheon, the Lyonses gave a party so that I could meet Ethel Merman, who was to portray the playwrights' conception of me in *Call Me Madam,* and Irving Berlin and Russel Crouse. I took Margaret Truman along to the Lyonses' home; Margaret always enjoyed being with musical and theatrical people.

Some of the guests, knowing that Ethel was going to satirize me in the play, were expecting sparks to fly when we met. But the moment she arrived and greeted me in that big, lovable, loud voice, I knew we were going to be good friends. I told Ethel I had never missed a play of hers. Then I noticed her earrings. "I have some just like those," I said. "I'll wear them more often." Ethel replied, "No, don't do that. I have some long earrings like yours and I'll wear them in the show."

As the party progressed, Irving Berlin played some of his great hit songs. When he began my favorite, "Remember," I sang along with him. Ethel nudged Margaret Truman.

"Get a load of that Mesta," she said to Margaret in a loud voice. "If she's going into my racket, I may ask your father for a diplomatic appointment."

Just before returning to Luxembourg, I saw the President again briefly.

"Can you give me any advice, Mr. President?" I asked. "I know our relations are good with Luxembourg, but maybe there is something else I could do."

The President thought for a moment. "How about taking some Luxembourg youngster and educating him over here?" he suggested. "It may be a small thing, but it could have worth-while results."

I went back to Luxembourg and conferred with Pierre Frieden, the Minister of Education, telling him that if he picked out a worthy student, I would pay his or her transportation and provide for support and college education in the United States. I attached only one string to my offer: his education completed, the student had to agree to return to Luxembourg and put his knowledge to work.

Mr. Frieden presently selected Pierre Reiff, one of six children from a family that could not afford to send the boy to college. Pierre wanted to study engineering, so I had a friend in New York check into the engineering schools. About this time, Purdue University's choral society came to Luxembourg and I gave a party for them. The university's vice-president was along on the tour, and I asked him if they had a good engineering school.

"We have one of the best engineering schools in the nation," said Dr. Frank Hockema. "In fact, some people say it is the best." And for the next ten minutes, he bragged up the Purdue engineers.

"That's fine, just fine," I said. Then I told him about Pierre Reiff, and added, "How about Purdue giving Pierre a scholarship?" Dr. Hockema immediately saw it as a fine opportunity to promote international good will. Within a week after he had returned to Indiana I received word that a scholarship had been awarded.

A short time after Pierre left for the United States, I established a fund to help educate deserving Luxembourg musicians. A competition was held, and Evalyn Schaus, a lovely youngster who had spent four years in a German concentration camp, was declared the winner. I placed Evalyn in the Sherwood School of Music in Chicago, for the study of piano and voice. Little did I foresee the ultimate result of the trip to America for these two youngsters, nor could I know how Mr. Truman's suggestion about international education was to broaden my activities in the years to come.

The news that Eleanor Roosevelt was coming to Europe and would visit us in Luxembourg threw our little household into somewhat of a tizzy. Though I had long admired Mrs. Roosevelt as one of the greatest and most influential women in the world, I didn't know her personally very well at that time. From the somewhat disparaging statements she had made to the press after my appointment, I knew she thought of me mostly as a party giver. I hoped to correct that impression. The problem that worried Marguerite and me most concerning Mrs. Roosevelt's visit, however, was George Tyson. George, the arch-conservative Boston Republican, still grows red in the face at the mere mention of F.D.R., and his opinion of all the Roosevelt family had never been very high. Marguerite and I decided to try to ward off trouble by arranging for my military aide, Colonel Albert Hoffman, also a confirmed Republican, to invite George to his apartment for the night. We figured George would be sufficiently calmed down by the next day to act civilly toward Mrs. Roosevelt. We miscalculated. He and Colonel Hoffman spent most of the night running down the New Deal and by the time we all got together at lunch, George was in fine Republican form. He lit right into Mrs. Roosevelt, telling her what a mess her husband had made of things.

Mrs. Roosevelt, bless her, just smiled and let him run on. Then she gently began to counter some of his arguments and to talk about interesting things she had been doing. She was so charming about it that George lost his belligerence. By the time she left Luxembourg, he grudgingly admitted that maybe there was at least one good Roosevelt after all.

I found that the Luxembourgers had a doubly warm place in their hearts for Mrs. Roosevelt, not only because of what her husband had done to help their country during the war, but also because Franklin Delano Roosevelt was a descendant of a famous Luxembourg family. The Delano family traces directly to the de Lannoi family, who were barons of Clervaux, in northern Luxembourg. While Mrs. Roosevelt was visiting us, I drove her to the ancestral castle. The town declared a holiday and turned out at the castle to honor Mrs. Roosevelt.

I was deeply gratified when Mrs. Roosevelt wrote an article in *Flair* magazine about her visit with us which showed she no longer thought of me as just a party giver. Among other things, Mrs. Roosevelt said:

When Perle Mesta was appointed to Luxembourg I am sure that many people thought as I did, that it was a personal appointment, since she had been such a warm friend of the President and Mrs. Truman. Now and then a President is allowed to recognize a friendship. He cannot do it too often, but there is not much criticism if a frankly personal appointment comes along occasionally, and I had thought of this as purely that kind of appointment. I shrugged and smiled a little as I wondered whether all the people of tiny Luxembourg could not be entertained in one week, and then what would be left to interest our Madame Minister?

How little I really knew and how shallow were my observations. Luxembourg is the seventh largest steel-producing country in the world, and when the President appointed Mrs. Mesta he knew she ran her own steel business and that she was familiar with the iron mines that belonged to her. It was no surprise to him, then, that immediately on arrival at her post she accepted an invitation by the miners in southern Luxembourg to come and see their mines. . . . She knew quite well when the President sent her to Luxembourg that he did so because he thought she could be useful in that particular place. He knew that she wanted to be useful, since the world was going through a crisis, and he feels that anyone who has brains and ability should use them for the benefit of the country. . . .

She has an arrangement with the guards on the roads entering this little duchy, and they not only let her know when an American enters, but they tell the American that Madame Mesta, the Minister from the United States, would be delighted to see them in her office. She sees every American who comes to Luxembourg, and even in Luxembourg, small as the country is, that means quite a number of people. . . .

I want to say here about this particular Madame Minister that she will not be found wanting in devotion to duty. I do not know enough to tell you about the situations our diplomats, particularly our women diplomats, are up against, but I do know that they are capable of giving every problem study, and of serving their country not as women but as able representatives of the United States, carrying out the policies of our Government with tact and wisdom and being helpful to every American citizen who comes to them for guidance. (Copyright © by Cowles Magazines, Inc.)

160

Late in June, 1950, the Korean War broke out. At home, President Truman was immediately criticized for sending American troops into action. In Luxembourg, the President's decision was lauded.

"We were very disheartened about the Korean situation until your President took this stand," Foreign Minister Joseph Bech told me. "Now it is comforting to know that the United States will step in at once when the small nations need help against aggressors."

I got on the phone and told Mr. Truman of the sentiments in Luxembourg. My news was a real boost to his morale, the President said, because he was hearing so much criticism on his side of the Atlantic.

That summer of 1950, despite the Korean War, thousands of American tourists arrived in Luxembourg. Many of them came to the legation, and whenever possible I would have them to tea or at least would meet them and see if we could be of any service. My workload at the office was also increasing. I had to supervise a staff of eighteen people. I insisted on seeing every document that went out of the office and personally signed every letter. There were contacts to be maintained with the Luxembourg Foreign Office. I had frequent meetings with the U.S. High Commissioner in Germany, John McCloy, both in Frankfurt and in Luxembourg. Junketing U.S. senators and representatives made our legation a port of call.

When my duties permitted, I continued my informal visiting around the country. On one trip I visited a farm where the wife was about to have a baby. She said if it was a girl, she wanted to name it Perle and asked if I would be the godmother. I said I would. It turned out to be a boy. Not to lose out entirely, I suggested that the mother name him William, after my brother—and she did. A short time later, another family named its twelfth child—a girl—Perle, so I was not disappointed after all.

There always were ceremonies going on. I vividly remember my first Fourth of July in Luxembourg. The holiday was American, but the celebration was delightfully European. Bright and early in the morning, there came a darling little civic band tootling its way up to the legation to serenade us. I invited the musicians into the garden and served refreshments. They played "The Star-Spangled Banner" for us and followed it with "Hemecht," the Luxembourg national anthem. After the concert, they marched tootling away. It was like a scene out of a Strauss operetta.

Jim and Bess Farley were visiting us that day, and in the evening we all went visiting the city's bands (each district has its own band and place to play). Each bandleader presented me with a big bouquet of roses (the Luxembourg national flower), and I gave each of them a kiss. We ended up in the municipal square, where the United States Air Force Band gave a concert and I made a little speech to the several thousand people who had assembled from all over the country. I told them about the American Fourth of July and what it stood for, and how both our countries had the same spirit of independence. Then we drank Coca-Colas in the park, handing them out free to the Luxembourgers (courtesy of Jim Farley, who had become vice-president of the company).

Each day brought new opportunities for helping in some way or another—such as the time when I found a cute little colored boy at an orphanage. He was the illegitimate child of a Luxembourg girl who had become too friendly with an American soldier. Because he was the only one of his race in the orphanage, the people who ran the home thought he soon would need to be among people of his own color. So I helped to find a suitable couple in America who were interested in adopting the child, and then worked to speed up the immigration and adoption procedures.

All during the summer of 1950 the Youth Argosy group made Luxembourg the arrival and departure point for their tours, having leased an old castle to house the over-nighters. A minor crisis arose early in September. A plane that had been shuttling the youngsters across the Atlantic was suddenly commandeered to fly troops and supplies to Korea. American students began piling up in Luxembourg. They all had their return tickets but no other airline would honor them.

I called Washington and made the emergency known. Then I got the Luxembourg Army to put up a large tent in the legation garden and furnish it with tables. Each day we served about two hundred of the students—the overflow from the castle—their noon meal and then tea cakes and sandwiches late in the afternoon. When the Luxembourgers learned of the situation they immediately opened their homes and gave the young Americans free lodging and breakfast.

After ten days of this, the plane returned from Korea and began flying the youngsters back to America in time for the opening of school. I think that most everyone involved considered it a rich experience. The Luxembourgers who took in the youngsters had an opportunity to see what American young people are like, and the youngsters had a chance to sample the simple wholesomeness of life in Luxembourg.

In October I was called home again by the State Department. It was probably a good thing I had to go back once in a while, because I found my viewpoint being swayed by my growing love for the Luxembourgers. I had been warned by experienced Foreign Service officers that this could easily happen. But the wisdom of the warning really came through to me when I made a tape recording at the State Department for use by the Voice of America and inadvertently spoke of Mr. Bech as *"our* Foreign Minister."

While in Washington, I was given a lovely tea by columnist Betty Beale and her sister Nancy Mann. I wore an exclusive Paulette hat from Paris—dove gray decorated with shell pearls and sequined veil. It was really a creation, and everyone had something nice to say about it. Then in walked Madame Bonnet, wife of the French ambassador, wearing my hat's twin. We both laughed and thought it was a great joke on us, but a wire-service story promptly intimated that the two of us had clashed and that we were both mad at Paulette. The following day a story from Paris quoted Paulette to the effect that Mesdames Mesta and Bonnet couldn't possibly expect to have absolutely exclusive hats for only fifty-five dollars. P.S.: Paulette still makes my hats.

It was during this visit back home that Mrs. Truman, Margaret, and I went to see *Call Me Madam*. People everywhere asked me what I thought of the play, most of them obviously expecting me to be indignant. Some of my friends thought it very unfair that the climax of the play had the lady ambassador being recalled from her job by the President after she got involved in "Lichtenburg's" internal politics—which was just what several State Department officials had predicted privately (and some reporters publicly) would happen to me. But instead of being offended, I was really flattered by all the attention. I remember being at a dinner party in New York a few nights after seeing the play. The Irving Berlins were also there, and all through dinner the talk was about his music. I noticed that everyone carefully avoided mentioning his current hit.

Just before the dessert course, I asked the host in a loud voice, "Isn't anyone going to talk about *my* play?" And from then on we had great fun discussing *Call Me Madam* and Luxembourg.

While I was still in New York, Bess Truman telephoned me early one morning to say she had heard from one of the President's press aides that my nephew had been reported missing in a small private airplane near the Mexican border.

"Why, that sounds ridiculous," I told Mrs. Truman. "Billy is at Harvard!" What I didn't know was that Billy had just finished his college work.

When I called Cambridge, no one there seemed to know where Billy was. At that point I began to get worried. Several hours later my telephone rang, and it was Billy, calling from Houston, Texas. He had seen the newspaper story and wanted me not to worry, and also to get in touch with his mother.

"Billy Tyson!" I exclaimed. "What are you doing in Texas? And what's this about an airplane?" And then he told me a story that practically turned me white-haired as I listened to it.

With a small inheritance from a relative, he had bought a tiny secondhand plane, had taken flying lessons, and gotten a student's license. He had then decided to fly to Syracuse to see a friend. Getting lost and running out of fuel, he had made a landing in a farmer's field, narrowly missing some high-tension wires. Refueling, he had got his bearings and gone on to Syracuse.

Having done that well, he had decided to visit his Uncle William in Oklahoma City. He had flown to Louisville and then headed for Memphis, following a railroad line. Becoming lost again, he had landed on a country road—to find that he had circled back almost to Louisville. The next day he had tried again, missed Oklahoma City, and landed at Dallas. Then on to Mexico and back into Texas. And so on until one night he had forgotten to notify anyone and to check in at the airport and was reported missing.

When Billy had finished telling me all this, I was not the least bit amused, as he seemed to expect me to be. I immediately telephoned my brother and got him to put an end to Billy's career as a barnstormer by advising him that a man in Oklahoma City was eager to buy a plane just like his for $3500 if he could have immediate possession. Billy leaped at the chance to make a profit of $1000, left his plane, and headed back to Boston. William had to pay a pilot $300 to fly the plane to Oklahoma City and then it took a year to get rid of it for $900. When William complained about how much it had cost him to get his nephew's feet back on the ground, I reminded him about the time when Father had paid off the farmer to buy his pet wolves.

I went back to Europe late in November, taking Billy with me. Marguerite and George and Betty and her little daughter met us in Paris. As soon as we got into my car after a dinner at Maxim's, my chauffeur, Frank, said he had something very important to tell us. He made sure all the windows were up. The Russians, he said, were getting ready to declare war on the Allies and Paris was very soon to be hit by A-bombs. Frank told us he had gotten this information from another chauffeur who drove for a high-ranking American general. I had heard nothing during my consultation at the State Department to indicate that such a thing might be coming, and I absolutely refused to take the rumor seriously.

Marguerite, however, said she felt Frank's information might very well have some truth in it. She insisted on rushing back to our hotel so that we could telephone Major Lewis Ellis in London. Lew, who had been a good friend of all of us when he had been a White House aide, was then Assistant Air Attaché to the U.S. Embassy.

Knowing the French telephone operators' fondness for listening in on conversations, Marguerite decided she needed to be subtle in her questioning. The conversation went something like this:

"How's the weather in London, Lew?"

"Fine," replied Lew sleepily, trying to figure out why Marguerite should have waked him at midnight to ask about the weather.

"Is *everything* fine?"

"Yes," Lew insisted.

"Is everyone getting ready to go back?"

"No," said Lew, thinking Marguerite referred to the tourists. "Most of the people have already gone home."

In her own gifted way, which I have never been able to figure out, my sister understood this as a warning. "Well, Lew, we're on our way and we'll see you soon," she said gaily and hung up with ashen face. Lew, figuring this meant we would be over in London in a few days, turned off his light and went back to sleep.

Marguerite was galvanized into action. Now certain that Frank's rumor was true, she insisted that we all take the next boat to London. Billy refused, deciding he would rather take his chances in war-torn Paris. I knew from experience that it was useless to try to talk Marguerite out of something like this, so I told her I would drive the rest of them to Calais and then go on to my duties in Luxembourg. We threw things into suitcases, checked out of the hotel at 1:30 A.M., and raced for the Channel. Marguerite and George, Betty and little Marguerite made it to London by early morning and checked into the Claridge.

"We're here," she announced to Major Ellis by telephone. "Can you get us a flight back to America right away?" Then she explained what she had heard the night before in Paris.

Lew tried to convince her that there was absolutely no truth to the rumor, but Marguerite's intuition was not to be denied. She and George rushed to Luxembourg to convince me I should leave while there was yet time.

Marguerite's last words to Lew Ellis, as she left her daughter and granddaughter in London, were, "Take care of Betty." And Lew did. So well, in fact, that within three weeks they were engaged! A few months later they were married at the legation in Luxembourg. By this time, Marguerite had decided that the danger of war in Europe had been exaggerated after all. I've never been quite sure that instead of just being a wacky Skirvin, as the rest of us assumed, Marguerite hadn't planned the whole thing to help Betty catch her man. Anyway, it has worked out beautifully. Betty and Lew have now been happily married for eight years; little Marguerite has two lovely sisters, and by the time this book comes out there should be one more member of the family (to be named Perle if it is a girl and I have anything to say about it—which I don't).

Each time I returned to Luxembourg after visiting the United States, I would make a series of calls on the Foreign Minister and other officials to tell them some of the things I had learned while home in the States. The Grand Duchess would also want to know the latest news from America. I always enjoyed my calls at the palace. Her Royal Highness was interested in all the things other women like to talk about. She loves gardening and gave me a great deal of helpful information when we were putting in flowers and new shrubs around the legation. We even exchanged recipes. Even though her position prevented her from ever getting genuinely friendly with any of the foreign diplomatic staff, the Grand Duchess was always warm and charming to me.

In the spring of 1950, when Marguerite and George had decided to stay in Europe, Garner and Edna Camper had come over to help me with the legation's housekeeping. Garner had immediately re-organized my household staff and replaced some of the help who were not performing their duties adequately. Knowing enough French to get along, he had also taken over much of the shopping and ordering for meals. Garner has a faculty of getting everybody to like him, and within a month he was on a first-name basis with most of Luxembourg.

One day Otto Hamilius, the burgomaster of Luxembourg, invited him to go on a wild boar hunt. Garner promptly spent a month's wages on a gun and costume: tight-fitting leather pants, a shirt and jacket, bright suspenders, and hat with a jaunty feather. For good measure he somewhere found some medals to pin on his chest.

A few days later he found himself in the woods with the hunting party. Each man was assigned an area to watch, and then hounds were loosed to flush out the quarry. All of a sudden, the yelping dogs chased a boar right at Garner. He got off two shots which missed, then turned tail and headed for a tree. "Shoot! Shoot!" cried the hunters nearest him, but Garner was much too busy scrambling up the tree. His skill as a climber became something of a legend in Luxembourg.

Garner was also a great hit with the servicemen at my G.I. parties. When he found out what my chef, a Belgian, was doing to the hamburgers, we had a change of command. The Belgian was making them thin, and dressing them up with truffles and spices. They *looked* beautiful but they weren't what homesick G.I.'s really wanted to eat. Garner built an outside barbecue grill, got himself a tall white hat, and installed himself as the hamburger specialist.

Then Garner decided we should have a soda fountain. He went all over Luxembourg and Belgium finding suitable dishes for sundaes and tall glasses for sodas. I bought some small tables, and we wound up with our own outdoor ice cream parlor, with Garner, of course, as chief soda jerk.

Garner even became an ex-officio labor mediator. On the day of one of my formal dinners, a spokesman for the waiters I had been using regularly informed Garner they would not appear that evening unless their wages were doubled. They knew I was having Luxembourg's hereditary Grand Duke, Prince Jean, at dinner that night, and they thought they could force me to pay more.

After determining that the men were adamant, Garner said, "We won't pay that." Then he came to me and we talked it over. We were sure that if we met their demands, we would be in trouble with the royal family and others who hired the same servants. Garner said he had a plan that ought to work, and when I learned what it was, I told him to go ahead. He went into town and lined up some women who were willing to do the work at the going wage. When the waiters found out they were about to be replaced, they dropped their unreasonable demands. Even so, Garner began hiring women once in a while just to keep the regular waiters in line.

My favorite story about Garner in Luxembourg concerns what happened one evening at Mardi Gras time, when each little town has a festival. Garner would try to take them all in. The sight of a colored person in Luxembourg is quite rare, especially in the rural areas where few visitors ever go. At one of these festivals, two women kept looking at Garner as he sat talking with a friend in a coffee house. Garner was wearing a harlequin costume, but no mask. Finally one of the women came over to him and said in good English, "You have a perfect mask." Far from being offended, Garner was delighted: "It ought to be perfect, lady—I've had it all my life."

In the winter of 1950, when we took a few days' vacation and went to St. Moritz, Garner bought himself some ski togs and cut quite a dashing figure parading around the grounds. He even brought along his "medals" to hang on the front of his sweater. He looked so impressive that Betty and Lew Ellis kidded him about looking like "the ambassador from Abyssinia." Someone overheard it and the rumor spread that I was entertaining the ambassador from one of the African countries who wished to remain incognito. And Garner, of course, did nothing to stop the rumor.

Garner wanted to get a picture of himself skiing—although he had never been on skis in his life. He rented some skis, stationed his wife at the bottom of the ski run with a camera, and grabbed hold of the tow. Halfway up the hill his skis started going in opposite directions and before you could say "Abyssinia" Garner had sprawled in the snow and dragged down the next three people on the tow. He was helped to his feet and finally made his way to the top of the hill carrying his skis. Then he put them on again and started down the slope. Once again his feet betrayed him. The next thing he knew he was head down in a large snowbank. Edna got her picture all right, but it is not one that Garner ever shows to anyone.

WHEN I HEARD in December, 1950, that General Eisenhower was going back on active duty to lead the organization of NATO military forces, the news was doubly welcome. Not only was this wonderful for Luxembourg and all of Europe, which had such confidence in its wartime hero, but I personally was glad because it meant I would be seeing more of Ike and Mamie.

Their first trip to Luxembourg was early in January, 1951, when Ike made a formal call on the Grand Duchess. I went with him to the palace, as did General Alfred Gruenther. Ike was a great favorite with the people of Luxembourg, having been Supreme Commander of Allied Forces when the country was liberated in 1945.

Two weeks later, Ike and Mamie returned for a weekend and I gave a small party for them at the legation. We were honored by the attendance of the Royal Consort, Prince Felix, who made one of his rare appearances at a party outside the palace. Prime Minister Dupong, Foreign Minister and Madame Bech, Grand Marshal of the Court and Madame Loesch, General Gruenther, Anthony Drexel Biddle, and Douglas MacArthur II were among the other guests at the dinner.

After the guests had left, Ike and Mamie and I stayed up for a while to talk. I told them of some of the difficulties I had been having with the one or two of my staff who still resented the fact that I would not let them run things. I had recently discovered that they had been sending adverse reports about me back to Washington.

"Sometimes I get sort of discouraged," I said. And then I told Ike about an experience the previous day when I had gone to the American Army post at Verdun. While I was gone, an important report had been sent to Washington signed by one of the staff, which made it look as if I wasn't on the job.

"I would get rid of these staff members immediately, Perlie," Ike said, and slapped his hand on the table. "You don't have to take that."

But it isn't that simple in the diplomatic service. These men were, for the most part, doing good work, and I couldn't just get rid of them for disagreeing with me.

Ike and Mamie came to Luxembourg frequently. Much as I'd like to think it was just to see me, I'm certain there were two other important considerations—the kitchen at the legation, where Ike could concoct his culinary specialties, and the Luxembourg golf course, one of the best in Europe.

A few weeks later, I had a meeting at the American Embassy in Paris, so I arranged to meet Mamie that afternoon and go shopping. We took in showings at Christian Dior and at Jacques Griffe and looked at hats at the millinery salon of Paulette. At Jacques Griffe's, Mamie saw a lovely short dinner dress and ordered it. I don't think Ike was very happy with me for encouraging Mamie to shop at such high-fashion places—with their high-fashion prices. The next evening I was at the Eisenhowers' for a Sunday buffet supper and I was sitting at a small table between Ike and General Gruenther, while Mamie was at another table. Ike started talking to General Gruenther about the ridiculously high prices of Parisian clothes. He didn't look at me or say anything to me, but he didn't need to—I squirmed. General Gruenther looked over at me and winked.

In April, Ike and Mamie flew down to Luxembourg on a Friday to meet the American High Commissioner for Germany John McCloy, who had driven over from Frankfurt. We were all out at the airport to meet the plane. General Eisenhower's pilot, Major Bill Draper, made a perfect landing, as usual, but as the big Constellation taxied up the runway toward us, something broke and one of the landing wheels suddenly came off and went spinning into the field. Major Draper was able to stop the plane without incident. Ike and his pilot immediately tried to determine the reason for the trouble, which might have caused a crash had it happened a few seconds earlier, or later at high speed on take-off. At first they suspected sabotage, but eventually they discovered that some maintenance workers back in the United States had installed a B-26 wheel on the plane by mistake.

Ike and Mamie seemed unperturbed by their narrow escape, and Ike greeted me gaily with his usual "Hello, Perlie." We didn't see much of him that weekend because he spent most of the time in conference with General McCloy and with General Lauris Norstad, who also flew in for the weekend. When Ike departed on Sunday, he left Mamie with us for the week. The following Friday, he flew back for another weekend, and as soon as he arrived at the legation he took off his coat, rolled up his sleeves, and started preparing the dinner. His specialties that day were to be soup, steak, and apple pie. Ike can fix steaks like nobody else in the world.

First, he rubbed the extra-thick steaks all over with garlic salt and brushed them with olive oil. Next, he rolled them in a heavy dough and put them not on a grate but right in the midst of the coals. Then he covered them with coals. At just the right moment, Ike dug the steaks out and scraped off the dough. I've never tasted a steak so good.

Ike takes his cooking seriously, and I learned a lot of good culinary tricks from him. Potato salad Eisenhower, which he taught me to make, was a great hit at my G.I. parties. This is the recipe:

Cook in a covered saucepan, until tender, 6 medium-sized potatoes in their jackets. Peel and slice while hot.

Sauté four strips of minced bacon.
Add and sauté until brown:
¼ cup chopped onion
¼ cup chopped celery
1 chopped dill pickle

Heat to the boiling point:
¼ cup water
½ cup vinegar
½ teaspoon sugar
½ teaspoon salt
⅛ teaspoon paprika
¼ teaspoon dry mustard

Combine all ingredients. Serves 6.

Ike served it hot, but for my G.I. parties, I let the salad blend overnight in the refrigerator and served it cold. It's delicious either way.

172

Ike tried to teach me to make an apple pie, but I never could get the knack of it. On the other hand, I have the touch for baking cakes, and that's one thing I could do better than the General.

Ike sometimes brought along his oils and tried his hand at a little painting. On one visit he asked Betty if he could paint her five-year-old daughter. Little Marguerite could sit still only long enough for Ike to make a rough sketch, but he finished the portrait on subsequent visits. He then presented it to Betty. My grandniece now has the distinction of having been lullabied to sleep by pianist Harry S. Truman and done in oils by portraitist Dwight D. Eisenhower.

It was in the spring of 1951, more than a year after I had taken my post as minister, that I had my first visit from a State Department inspector. He spent several days with us. I was on pins and needles because I had been running things the way I pleased, and was afraid he might find things wrong and give the State Department some reason for recalling me. The day he was to leave, the inspector relieved me by saying he was quite satisfied with the way I was running things.

On my next trip home, I persuaded Helen McLean, my lifelong friend, to return with me to Europe. She has a fine sense of humor and is always fun to be with. I don't know why she never got married—I guess she was just too choosy—but I've never given up trying to find a man for her. I figured a trip to Europe might help. I had in mind an attractive Luxembourg gentleman I wanted her to meet. We took a Pan American airliner to Paris. Since Helen had never been in a plane before I wanted to make her flight memorable in every way, and arranged for her to have a berth. Helen was so nervous, however, that she insisted on sitting up all night. "If the plane is going to crash in the Atlantic, I want to have my clothes on," she said grimly.

In Paris the first thing I did was take Helen to my coiffeur for a new hair style. Not that Helen didn't look very nice the way she was. I simply felt she ought to look more chic for her stay in Europe. Her hair was on the mousy side, so I told the hairdresser to tint it a warm reddish blond. Helen made a terrible fuss. But I told her she would look much more glamorous and that, anyway, it was too late to do anything about it. After they had reshaped her eyebrows and given her a professional makeup, I thought she looked lovely. I then took her to couturier Jacques Griffe and ordered her a couple of stunning outfits, then had her take some dancing lessons to catch up on the latest steps.

By the time we reached Luxembourg, Helen was in a daze. Marguerite took one horrified look and said, "Perle! What have you done to Helen!" And then, to make things worse, the "new" Helen and the Luxembourg man I had picked out for her didn't hit it off at all when I got them together at a party.

Me and my big ideas about matchmaking! But Helen didn't mind. And I don't think Helen's sprucing up was a complete failure because she herself found a French beau in Paris a few weeks later without any help (?) from me.

The next two years were busy ones in and out of Luxembourg. I received invitations to speak in many of the Western European countries. At first I stuck to scripts written for me by the Foreign Service officers on my staff, but as I gained confidence, I started putting in things that I particularly wanted to say. One of my favorite topics was women's rights. Of course this was not overly popular with the men, since they cherished their custom of keeping wives busy with household duties, but I felt I had a perfect opportunity to tell what our comparatively new country had done to increase the prestige of women.

"The woman who lives by the democratic principles rises up and lets herself be heard in no meek terms," I said in a speech to clubwomen in Wiesbaden, Germany. "In America, a woman is not merely expected to say pretty things and smile sweetly for special occasions. Her rights begin in the home. There she is the voice of final authority. She is her household's prime minister and economic expert. And she votes the way she wants to, not the way her husband would like her to."

I was scheduled to give a speech of this sort in Switzerland, but the sponsors, who had seen newspaper accounts of my previous talks, told me I must not mention women's rights. Women did not even have the vote in their country, they said, and there was no use in reminding them of the fact. I replied that if I could not speak about women and women's rights, I wouldn't speak at all. And I didn't.

In Luxembourg, in 1951, at a formal ceremony at the military cemetery in Hamm, I signed a treaty with Foreign Minister Bech which gave the United States perpetual use of the land where five thousand American soldiers are buried. A large crowd was on hand, and I thanked the people of Luxembourg for creating this "little America" on their soil. And then, thinking of Soviet Russia, I added: "Today this countryside is peaceful, but there can be few among us who are not wondering how long it will remain so. Is there another tyrant in the name of some other new order preparing to overrun Europe and oppress the people?"

As if on cue, Luxembourg's Communist newspaper came out next morning with an editorial entitled, "Be Silent, Madam Minister." It told of American women supposedly holding mass demonstrations in front of the White House against Truman's war policy. "It is the progressive women of America themselves who are active in the world fight against American war mongers," the editorial went on. "Truman's minister, however, is of another sort. She is not entitled to speak in the name of the progressive people of America. And that is the reason her speeches do not find an echo in the hearts of the Luxembourg workers and peace fighters."

A short time later, the Communist paper took another swipe at me: "The numerous parties and arrogant appearance of the minister in public cannot be traced to a harmless popularity craze only. While Mrs. Perle Mesta waves to the Luxembourgers like a magnanimous benefactor and has occasionally distributed a few scholarships, thousands of young Luxembourgers are being drilled for war."

I was reliably informed that few people in Luxembourg were taken in by this sort of propaganda. The point seemed clear at the next general elections when the Communists lost two of their five seats in the Chamber of Deputies.

We continued to have a stream of American visitors to Luxembourg. Whenever I made a speech back home, I would say, "Come visit me in Luxembourg." And many, many people did. I was glad to see every one of them.

India Edwards came over and spent a week with me. I guess she wanted to see for herself how I was getting on. Margaret Truman stopped by on a trip around Europe and I took her to call on the Grand Duchess. Some of our other visitors included Mr. and Mrs. Roscoe Drummond, Georgia Neese Clark, John Snyder, William Hillman, Nellie Tayloe Ross, Verbena Hibbard, Dr. and Mrs. Francis Griffin (Irene Dunne), General and Mrs. George Marshall,

175

General and Mrs. Hoyt Vandenberg, and General and Mrs. Anthony McAuliffe. General McAuliffe was practically a national hero in Luxembourg because of his record in the Battle of the Ardennes.

All these activities I have described naturally cost money, and I can agree with the State Department that the entertainment allowances for diplomats overseas are far too small. I was given six thousand dollars a year for entertainment and drew a salary of seventeen thousand, but while I was in Luxembourg I spent an additional sixty thousand dollars of my own money for entertaining.

In late April of 1952, Ike and Mamie made their last trip to Luxembourg (Ike was resigning his NATO post on June 1). This was an official farewell visit, and the newspapers estimated that almost half the population of Luxembourg lined the ten-mile route from the airport to the capital to greet Ike with shouts of "Hurray General Eek!"

Ike's first official act was to go to the Hamm military cemetery and lay a wreath of white and red tulips at the entrance, then place another wreath on the grave of General Patton. Later he placed a third wreath at the war memorial in Luxembourg City and then reviewed a part of Luxembourg's twenty-four-hundred-man army.

"That is excellent, sir, they look very good," Ike told Colonel Aloys Jacobi, the Chief of Staff. Foreign Minister Bech beamed as he heard the praise. No wonder Ike had the gratitude and love of all of Europe. He could make even this smallest of the NATO nations feel that it was a vitally important part of the organization.

The Grand Duchess gave a state dinner in honor of General Eisenhower. It was a small affair, including only the Grand Duchess and her family, her guest of honor, Mamie and her sister, Mrs. Gordon Moore, Foreign Minister and Madame Bech, and George and Marguerite and myself. I gave no party for Ike during that visit. However, we discussed many things, including my conviction that Ike should run for President as a Democrat. I did most of the talking on this point. Ike just smiled.

In my speeches on both sides of the Atlantic I always talked about the wonderful job General Eisenhower was doing to build up morale in Europe. When I returned to America in late May of 1952 on an official visit, I was surprised to discover that some Democratic leaders were criticizing me for giving aid and comfort to the probable Republican candidate for President. As soon as I got to

Washington, I went to see President Truman. Mentioning the criticism and pointing out that I had speaking engagements planned for women's organizations in several parts of the United States, I asked him what I should do.

The President thought for a moment. "You go right on saying what you have been saying," he said finally. And it was clear to me that he regarded the peace and unity of Europe as more important than any minute political help my speeches might give to the opposition.

The rebuilding of the White House had been completed shortly before I returned to Washington, and while the Trumans had given some official luncheons there, they had not yet had a formal dinner. A few days after my arrival, Mrs. Truman called to say that they wanted to have a dinner for me. On the evening of May 30, I arrived at the White House and stood with the rest of the guests in the Red Room waiting to go through the receiving line. All of a sudden Colonel Don Lowry, the senior White House aide, came into the room and said that the President and Mrs. Truman wanted to see me. To my surprise, I discovered that they wanted me to stand with them in the receiving line in the Blue Room. Inasmuch as many of the guests—Vice-President Barkley, the Cabinet members, and the senators—outranked me, protocol required me to sit far from the President at the dinner table. Nonetheless it was very flattering to have the President and Mrs. Truman give this first dinner in the rebuilt White House in my honor.

While on this trip home, I received an award I hardly think I deserved. I was made an Honorary Doctor of Laws by Fairleigh Dickinson University of Rutherford, New Jersey. Just why Perle Mesta from Oklahoma City, who never had gotten a college degree, should now become a Doctor of Laws, I will never know. But it happened, and I was certainly not displeased. Because school was then out and I was keeping office hours at the State Department, the ceremony took place there in the fifth-floor reception room. Dr. Peter Sammartino, president of Fairleigh Dickinson, and other faculty members were there, as were some of the State Department chiefs, representatives from several foreign countries, and some of my close friends: Joe Martin, India Edwards, Edith Nourse Rogers, and Mrs. Tom Connally.

Just before he handed me the degree Dr. Sammartino gave me

a very flowery tribute (I guess he had to justify the award somehow):

"You have served your country well. You have sought during every day of your work to know the people of Luxembourg, the farmers, the miners, the business employees, the industrial leaders, the government officials . . . you have brought to your job a warmth, an affection that has touched the hearts of Luxembourgers . . . that is the true essence of international relationship, the friendship and love that is generated between one people and another."

Accepting the award, I said I really felt a little guilty about being honored for just doing what any friendly, energetic, normal American woman would do if she had the same opportunity. Then I exchanged the mortarboard for my new Paulette hat and invited everybody over to the Sulgrave Club for a party. Later, Senators John Sparkman and Bill Fulbright and several others from Capitol Hill came over, and we demolished a magnificent cake that had been sent by William Seiter, my faithful friend of the *America,* who had heard about the occasion and wanted to do his part.

During the party, Hope Ridings Miller kept addressing me as Doctor Mesta. Each time, I found myself looking around to find someone else. Then I wondered what Father would have thought about his doctor-daughter. I decided he would have been astonished, even suspicious, but proud. Mother, of course, would have been pleased with me, even though I had gotten my degree the easy way.

Before returning to Luxembourg I took in the Democratic convention in Chicago. For the first time in twenty years, I did not attend the Republican convention. Because of my connection with the Democratic administration, I felt I could not be seen there without its causing undue comment.

Arriving in Chicago a few days early, I got in touch with Evalyn Schaus, my Luxembourg scholarship student at the Sherwood School of Music. Evalyn had been getting along fine with her music, but hadn't yet been active socially. Perle the matchmaker got busy. I took Evalyn out and bought her a wardrobe that was really something. She is a naturally attractive girl, but when we got through, she looked like a movie star. Then I phoned my other Luxembourg student in that area, Pierre Reiff, and asked him if he would escort Evalyn to my convention party. He agreed to do so.

The second day of the convention was "Ladies' Day," and I was one of three Democratic women asked to address the afternoon session. My speech on that July afternoon was not any great oration, although I worked hard on it. I wish I had known more about public speaking and had not needed to read the speech. That night, when I heard Eleanor Roosevelt give her talk—which was to me the highlight of the whole convention—I realized how important it is for a woman to learn how to express herself well. Just having ideas isn't sufficient: one has to be able to present them so that every listener can grasp the ideas. What I offered in my speech, though, did come from my heart. Some of my points seem to me as timely in 1960 as they were then:

"In America today, women have a lot to say about what goes on and how it shall go. And unless I miscalculate, we will have more to say as the years roll on. I do not mean by this that we will, or want to, dominate. We want only to be equal partners on the team. We want to see our knowledge, our talents, our thinking, put to work. We want to help our men shape society.

"Together, men and women are a tremendous force. And I feel certain that when our forefathers said that our society should be based on equal rights for all *men,* they did not mean it just that way. They meant equal rights for all men—and women.

"Women everywhere are deeply interested in the foreign policy of their country. They want to know about it. They want to know what they can do to make it work. And I find that women appreciate very deeply that this foreign policy of ours is seeking peace. And peace is very precious to us. It is something we want with all our being. But we know that peace, to be permanent, must be based upon freedom and justice. These are things that give meaning to our lives and which we acknowledge to be greater than ourselves.

"What the immediate future will bring, no one can say. At the time of great crisis in our early history, George Washington said, 'the event is in the hands of God.' I think women have always realized that 'the event is in the hands of God.' But we have never felt that He meant for us to stand idly by and let Him do all the work. We have God-given intelligence to see what work needs to be done. So we must be alert and work through the right principles. And in the present grave emergency, our country needs the efforts of all its people. There can be no excuse for any one of us shirking his or her duty."

Later, I made one of the seconding speeches when the name of India Edwards was placed in nomination for Vice-President. India's nomination was mostly a gesture of appreciation for her great work, and all of us knew she didn't really have a chance. All of us, that is, except one naïve woman from Florida who came up to Sam Rayburn, almost sobbing, to ask, "Is it true that India is going to withdraw?" Sam gave her one of those glowering looks that only he can give and replied, "You are damned right she is going to withdraw. If she hadn't agreed to, I wouldn't have let her name come up in the first place."

I gave a party after the convention's second evening session. I took over the Mayfair Room at the Blackstone and started out to have only two hundred guests. But once again I just couldn't shut off the guest list. I kept running into old friends I didn't know were in town and I wound up with more than five hundred guests. Although the Mayfair Room was jammed, everyone seemed to have a good time. Quite a few people managed to dance despite the crowd. I had put my Luxembourg students, Evalyn and Pierre, at a table with my brother and Helen McLean, and from time to time I would drop by to see how my young charges were doing. But there was such a mob, there was little opportunity for me to encourage romance.

About midnight, Phil Regan grabbed the microphone from the orchestra leader, Lou Breese, and started to organize some impromptu entertainment. Phil first called on Senator Happy Chandler, who rendered "My Old Kentucky Home." When former Democratic party treasurer Lawrence W. (Chip) Robert was called to the mike, he said he couldn't sing and instead gave a hilarious campaign speech for Senator Richard Russell. Next, Marny Clifford, Clark Clifford's beautiful wife, sang a couple of numbers. Regan then called up Martha Rountree, and she got Lawrence Spivak, her co-producer of Meet the Press, to help her put on a mock Meet the Press program right then and there.

Ethel Merman happened to be passing through town en route to Denver and she stayed over for the party. When the amateurs had finished with their show, Phil Regan called on Ethel to come and take a bow. She did more than that. She donned a waiter's coat, sang several numbers, and did a dance. It was quite a show and quite a night.

The day after the party I called Pierre Reiff and said I had an extracurricular project I wanted him to undertake for me.

"Anything you want me to do, Madam Minister, I will be glad to do," said Pierre.

"I want you to continue to take Evalyn Schaus out," I said. "Take her to the concerts and the theater. I will pay for it."

"Aw! Do I have to?" Pierre replied.

"No, of course you don't *have* to do it," I said.

"Well, all right. For you, Madam Minister, I'll do it," said Pierre somewhat dejectedly. But he discovered it wasn't such a bad assignment after all. Two years later I had an announcement from Luxembourg of the marriage of Evalyn Schaus to Pierre Reiff. To the tireless matchmaker, success had come at last!

Having to return to Luxembourg immediately after the convention, I did no work on the campaign beyond a little fund raising. It was just as well, for I found myself in a difficult position. I wanted the Democrats and Adlai Stevenson to win, but I didn't want to campaign against my close friend, General Eisenhower.

After the Eisenhower victory I continued my ministerial duties, not knowing how long this would be permitted. I was especially busy that fall assisting in the organization of the European Coal and Steel Community, which had its headquarters in Luxembourg. Although the United States was not directly involved in this joint economic effort that drew together Germany, Belgium, France, Italy, Luxembourg, and the Netherlands, I was able to help coordinate the activities with the coal and steel industry in America, and I met frequently with Jean Monnet, president of the Coal and Steel Community High Authority.

Toward the end of 1952, I submitted my resignation to President Truman, as is customary for political appointees when an administration is due to change. But President Truman refused to accept my resignation. (It was reported that he said, "Let General Eisenhower fire her if he wants to.") Hearing nothing from Ike, I continued with my duties. In February, John Foster Dulles and Harold Stassen arrived in Luxembourg for an important NATO defense meeting. After the session, Mr. Dulles took me to the side and said, "Ike wants you to stay on indefinitely." I said that was fine with me.

In the middle of March, 1953, I had a surprising telephone call from Brussels. It was from the new Russian ambassador there. He asked if he could call on me the following week. Of course I said yes, though I wondered what he could possibly want. This was the legation's first official contact with a Russian in almost four years, even though the Russian ambassador to Belgium was also accredited to Luxembourg.

On the agreed day Victor Ivanovich Avelov arrived at the legation. We talked for a half-hour about the weather and about his family and about the United States, which he had never seen. Out of the blue, he then said, "We would like to have you visit Russia." I was taken completely by surprise. Since the dropping of the Iron Curtain, Russia had allowed few Western visitors, except for specific missions. And I couldn't imagine why they would want *me* to come—especially since I had not troubled to hide my dislike of the Communists in Luxembourg. I thanked Ambassador Avelov and said I would think it over. On that particular day, however, I had not the slightest idea of accepting.

But the very next day something happened to change the situation. I received a perfunctory cable from John Foster Dulles saying that my resignation had been accepted, effective April 13. I had been fired with the minimum two weeks' notice—although Luxembourg was not sent another minister for eight months. Later I found out that President Eisenhower had been under heavy pressure from the women's division of the Republican National Committee to get rid of me. I couldn't blame them: they all knew what a Democrat I was. Nevertheless, the suddenness of my dismissal did take me by surprise. The reason for this, I determined later, was that the Republican women's organization didn't want a Democratic appointee to be representing the U.S. Government at the coronation in England the first week in May.

That weekend, Congressman James Fulton, from Pittsburgh, visited us at the legation. I had known Jim Fulton for several years. When I told him about the Russian invitation, he exclaimed, "Go, by all means, Perle! Why, I've been trying for years to get into Russia. And tell them you would like to have some companions and Bob Corbett and I will go with you." The two congressmen were then on a committee tour of Europe. I thought about it a while and decided it might be interesting, at that, to see what was going on behind the Iron Curtain. I called Ambassador Avelov, told him I would be happy to accept the invitation, and asked if my secretary, Pat Ventura, and the two congressmen could go with me.

"Why not?" Avelov said, and then hung up, leaving me without definite permission.

I checked with the State Department and was told I could make the trip, but not on my diplomatic passport. This was fine with me. That way I wouldn't be responsible to the State Department for anything I might do or say.

Congressmen Fulton and Corbett went on through Europe, completing their inspection trip, and then returned to Luxembourg. I had called Ambassador Avelov several times but still had no definite permission for the congressmen. Reluctantly, they gave up on the Russians and returned to the United States.

My last few days in Luxembourg were hectic but satisfying. A royal wedding had been planned for the marriage of Prince Jean of Luxembourg to Josephine-Charlotte, the sister of King Baudouin of Belgium. The day of the wedding, April 9, I had a call at 8:00 A.M. from the palace, requesting my presence there in two hours.

Having no idea what was in store, I arrived at the palace at ten and was immediately ushered into the private sitting room of the Grand Duchess. After telling me how sorry she was to hear I was leaving, she said she wished to present me with a token of her country's appreciation for my services as minister. The token proved to be the Grand Cross of the Crown of Oak, Luxembourg's highest honor, and a decoration never before given to a woman. I was, of course, overwhelmed. But the thing I will always remember even more than the decoration was the thoughtfulness of the Grand Duchess in taking time from that busy day so that I might have the decoration to wear at the wedding dinner that night.

Three days before leaving Luxembourg, I broadcast a radio farewell message to the citizens. The next night, some of the Luxembourg government officials put on a radio program expressing their thanks to me. On Sunday, my next to last day as minister, Marguerite and I took one last trip to visit some of our burgomaster friends, and to say good-by to my many Luxembourg godchildren, which group now included several Perles. That night the good people of Luxembourg held a torchlight parade around the legation and the Limpertsberg band again serenaded me. The Court Chamberlain presented me with a large leather-bound scrapbook made up of pictures of Luxembourg and signed by the burgomasters, by all the Chamber of Deputies (except the Communist members) and by the Prime Minister and the Foreign Minister.

On the day I left, I was given the most moving farewell of all. Two hundred orphan children, dressed in their best, with faces scrubbed and hair neatly combed, came to the legation to present a gift to their American "auntie." It was one of the most touching presents I have ever received: two little farewell poems they had written themselves, one recited by the girls and one by the boys.

Drying my eyes, I drove off toward London for the coronation of Queen Elizabeth II.

FIFTEEN: *Without Portfolio*

ENDING MY ASSIGNMENT as Minister to Luxembourg, I planned to relax for a while. But it was not to be, for I immediately entered the most active period of my life. In the seven years since leaving Luxembourg I have traveled more than eighty thousand miles, talked with the heads of nineteen governments, continued to work for a Constitutional amendment to give American women equal rights with men, and helped start a dairy business in Nevada. Of course I also have continued to give parties.

When I arrived in England from Luxembourg, London was agog with excitement over the coming coronation. I stayed with Marguerite and George in the large apartment in Grosvenor Square they had taken two years earlier, after Betty's marriage to Lew Ellis. Marguerite visited in London often, especially after the Ellises' child, Betty Lou, was born in 1952. One night shortly after I arrived in London, I suggested to Marguerite that it might be fun for us to give a little party for President Eisenhower's official representatives to the coronation and a few other Americans we knew would be coming over for the event. We decided we would give our party the evening of June 3, the day after the coronation. I went to see Ambassador Winthrop Aldrich. He thought it a wonderful idea and asked if he could assist with the guest list. I think he was relieved to have a party going that night because it took him out of a difficult protocol jam. It seemed that June 3 was also the night of a state dinner at Buckingham Palace, and of the Americans only General George Marshall, head of the United States Diplomatic Mission to the Coronation, and General Matthew Ridgway, then Supreme Allied Commander in Europe, had been invited—and without their wives. Marguerite and I gladly asked to our party the other three members of the mission to the coronation

—General Omar Bradley, Governor Warren, and Mrs. Gardner Cowles—as well as Mrs. Marshall, Mrs. Ridgway, Mrs. Bradley, Mrs. Warren and the three Warren girls, and Ambassador and Mrs. Aldrich.

We started out just to have a small crowd for dinner. We rented Londonderry House, a magnificent mansion on Park Lane that had been Lord Londonderry's town home, and which had fine large reception rooms and a big gold ballroom. When more and more friends kept arriving in town, and when Ambassador Aldrich asked to make some additions to the list, we decided to enlarge our plans and hold a dinner party with a supper dance afterward for those we could not accommodate at the dinner. The list kept growing until we finally had a hundred and twenty-five guests at dinner and an additional five hundred and seventy-five invited for the supper dance. We called it our Coronation Ball, and it turned out to be the most lavish party Marguerite or I have ever given.

Londonderry House practically bulged that evening. After the dinner, which was held in the large dining room downstairs, Marguerite and I stood at the top of the wide staircase to greet the rest of our guests. In addition to General Marshall and General Ridgway, several of the other guests at the Queen's dinner party came straight over afterward to join our fun. We greeted Crown Prince Olav of Norway, his wife, Princess Martha, and their daughter, Astrid; the handsome Marquis of Milford-Haven; Prince Bernhard of the Netherlands; the Lord Mayor of London, S. R. Rupert de la Bere (adding a medieval touch with his gold chain of office and his knee breeches); Prince Jean of Luxembourg and his bride, Princess Josephine-Charlotte, and his sisters, Princesses Elizabeth and Marie-Adelaide.

Other guests at our party included Mrs. Cornelius Vanderbilt Whitney; Elizabeth Arden and her sister, Viscountess de Montblanc; Prince Serge Obolensky, Mr. and Mrs. Robert Sherwood and Mr. and Mrs. Douglas Fairbanks, Jr.; General and Mrs. Anthony Drexel Biddle, Mrs. Lucius Boomer, Ambassador and Mrs. Joseph E. Davies, and Mr. and Mrs. William Randolph Hearst, Jr.; Mrs. Robert Low Bacon, the Paul McNutts, the Ray Henles, and Jack Logan from Washington; Mr. and Mrs. Whitelaw Reid, Mr. and Mrs. Jules Stein, Jinx Falkenburg and Tex McCrary, and Lauren Bacall and Humphrey Bogart.

The Bogarts almost didn't make it. He had announced to his wife that he had gone through life without ever wearing tails and he'd be damned if he was going to do it now. But Mrs. Bogart is a very persuasive woman—her husband showed up wearing a full dress suit borrowed from the Earl of Warwick. And the actor looked miserable. Every time I saw him he was grimacing, stretching his neck, and pulling up his coat sleeves that were two inches too long.

Along about midnight, Bogart was dancing with his wife when he spotted movie executive Spyros Skouras, the only man present in a tuxedo (Skouras had arrived in London too late to arrange for a full dress suit). Bogart stopped dancing right in the middle of the floor, pointed at Skouras, and grumbled to his wife, "See—I told you there was no need to get me into this damned monkey suit!"

The guests circulated between the huge ballroom and the large library, where champagne and cocktails were served, and then to the dining room downstairs where supper was served all night. What a sight it was to see all the distinguished and handsome people, the colorful gowns and sparkling tiaras! Princess Martha wore a magnificent diamond and sapphire tiara at least four inches high. There were military uniforms of scarlet and blue and gold, and the diplomats and nobility all wore their colorful decorations across their chests. Scotland Yard sent out five men to keep an eye on the millions of dollars' worth of jewels. I heard one woman remark, "I feel absolutely naked here without a tiara."

There had been so much pomp and ceremony the previous day that it took a while for our guests to unbend and enjoy themselves. But before long, Tim Clayton's music had the gorgeously gowned ladies and bemedaled gentlemen whirling around the room. I prepared no formal entertainment, hoping that the guests would feel like providing their own. About 1:00 A.M. they began doing so. Billie Worth, then playing the Ethel Merman part in the London company of *Call Me Madam,* put on several numbers, and Charles Bangs, from the original *Oklahoma!* cast, sang for us. Then Lord Foley played the piano. While these impromptu performances were going on, many of the guests just sat down in the middle of the dance floor, ball gowns and all. They moved quickly out of the way when Prince Jean of Luxembourg led me to the center of the floor and swept me around the room to the strains of "Hostess with the Mostes' on the Ball." The other guests joined us and the dancing continued. About two o'clock I saw Virginia Warren, foot-weary but still gay, dancing in her stocking feet. We started serving scrambled eggs and sausage about three o'clock. When I started down the stairs at five, after dismissing the orchestra, I met Prince Jean of Luxembourg and his bride rushing up the steps. "May we have just one more dance?" they begged. So I went back and persuaded the orchestra to play a final number.

The day after our ball, I received an unexpected call from a secretary at the Soviet Embassy who seemed to have had no difficulty in getting Marguerite's unlisted telephone number. The secretary informed me that a visa was waiting for me. When I arrived at the embassy, the second secretary, Alexander Startsev, handed me a visa valid for three months in the Soviet Union. I asked about the visa for my secretary, and for good measure, those for Congressmen Fulton and Corbett.

"There is a visa only for you," Startsev said. "You go alone."

"Very well, I will go alone," I said. I wasn't going to let them scare me out of the trip.

"Fine," said the Russian. "Our people will meet you in Moscow and take charge of you."

I figured it was time to get one thing straightened out right then and there. I was not going on the trip simply to be used for their propaganda purposes. I wanted to see Russia through my own eyes, not through Russian eyes.

"Thank you," I said. "But I will not need to be met. *My* people will meet me."

"Very well," said Startsev. "But we will furnish an Intourist agent to guide you and interpret for you."

"I will let your people in Moscow know if that is necessary," I said. Of course, I knew I would sometimes need the guide, but I had been promised I could have an American interpreter from the U.S. Embassy. Before I left Startsev's office, I made a specific request.

"I would like to visit the Zaporozhe steel plant," I said to the Russian official. George Mesta had once told me that the Zaporozhe plant was one of the biggest in the world, and I knew that no Western visitor had been allowed to inspect it since the outbreak of World War II.

"Why not?" answered Startsev, smiling. His reply was an echo of Ambassador Avelov's. It didn't leave me hopeful about seeing the steel plant.

I packed only a few bags, so as to be able to move freely by myself. Into my luggage went several bottles of perfume as gifts from the outside world to some of the women I expected to meet in Russia.

A few days before I was to leave, I was invited to a reception given by the Duke and Duchess of Marlborough at Blenheim Palace. There I met Jacob Malik, the newly arrived Russian ambassador to England. He said he hoped I would have a pleasant visit in his country.

I was also introduced to Sir Winston Churchill, who raised his brows and said expansively, "Ah, Miss Call-Me-Madam!"

"Oh, Sir Winston," I said disappointedly, "I hope you don't always connect me with that. I do other things."

"I know you do," said Mr. Churchill. "But you shouldn't mind— it was a good show." Then he told me he had seen it twice.

On June 10, I left London by plane for Helsinki. There I changed to a battered Soviet airliner: an old twin-engined Dakota which the Russians had received as lend-lease from the United States and which they apparently were determined to keep flying until it fell apart. The take-off was in what I came to appreciate was the typical Russian style. We didn't have to fasten safety belts because there were none. Some of the Russian passengers lit cigarettes as if that were a signal that all was ready. The pilot, without bothering to warm up his engines, suddenly lifted us into the air with a roar. He flew very low over the ground, as if he were following the road below. We made it to Leningrad, changed to an even more alarming Dakota, went through the same take-off procedure, and finally landed intact at Moscow.

I was certainly glad to see the smiling faces of Ambassador and Mrs. Charles Bohlen as they met me at the airport. Chip and Avis Bohlen are two of the most gracious people in the entire Foreign Service. I had the pleasure of staying with them a few days at Spaso House, the American residence, before moving to the National Hotel.

Realizing that I might have a chance to see things no other American had been allowed to see, I was determined to make a detailed record of all that I saw and heard. I had brought along a Brownie camera and four dozen rolls of film. Also, I carried a little black notebook. It was soon too full of precious data to be left around, so it went with me wherever I went, tucked into my bosom.

One of my introductions to life in Russia was the high cost of taxi rides. I had walked six or eight blocks looking in shop windows, when I hailed a taxi. It was old and decrepit. In about three minutes we were back at Spaso House. The driver thrust out his hand and asked for twenty-four rubles, which amounted to six dollars.

"Why, that's ridiculous!" I exclaimed. "We only went a few blocks. I'm not going to pay you twenty-four rubles."

The driver either could not, or did not want to understand.

"Twenty-four rubles," he repeated, and kept his hand out.

I appealed to the uniformed Russian policemen in front of Spaso House, but they merely shrugged their shoulders. So I marched into the embassy and appealed to the first person who could speak both English and Russian—the telephone operator. "Please come outside with me," I said, "and explain to the cab driver that he's asking a preposterous price for his ride."

The girl came out but the driver wouldn't budge. "That's the price," he insisted. He was getting angry, so I gave him his twenty-four rubles and said I was going to report him. I soon learned that the driver was innocent. The guilty party was the Soviet economic system that produced such a price scale. Not many Russians, I found out, are rich enough to ride around in taxis.

When I told Ambassador Bohlen I wanted to visit the Zaporozhe steel plant, he said I hadn't a chance in the world. "No American has been allowed to go there since the war," he said.

But when I told him of my conversation at the Russian Embassy in London, and how the second secretary had left it at "Why not?," Chip said he would try to obtain permission for me.

"But I think it would be easier if you wanted to see an ice cream plant or a hosiery mill," he added. I told him I hadn't come all the way to Russia to see an ice cream plant.

Three days after Ambassador Bohlen put in the request, permission was granted for me to visit Zaporozhe. Surprisingly, I was even allowed to take along a secretary from the embassy, David

Kline, who spoke excellent Russian. To cap it all, David's wife, Ann, was also allowed to go with me.

It was a twenty-four-hour train trip to Zaporozhe, situated about five hundred miles south of Moscow. We arrived just before midnight and were met by N. P. Moisenko, deputy director of the plant, and A. M. Pisachenko, an official of the city of Zaporozhe. They were most cordial. We were driven to the private dacha (villa) belonging to the steel plant, and there, in comfortable quarters, we spent the night.

The next morning we were taken into the tremendous plant and presented to its director, A. L. Boboreikin. "If there is anything you want to see, you need only ask," he said graciously enough. He volunteered the information that there were ten thousand employees, working around the clock in eight-hour shifts; that everything was new, since the plant had been razed during the war; and that they were producing steel for the manufacture of automobiles, tractors, agricultural equipment, and excavators.

"What is your production?" I asked.

Mr. Boboreikin, a big, ebullient sort of man, suddenly fell silent as a mouse.

"Well," I said encouragingly, "I would guess your tonnage is about—"

"Madam Mesta," he interrupted, "you are guessing too much." And he stood up to indicate the interview was over.

Guided by the two men who had welcomed us the night before, we now toured the plant. Mr. Moisenko proudly pointed out such features as the automatic furnace stokers. One man, by operating a lever, controlled the loading of ore into the furnaces—a job that would ordinarily take many men.

The plant, with its spacious, well-lit, and clean premises, seemed as modern as some of ours in the United States. But there was one striking difference in the working force: the presence of women. And I noticed they were assigned the dirtiest and heaviest jobs, such as lifting back-breaking pieces of metal.

As I walked through the plant, I identified an American-made (United Engineering) rolling mill and noticed other equipment that looked like copies of Mesta machinery.

The Klines and I stayed in Zaporozhe several days. We visited the village nursery and the Pioneer Camp where they were teaching the children to be Communists—children seven or eight years old. All the children had red kerchiefs around their necks. One little girl came up to me and put a red kerchief around my neck. I took it off at once, suspecting there might be a photographer around, waiting for just that sort of propaganda shot. The little girl commenced to cry. I tried to tell her that it was not because I did not want to accept something from her, but because I didn't believe as she did—and therefore could not wear her kerchief.

The last night of our stay at Zaporozhe we were given a banquet in our dacha. We were served all the best Russian foods and, of course, vodka, vodka, vodka. I drank tea, and the Klines were wise enough to drink very little vodka. Our two hosts drank vodka until one or two in the morning—and we were supposed to be on the train at seven. Finally, the Russians brought me a guest book and asked me to write in it. David Kline read me some of the things that were in it: enthusiastic comments by delegates and visitors from Czechoslovakia, Hungary, Rumania, and East Germany. "You have the most wonderful steel plant in the world." "We have never seen better treatment of employees." "The workmanship is superb." It went on and on, page after page of lavish praise. So I took the book. I knew that whatever I wrote would most likely be used all over Russia.

"To whom shall I address these remarks?" I asked.

"Write 'Dear Comrades,' " our hosts said in unison.

"Oh, no," I said. "We don't use that term in America. We would say 'Dear Friends'."

When they saw I wouldn't budge, they said, "Well then, address it 'To the Director of the Zaporozhe Steel Plant."

I closed my eyes and prayed silently for a moment to know what to write. Then, as I wrote, I said each word aloud:

"To the Director of the Zaporozhe Steel Plant. Thank you very much for your hospitality in allowing us to visit your plant. Thank you very much for the use of your residence and thank you for the use of your car during our stay. Thank you. Perle Mesta."

Mr. Pisachenko's face turned white as a sheet. Mr. Moisenko, whose conversation had been flowing as generously as the vodka, was so shocked that he sobered up immediately and fell silent. The party broke up soon after.

The Russians obviously had been instructed to secure a glowing

192

tribute from me. Their resentment was evident the next morning when the Klines and I had to make our own way to the railroad station. And although I was in Russia for two more months and traveled twelve thousand miles through the country, I was never again asked to be a guest of the Soviet Government.

When I returned to Moscow I made an embarrassing discovery about the perfume I had brought to Russia. One of the bottles was empty. I decided that the perfume must have evaporated while I was flying in on those old unpressurized Dakotas. Then suddenly I remembered that I had presented Mr. Moisenko one of the bottles for his wife. It had been bad enough for him that I had not written a flowery tribute in his guest book. If my present turned out to be only an empty bottle, Mr. Moisenko would certainly have a low opinion of me—and probably of Americans in general.

During the rest of my stay in Russia I visited Kiev and took a boat trip down the Dnieper; I went down the Volga from Stalingrad to Astrakhan on a boat called the *K. S. Stanislavsky;* I visited Leningrad, saw the Baku oil fields, went to the Black Sea and to the Ukraine. Every place I went, I would sneak out my little black book and scribble my impressions. And thanks to my Brownie camera, when I left Russia, I had 256 good pictures. It would take another book to detail all I saw and heard, but here are a few experiences that stood out more than others and gave me new insights about the Russian people.

One day in Stalingrad I spotted a shoeshine woman on a street corner. While she was shining my black walking shoes, I discovered she could speak a little English. She was a typical fat Russian woman, about forty-five, with dark hair and a babushka around her head. I asked her if she had a family. She told me her husband was a soldier in the Red Army and was away and that their children were grown.

She asked if she might take one shoe off my foot and look at it. She felt the material and examined the inside to see how it was made. "Good shoes," she said. As we chatted about the type of business she was in, it occurred to me that this woman was about the only person I had yet met in Russia who was engaged in private enterprise.

When I visited the Kremlin, a group of Americans from the embassy came along. Several of us hopefully took our cameras, but we were ordered to leave them at the entrance. On a later visit, however, permission to photograph was granted and I took numerous pictures.

David Henry, of the American Embassy, and I were walking near the Kremlin one afternoon when I saw a beautiful scene of the Kremlin's minarets and domes. As I aimed my Brownie, a burly policeman rushed up, shouting in Russian and gesturing for me to stop. Mr. Henry told the policeman that I had been invited to Russia by the People's Government. It did no good. The man threatened to arrest me. Since I didn't want to take the chance of being jailed and perhaps losing my visa, I put away my Brownie and, with a smile, offered to shake hands. The policeman merely glared, warning me that any further use of the camera would mean instant arrest. After that, I asked for and received permission to use my camera in the cities I visited.

I went to a performance of *Swan Lake* at the Bolshoi Theater, with Struchkova as principal ballerina, and I was just dazzled by the spectacle. It seemed to me that the Soviet ideology had taken nothing from the beauty and other-worldliness of the melting lines of wraithlike dancers. Yet I presently came to see that Russia's great classical ballet, like her other arts, had been made a means of spreading Party doctrine. New ballets had been written and old ones revised to dramatize in dance the themes of revolution and the struggle against capitalism. My program announced that *The Red Poppy* would be danced later in the season. This, I was told, was a new version of the ancient Chinese story in which the long-heralded Chinese revolution suddenly breaks out.

I talked to several Russians during the intermission. It was apparent they love pageantry and spectacle. Their faces lighted up as they spoke enthusiastically of *Swan Lake.*

"Do you come often to the ballet?" I asked a girl of about eighteen.

"Oh, yes," she said. "I save up my money to come. Every Russian girl dreams of being a ballerina. We love to dance."

I later paid a visit to the Moscow Ballet School with Mrs. Bohlen and several others from the embassy. This is the state school that trains dancers for the Bolshoi Theater's *corps de ballet*. After climbing up four flights of stairs lined with prints of famous Russian ballerinas of the past, we met the director, Madame

194

Bocharnikova, a woman of about forty-five, a former ballet dancer and teacher.

To my surprise, she informed me that children were not admitted to the school until they reached the age of eleven. "I thought Russian children danced from the time they were five or six years old," I told her.

"Oh, no," she said. "We do not wish them to have danced before they come here."

"How do you choose them then?" I asked.

"We choose them for their general intelligence and their sense of music and rhythm. We do the rest," she explained.

The students, I gathered, came from all over the Soviet Union. They have regular school classes for several hours a day, in addition to their dancing classes. Their physical development is carefully watched.

"They work very hard," the director told me, "but they enjoy every minute of it."

The senior classes presently put on a demonstration for us. There are nine grades of dancing classes. We watched, entranced, as the upper three performed extracts from classical ballets. Between these, they did the national dances of the Ukraine and Georgia. They danced with a sense of concentration. One felt these young people were wholly dedicated to their art. They were relaxed and happy when doing a gay dance; they changed entirely in a serious dance. Their pantomime and their poise were faultless.

My afternoon at the school was a wonderful treat. It was good to see such joyous self-expression. I went away feeling lifted out of the depression that I had acquired from some of my other experiences. I felt I could now understand why the Russian people flocked to the theater. The youthful spirit and the beauty of the Bolshoi spectacles doubtless provided a wonderful escape from the drab, colorless uniformity of everyday life.

I saw still another side of Russia when I visited the "birth house" of a Leningrad hospital. When I arrived, the superintendent explained how the system operated. Each such birth house served a number of surrounding districts. In each district there was a consultation station to which women went regularly after their first two months of pregnancy. In addition to the routine examinations they were expected to attend a course of health lectures. If the mother-to-be was working, she got thirty-six days off before her child was due. The mothers paid nothing for their care. On the contrary, the Soviet Government paid them cash sums ranging from three hundred rubles for the first child up to five thousand for the tenth. After the child was born, the mother stayed nine days in the hospital—though longer if there was any trouble in the delivery—and then had forty-two days off from her work.

After this briefing, I was taken into a large room containing perhaps fifty beds. Most of them were occupied by women in labor. I noticed one who lay near me. Except that she was breathing heavily, she was making no sound whatever. A nurse or midwife moved to her side and the next thing I knew Russia could boast one more citizen. I was appalled to see a baby come into the world with no more attention than this. When I looked over at another bed, the same thing was happening again. Three babies were born in the few minutes I was there. And I was told that the hospital had several more such delivery rooms.

Another disturbing visit I had was to a state nursery. With obvious pride the officials roused a group of four- and five-year-olds from their afternoon nap so that they could sing this song for me:

> We cannot read or write
> But we thank Lenin and Stalin
> For the books that are going
> To teach us to read and write.

My interpreter read me typical passages from some of the school-books these brain-washed children would soon be studying. The Russians boast about their high rate of literacy. It's no wonder they teach everyone to read: all the books I saw were filled with propaganda designed to make their readers follow the Communist rulers unquestioningly.

One day in a Moscow park, I struck up a conversation with a seventeen-year-old boy. He was studying English in school, and was eager to try it out on me. When I ran into him, he was studying one of the many propaganda posters on view in the park. This one pictured a monkey, and the youth explained that it showed man's descent from his original ancestor.

"Do you really believe that?" I asked.

196

"Yes," he said.

"Are you an atheist?" I asked.

"Of course I am," was the reply.

"How in the world can you believe that you are descended from a monkey?" I asked.

"I can prove it," the youth said. "We are taught to prove what we believe."

Then he started telling me what was wrong with America. I could see that he had a completely false picture of our way of life. Patiently, I explained that in our country, each individual was free to choose his own career; he could read any newspaper or book, and he could criticize the government without fear of punishment. And underlying our whole American system, I told him, was our freedom to worship in the way of our choice without interference from the government. I'm sure the dent I made in that boy's Communist armor was not large, but at that I may have given him something to think about.

Just before leaving Russia, I wangled an invitation to a meeting of the Supreme Soviet in the Kremlin. There was intense interest in what might be disclosed during this session inasmuch as it was being held soon after Beria's arrest. All the foreign observers in Moscow were wondering if there would be a detailed report on the arrest or an announcement of future Soviet policy. I had a good seat in Box No. 2, reserved for diplomats. A diplomat sitting next to me was kind enough to explain what was going on.

I looked down over the vast gathering of some two thousand delegates. It was a colorful sight, for many of them were in the costumes of their native areas, and many of them were women. There were red shawls and green shawls and all varieties of caps —round, pointed, and square. It looked more like a folk dance festival than a parliament meeting.

Suddenly the delegates surged to their feet, applauding. Watching the high Soviet officials file in, I was puzzled to see them join in the clapping. My friend explained that the leaders were clapping to thank the audience for clapping.

"There's Molotov, the one with the glasses," he said. "Next to him is Voroshilov. Then Malenkov, then Khrushchev and Kaganovich."

The Soviet leaders sat in a group to the rear and left of the platform, behind a row of ten minor functionaries seated at a long table that ran across the width of the carpeted stage. Directly behind Molotov and Voroshilov were Bulganin, in his marshal's uniform, and Mikoyan. I pulled out my opera glasses for a better look at these seven leading stars of the Kremlin.

I nudged my diplomat. "Do you see how Kaganovich keeps rattling his fingers on the desk as if he were playing a piano? Some of the others are doing it, too, but none as much as Kaganovich. What do you think makes them so nervous?"

"Wouldn't you be nervous," he replied, "if you had done all the evil things they have done in their lives?"

The principal event of the session proved to be a long—in fact nearly endless—speech by Malenkov. Rather, it was a reading, for the speech had been carefully prepared. Beria was dismissed with a brief denunciation, disappointing at least all the foreign observers. After an hour or more of his monotonous reading, the pudgy Malenkov launched into a violent attack on the United States. The two thousand delegates rose as a body and applauded vigorously. I decided I had had enough. Ambassador Bohlen and another member of the American Embassy staff also left the meeting. We would not be a party to such a demonstration.

The next day, as I prepared to leave the Soviet Union, I stopped at the Intourist office to see whether my exit permit had arrived. A young clerk asked me how I had liked Malenkov's speech.

"I didn't like it at all," I said. "How would you like it if someone attacked your government the way he did ours?"

"But we don't like your system," he replied.

"We don't like yours, either, so we are even," I retorted.

"No one has a chance in your country," the Intourist man continued.

"How do you know?" I asked. "You're not free to travel or to read foreign newspapers. How do you know anything that is really going on in the outside world?"

We really had it back and forth. "Now let's get the record straight," I said to him at last. "You're trying to rule the world and we Westerners don't approve of that."

I had no difficulty in obtaining my exit visa and getting my passport returned. Maybe they were glad to get rid of me! After three months in Russia I was unspeakably grateful to breathe again the free air of the Western world. I came away with some definite impressions. Most of the people I had talked with—stallkeepers and women shoppers in the market places, workers, young people in the schools and parks—were friendly. Though they obviously were convinced their system was better than ours, I had detected no animosity toward Americans as individuals. However, I had gained an awed respect for the ability of the Soviet leadership to achieve its economic and military goals. And I was convinced that Russia was determined to force the rest of the world to come under its system—by resorting to war if necessary. In the years since leaving Russia, I have seen nothing that changes my opinion. I still believe the only safety for the West lies in being constantly alert to the dangers of the Soviet military and economic threats. They continue to exist despite all the smiles and glad-handing of Mr. Khrushchev and Mr. Mikoyan.

SIXTEEN: *I Do Some Fast Talking*

AS SOON AS I landed in England, I started writing up my trip. I was ably assisted by Joseph Newman of the New York *Herald Tribune's* London staff. I had my pictures and also my little black notebook crammed full of scribbles. In a month's time, my scribbles had been transformed into ten articles. These were syndicated by the *Herald Tribune* in newspapers throughout the United States and Europe. They were also printed for use in schools as supplementary material. I didn't win any journalism awards for the series, but I think the articles portrayed fairly well an average woman's view of the Russian people and Russian system after a three months' acquaintance with them. The only real criticism for my literary efforts came from Communist newspapers. If what they wrote was taken seriously in the homeland, I'm willing to bet that the man who was responsible for inviting me in the first place was shunted off to the salt mines. When my articles appeared in the Luxembourg *Wort,* the Communist *Wochen-Zeitung,* which had scalped me many times in the past, had this to say:

> Seldom has anybody written such a childish nonsense as Mrs. Perle Mesta, whose reports about her Russian trip are being published in the "Wort." . . . There is no use to discuss in detail the gossip and nonsense which fill the report of Perle Mesta. With her stupid writing, she unmasks herself in each line. She is called Perle, but she is none, especially not a pearl of the truth. On the contrary: Perle Mesta lies, and even ridiculously.

When I returned to the United States late in November of 1953, I met Marguerite and William in New York. I had signed up to go on a lecture tour, but when I had agreed to the tour, I had not been fully aware of all that would be demanded of me. I had just known that I wanted to tell people about what I had seen in Russia. Shortly after I arrived in New York, I had a conference with the booking agent.

"Well, now I've got to prepare a speech to read," I told him.

He looked at me in amazement. "*Read* your speech?" he said. "Don't you know you can't read speeches in this day and age? You've got to deliver them. People won't go to hear you read a speech. No indeed."

Just the thought of talking extemporaneously for an hour made me want to quit right then, but Marguerite and William and I took the problem up in a family conference. William said he could break the contract if I desired it. Marguerite said, "Maybe it would be easier for us to do a sister song-and-dance act instead." Neither of them thought I could ever prepare and deliver an hour-long talk.

My second thoughts on a problem are often more optimistic than my first. I finally decided that there was no reason why I couldn't learn to deliver a lecture properly. A friend gave me the name of an excellent speech teacher, Lester Pridgen, and I went to work. Mr. Pridgen saw to it that I worked all day every day, and then at night I would practice by myself. At the end of the first week I still didn't think I could do it, and my teacher was not much more confident than I was. But we kept plugging away. It was now mid-December, and my first lecture was scheduled for January 16 in Houston, Texas. I discovered that it wasn't enough just to describe incidents—that I had to find some way of imparting the ideas I felt inside of me. And while some of my friends had accused me of being overly dramatic at times, I found I really didn't know the first thing about dramatizing an experience to make it interesting. How I wished that it was Marguerite who was doing all this, for she was already a wonderful speaker.

The week before I was due in Texas, we rented the ballroom of a New York hotel and I started practicing in the empty hall. I kept several "cue cards" handy—small cards with one or two key words written on them in large letters—in case I went blank. I managed to get through my hour's lecture without breaking down, but I knew that talking in an empty hall was hardly the real test.

The night of January 16, as scheduled, I walked out onto a stage in Houston. I looked at the microphone. It seemed to stare right back at me. I looked at the seven hundred people who had turned out to hear me, and I could hardly breathe. I honestly didn't know what would happen. Neither William nor Marguerite had had the courage to come to Houston with me. They just couldn't bear the thought that I might make a fool of myself.

The welcoming applause stopped and all was silent for a moment. Then all at once I realized I was talking. The words seemed to come tumbling out effortlessly. I knew the ideas I wanted to express. Even when I couldn't think of the exact words I had prepared, other words came out to take their place. I felt that I had been well taught. The question period at the end of the lecture turned out to be a challenge. I never knew what would be asked next. On a number of points I was unable to give authoritative answers. When a question stumped me, I just admitted I didn't know the answer, and went on to the next. If I do say it, my lecture was well received.

An even bigger test awaited me: Town Hall, in New York, January 27. Some of my Newport friends were in the front row and Marguerite was in the second row on the aisle (so she could leave if my performance embarrassed her too much). Jim and Bess Farley were there, as were Mrs. Ogden Reid, the Countess de Kotzebue, Norman Thomas, and Lawrence Langner. Marguerite later said that when I came out on the stage, all she could do was stare at her feet—she was afraid to look at me. But as I started to talk and the people didn't laugh at me or get up and leave, she began to relax a little. Toward the end of my lecture, she said, she was listening to what I was saying about Russia instead of reminding herself constantly that it was her sister, Perle, who was doing the talking. I considered that one of the finest compliments possible.

After giving several other lectures around the country, I returned to Washington and took an apartment at the Sheraton Park. I was so happy to be back and free of obligations that I just had to celebrate. I decided to have a big party in honor of the ladies of the fourth estate—those of the Women's National Press Club and the American Newspaper Women's Club. Some of my friends kidded me about giving this party because I had written a magazine article two years earlier entitled "I'm Through With Plush Parties!" But the friends who know me best realize that just as sure as I say I'm *not* going to do something, it's a sign that I'll probably do it. Anyway, I already had broken this 1952 resolution with the Coronation Ball—the plushest party I've ever given.

For my Washington party, held at the Sheraton Park Hotel, I engaged Sidney and his orchestra. A few days before the party I called Sidney and asked if he could hire some extra violins for the evening. I had seen strolling violins at Monseigneur's in Paris and thought it would be fun to try the same thing at a Washington party. After Sidney had obligingly hired six extra violins, I decided six weren't enough. I continued to have second thoughts and finally wound up hiring twenty-four extra violins. Sidney had to search all over Washington and Baltimore to find that many who were available. At the stroke of ten, the lights dimmed and a spotlight illuminated a side door. One by one the violinists came into the room playing gypsy music, and with the lighting effect, it looked as if there were a hundred. It was quite an exciting moment.

As usual, when the party got rolling, the guests began to perform. The lovely composer and singer Eleanor "Hank" Fort introduced a song she had made up for the night called "Protocol"; it spoofed me and Washington parties. Celeste Holm sang several numbers, and was followed by Janet Blair and then by Billie Worth, who had just come over from England.

In the receiving line with me were Hazel Markel, president of the Women's National Press Club, and Ruth Crane, president of the American Newspaper Women's Club, and among the guests that night were Chief Justice and Mrs. Warren and their daughter Virginia, and Justice and Mrs. Sherman Minton; French Ambassador and Madame Bonnet, Norwegian Ambassador and Madame Morgenstierne, Chinese Ambassador and Mrs. Koo, Italian Ambassador and Signora Tarchiani, and Swedish Ambassador and Mrs. Boheman; Swiss Minister and Mrs. Bruggman; Senators Alexander Wiley, Dennis Chavez, Clinton Anderson, Homer Ferguson, Edward Martin, William Fulbright, and Barry Goldwater and their wives; Secretary of Interior and Mrs. Douglas McKay; Colonel and Mrs. Gordon Moore; Representatives Katharine St. George and Jim Fulton; Admiral and Mrs. Robert Carney, former Ambassador and Mrs. Joseph E. Davies, and Mrs. Robert Low Bacon. The press was well represented. Hedda Hopper came from Hollywood, Bob and Millie Considine, Earl Wilson, Danton Walker, and Nancy Randolph came from New York, and of course

I had invited most of the Washington news and society writers. I had a marvelous time and I felt it was a successful party. I was delighted to be back in business again at my old stamping grounds.

At about this time Marguerite and George started looking for a house in Washington. After several months of searching they found a French château-type house in Spring Valley that, as Marguerite said, "had possibilities." If Marguerite ever bought a house that was perfect as it stood, I believe she would have been too disappointed to move in. As it turned out, she left little more than the foundation and outside walls intact in her "redecorating." The changes were so extensive that it was more than a year before she could move in.

While this project was proceeding, I decided to go traveling again. I had never visited the Far East and Middle East, and since I had observed the Soviet system at its source, I thought it might be interesting to see what influence communism was having in other parts of the world. When Bob Murphy at the State Department heard about my trip he reminded me that even an ex-minister has some importance to her country, and that there would inevitably be courtesy calls on heads of state as I went along. Bob suggested I visit as many of the current hot spots as possible and keep my eyes open. He said the State Department would notify our embassies to assist me in any way possible.

I traveled for most of the trip with Marjorie Pridgen and Jean Anderson. Over a period of four months I visited Hawaii, Japan, Korea, Formosa, Hong Kong, the Philippines, Vietnam, Singapore, Thailand, Pakistan, India, Ceylon, Egypt, Lebanon, Israel, Syria, Turkey, Greece, Italy, and Luxembourg. In sixteen of these countries I had opportunities to talk with the head of state or other high officials. Although I observed much that was interesting to me and later was of considerable interest to the State Department, I'm going to concentrate here on the high points of my trip: my experiences in Saigon, New Delhi, and Cairo.

I had received conflicting advice about visiting Saigon, the capital of South Vietnam. Everyone agreed the situation there was dangerous because of the Red Chinese invasion of North Vietnam and the somewhat tenuous truce between the French and the invaders. In Hong Kong, Associated Press correspondent Forrest Edwards, who had just returned from Saigon, assured me we would be perfectly safe because the French Colonial Government had things under control. But in Manila a few days later, American Ambassador to the Philippines Homer Ferguson told me of a recent bomb scare in an American office in Saigon. He urged us to bypass South Vietnam. Having all this expert advice, we did what we had been planning to do all along: we took the plane to Saigon.

When we arrived there on July 18, 1955, it was so hot we stayed in our rooms at the Majestic Hotel all afternoon. Late in the day loud-speakers began to blare in the streets. I phoned the American Embassy to find out what it was all about and discovered the anti-Communists were protesting against the International Truce Commission. This commission, which had just arrived in the city and was also staying at the Majestic Hotel, was composed of Canadian, Indian, and Polish representatives. It was trying to force an immediate election in Vietnam. The anti-Communists, hoping to counter the intensive Communist propaganda campaign then going on, were determined that the election would not be held.

That night in front of the hotel I ran into two friends from New York, Angier Biddle Duke and Alfred Katz. Angie was then in charge of the International Rescue Committee and was in Saigon working with one of the camps for refugees. He and Alfred asked if I could go to the camp the next day and talk to the boys about America and democracy. I said it wouldn't be possible because I had several appointments to keep. I did have a couple of hours free at noon, but I had been warned not to go out in the intense noonday heat.

"I'm sorry you can't go, Perle, because you could certainly help us by talking to those boys," said Angie. "They are the children from North Vietnam who have seen their parents killed by the Communists. They are now down here organizing to fight for their freedom."

Angie made me see the importance of his cause, and I told him I would somehow find a way to go with him.

The next morning I had a ten o'clock appointment with Ngo Dinh Diem, President and Prime Minister of the Republic of Vietnam. Miss Anita Lauve from the American Embassy went with me to interpret. At one point in the interview I asked Diem about the loud-speakers. He said the demonstration wasn't anything serious—just students making a verbal protest against the International Truce Commission.

At the peak of the day's tropical heat, I left with Angie and Alfred Katz for their rescue camp, about fifty miles to the north. There were many little tents scattered around the area, and groups of the refugees were squatting around fires preparing their noon meal. Angie Duke called them all together. There were a hundred or so, some of them only thirteen or fourteen years old—tragically young to be training for guerrilla warfare. With Angie interpreting, I talked to them about the young people in America and what the boys might see if they could some day visit our country. Then they sang some of their native songs for me, and one of the leaders requested me to relay their greetings and their avowals of friendship to the youth of America when I returned.

That evening, back at the hotel, all seemed peaceful. My two traveling companions and I could see an American warship in the harbor, so we felt a sense of security.

At nine the next morning we heard shouts and gunfire and then bedlam broke loose. I happened to be in the lobby and saw hundreds of young men coming swiftly toward the hotel.

"You'd better go to your room, Madam Mesta," said the desk clerk. "The students are demonstrating against the Truce Commission."

I hurried upstairs, and a few moments later the mob burst into the hotel and began wrecking the lobby.

Our rooms were in between those occupied by the various Truce Commissioners, and the rioters soon headed for our floor. I glimpsed other hotel guests running around wildly, trying to get out. We bolted the door and I tried to call the American Embassy, but the switchboard had been knocked out. Someone commenced throwing stones through our windows and I could hear shooting right outside. Finally, screaming and shouting, they started to break down our door. I ·had been praying, knowing that God would take care of us in His own way. Now I knew it was time to take action. I told my companions to go over to a corner and pray as they had never prayed before. Then I threw open the door and faced the rioters.

"We are your friends! We are Americans!" I protested.

"No, Canadians," said one of the rioters, brandishing a knife.

Just then a colored girl, screaming, her dress almost torn off, came down the hall with her baby in her arms. I recognized her as the wife of an American I had met the night before. He had just come to Saigon to work for the United States Overseas Mission.

"They think you're an Indian—tell them you're an American," I said. But she was too frightened to help herself. I managed to get her into our room and told her to join the other women and start saying the Lord's Prayer.

I turned back to the rioters. "We are Americans, we are your friends," I said again and held out my hand as if to shake hands. They paid no attention. Suddenly, one of the youths rushed at me, his eyes glassy, his knife raised.

In desperation, I cried out: "I'm Perle Mesta!" I thought at least he ought to know the name of the person he was about to kill.

The boy stared at me a moment, and then his expression changed. In that one frightful instant he recognized me as the woman who had spoken at his camp the day before. He put his hand on my shoulder and said, "Ahhh . . . Mesta . . . camp . . . talk." Then he shouted an explanation to his friends and they saved us from the other rioters.

A short time later some French troops arrived, and then we felt a little safer. The embassy's Miss Lauve had performed beautifully when the rioting broke out. Our ambassador being out of town, she had called the French governor and told him he had to get troops to save the Americans in the hotel. General Harris, an American Army officer, and Francis Meloy, one of our embassy officials, arrived soon after the French troops. General Harris took charge of the girl and her baby, and Mr. Meloy hustled my companions and me down through the ruined lobby into an embassy car. When we got to the sidewalk, in the midst of all the confusion, the Foreign Minister of Vietnam arrived with a message from Prime Minister Diem regretting that we had been caught in all this.

We had no time for social amenities, because firing suddenly broke out again, and we sped off to the embassy, the three of us women huddled in the bottom of the car. Early in the afternoon we flew on to Singapore. Later we learned that two persons had been killed and sixty injured in the riot that day.

When I arrived at Singapore, I found that everyone wanted to know what had happened. All communications had been out with Saigon. And I also discovered that a report had gone out that I had been killed. I managed to get a call through to Oklahoma City to let William know I was still alive, and to tell him to get in touch with Marguerite. Then I got the following cable from Hong Kong:

MY SINCEREST APOLOGIES IF OUR CONVERSATION HONG KONG
PROMPTED YOUR CHANGE OF PLANS AND VISIT SAIGON STOP TOLD
YOU IT WAS HOT SOUTHEAST NEWS SPOT BUT UNKNEW IT WOULD
BE THAT HOT STOP GRATEFULLEST PROVIDENCE YOU ESCAPED
UNHARMED BEST REGARDS

EDWARDS, ASSOCIATED PRESS

Later I was amused to see how the *Daily Oklahoman* treated the story. The headline was: PERLE TALKS WAY OUT OF SAIGON RIOT. One of my Oklahoma newspaper friends, Mary Goddard, summed up the incident this way: "Perle proved she can talk her way out of anything."

My interview two weeks later with Prime Minister Jawaharlal Nehru in New Delhi was certainly one of the oddest experiences of my entire trip. I was taken to his office by a young lady from Ambassador John Sherman Cooper's staff. Nehru came to the outer office and greeted me cordially. When I got into his office, I sat down and he sat down. But he said nothing. Several moments passed. Finally, I decided to break the ice.

"Mr. Prime Minister," I said, "you have been having some very bad storms. Do you have these often?"

"Not often," he replied. And not a word else. More time elapsed.

I looked at his inscrutable face and wondered: Doesn't he like me? I certainly haven't said anything that could make him dislike me. Since I regarded Prime Minister Nehru as one of the great statesmen of his time, his conduct struck me as being very odd. I decided to try again.

"We enjoyed your sister Madame Pandit when she was your ambassador to the United States," I said. "It was wonderful for you to send her over to us and we would like very much to have her return. But I suppose it wouldn't be your policy to send her again soon."

208

"It might be," he replied.

Another long silence. I wondered what I could talk about next. I usually am not at a loss for words, but then I usually get some help. I had wanted to talk about Russia, since I knew that Nehru had just been there, but Ambassador Cooper had asked me not to bring that subject up. Then I remembered hearing that a law had been passed in India allowing women to get divorces. I grabbed at that straw.

"The women in America were so interested in that law you just passed about divorce," I said.

He didn't answer, but pressed a button and called in an aide and asked to have something brought in. When a document was handed to him, I gathered it must have been the law I had asked about. He sat there and read it and never said one thing. And the time went on. You always wait for a head of state to make the first move before you leave. But this was too much. He didn't make a move for me to go, so I made it.

"I don't want to take any more of your valuable time, Mr. Prime Minister," I said, and got up to leave.

Without a word, he got up and came to the door with me. And just as soon as we crossed the threshold, he became just as pleasant as could be. "So happy to have met you, Madam Mesta," he said warmly. "I hope we may meet soon again."

When I got back to the American Embassy and told Ambassador Cooper about my puzzling experience, he couldn't figure it out either. One possible solution, we decided, was that the Prime Minister, who had just returned from Russia, might have assumed I was going to question him about his friendliness with the Soviets and didn't want to give me an opening. But then, who knows? Perhaps Nehru was just in a bad mood that day.

The next national leader I met was an entirely different sort of host. As I walked into Gamal Abdel Nasser's office in Cairo, the Egyptian Premier spread his arms wide and gave me the same greeting Sir Winston Churchill had given: "Ah, Call Me Madam."

What a handsome man that Nasser is—by far the most attractive man I met on my entire trip. He is very tall, very masculine, and very forceful, and those beautiful brown eyes and that flashing smile are hard to resist. He just oozes charm. He greeted me in English, but from then on spoke through an interpreter. Colonel

Nasser was very enthusiastic as he showed me pictures and models of schools and factories and dams, and told me about the great accomplishments he had made and his ambitious plans for the future of Egypt. At the time of my visit, the Premier was courting American financial support for his Aswan dam, and it was obvious to me that he was trying to make a big impression. After he had talked for almost an hour, he offered to have some of his industrial, agricultural, economic, and educational experts take me around and show me at first hand the new Egypt. I accepted the invitation. Then I said I had something to ask him.

"Are you not buying arms and machinery from Russia?" I asked. Nasser admitted he was.

"When the Russians send their machines and weapons to you, do they not also send men to teach your people how to use them?" I queried. Nasser nodded agreement.

"And do you mean to tell me these Communists are not teaching your people more than just how to operate these machines?" I asked.

"Certainly not, Madam," Nasser replied indignantly. "You have been misinformed about Russian intentions. And besides, Egypt can take care of itself." He rose to indicate the interview was over.

During the next week, I saw many examples of the progress being made in Egypt. I was impressed by what I saw, even though I was aware that I was being shown only what Nasser wanted me to see. And even when I was on my own for meals or simple sight-seeing, I was aware that I was being kept under constant surveillance. I left Colonel Nasser's land of change feeling uneasy about its future.

After leaving Egypt, I continued my travels and wound up in Luxembourg, where I had not been for two years. It was like going home. People would wave to me on the street, and when I visited Namur's for the customary late afternoon tea and cakes, many of the patrons stood up to greet me. I went to the palace for a visit with Grand Duchess Charlotte and stayed several days with Ambassador and Mrs. Wiley Buchanan and their three lovely children. I was so glad that the people of Luxembourg could have such a wholesome example of an American family representing the United States, and was also pleased that President Eisenhower had seen fit to raise the post from that of Minister to Ambassador.

SEVENTEEN: *Fifi's Conquest*

WHEN I RETURNED from my round-the-world trip late in 1955, Marguerite had almost completed her renovation of Les Ormes (The Elms), as she had decided to call her new house in the Spring Valley section of Washington. The house was the culmination of several years of planning. She had collected many of the furnishings while in Europe from 1949 to 1953 and had just been waiting for an opportunity to put them all together. In fact, the one thing that caused her to select this particular house was that the drawing room was exactly the right size for her Aubusson rug. Marguerite had spent two years looking for this lovely rose-toned original of the Louis XV period. She had also scoured Europe for signed pieces of furniture. The antique parquet floors came from a château near Versailles, and the walls are covered with rose-toned silk brought from another château. The crystal chandelier in the drawing room once hung in the London house of Lord and Lady Beatty. The chairs were designed by cabinetmakers of Louis XV and XVI, and some of them still have their original silk velvet upholstery.

The entrance hall of Les Ormes has a black and white inlaid marble floor that makes it a wonderful place for eight or ten couples to dance. The dining room seats twenty-four and looks out onto a French-style terrace. Around the walls of the dining room are murals that were found in a palace in Venice. They are the original tempera paintings on canvas that served as designs for tapestries. Marguerite chose these murals, which depict French figures playing games, because they give a lighter, less stuffy feeling than tapestries. A small dining room adjoining the main dining room can seat an additional fourteen guests. Also on the ground floor is a cheery sunroom and a small Louis XV drawing room.

211

Upstairs there are four large bedrooms, a sitting room, and a library.

I had been staying at the Sheraton Park Hotel when in Washington, but when Les Ormes was completed Marguerite and George wanted me to stay with them. It is a beautiful house and lends itself perfectly to either formal or informal entertaining. And in late January of 1956, Marguerite and I started our social activities in the new house with a luncheon for Mamie Eisenhower and a large reception for Adlai Stevenson's sister, Eleanor "Buffie" Ives.

At the 1956 Democratic convention in Chicago I worked for the National Woman's Party in helping to keep the Equal Rights for Women plank in the platform, and I also tried to get a Lyndon Johnson for President boom started—but I didn't get very far with that. I guess I was four years too early. I held my usual convention party at the Blackstone Hotel. Three secretaries and the doorkeeper of the House of Representatives, William "Fishbait" Miller, stood with me at the entrance to the Mayfair Room to guard against crashers. We discovered later, however, that two Harvard Young Republicans had managed to get in by dressing up in busboy coats and entering through the kitchen.

I had invited some six hundred guests, including Harry and Bess Truman, Adlai Stevenson and Buffie Ives, the Averell Harrimans, the Estes Kefauvers, the Stuart Symingtons, the Hubert Humphreys, the Jack Kennedys, and the Lyndon Johnsons. When Fishbait announced Senator and Mrs. Johnson, I turned to some reporters who were grouped around the receiving line and said determinedly, "Here comes my candidate for President." Lyndon heard it, and as he greeted me with a kiss, he said, "Aw, now, Perle, quit your kidding."

Among my other guests were Oklahoma's Governor and Mrs. Raymond Gary, along with the Oklahoma official state hostess, Mrs. Hallie Johnson; and Joan Blondell, Spike Jones, Carmine De Sapio, Will Rogers, Jr., Sue Ruble, N. G. Henthorne, Loyd Benefield, Edith Gaylord, Mark Weaver, Mrs. Glenn Frank, George Jessel, Marvin Braverman, Philip Perlman, Mr. and Mrs. James Bruce, and the Ed Pauleys.

The guests seated themselves at tables around the dance floor, and it was noticeable that Harry Truman and Adlai Stevenson had

212

chosen tables at opposite sides of the room. Relations between them were a bit strained because of Mr. Truman's backing of Harriman's candidacy. Everyone was eager to see what would happen when Governor Harriman arrived on the scene. But we waited in vain, because when Mrs. Harriman arrived, she brought news that her husband regretted he would not be able to attend the party.

I had not planned any formal entertainment, but as usual, along about midnight, things started to happen. Phil Regan went to the mike and called on Hank Fort to sing "Mr. Sam," a song she had composed to honor Speaker Rayburn. Vaughn Monroe and Johnny Desmond sang a few numbers. Martha Rountree called Jim Farley, Frank Clement, Paul Douglas, and Hubert Humphrey to the center of the floor, and, as she had done at my 1952 party, staged an impromptu Meet the Press program. And to top things off, H. V. Kaltenborn poked fun at himself by imitating President Truman's take-off of the famous Kaltenborn "Dewey sure to win" broadcast on election night of 1948.

During the convention, I had a run-in with Happy Chandler, then Governor of Kentucky, who had surprised everyone by announcing he would try to get the presidential nomination.

"Now, Happy, what's all this nonsense about you running for President?" I joshed when we met in the Blackstone dining room. "Why don't you just stop this foolishness and go on home?" I said. "You're never going to be President."

Chandler was furious. He went right up to see Harry Truman and said, "Make Perle keep her mouth shut." Mr. Truman laughed and replied, "I can't do a thing with her myself."

A few weeks after the convention, while I was staying at the Sheraton Russell in New York, Marguerite sent me a toy poodle. She had become interested in breeding these dogs a few years earlier, and one of her miniatures, Adastra Magic Fame, had won fifty-three best-of-show awards, setting a new world record for poodles. That summer of 1956 one of her new white toy poodles didn't turn out well: she was healthy and had an excellent pedigree, but was too long and too bowlegged to become a show dog. This was the dog that came to me. Her registered name was Ty-del Dancing Girl; I called her Fifi. I suspect Marguerite thought I would soon pass Fifi along to someone else, or she might have sent me a more valuable dog. As a child, you see, I had never had a

213

high opinion of William's or Marguerite's dogs. They had always seemed so silly, so *underfoot*. It was like old times again when Fifi entered my life: I was definitely not impressed with Marguerite's sisterly gesture. In fact I even telephoned my good friend Mrs. William Randolph Hearst, Sr., to see if she didn't want to be given a *very* nice poodle. Millicent thanked me for thinking of her, but said that her one dog was enough.

Fifi and I didn't get along at all. She nipped at me. I scolded her. She barked constantly and chewed up the hotel's rugs and furniture. The manager informed me that I would either have to get rid of Fifi or move out. By this time, the issue between Fifi and me as to who was to be the boss had become a real challenge. Taking the poodle with me, I went to Elizabeth Arden's Maine Chance Farm, near Phoenix, Arizona, intending to lose a little weight while our battle continued. The first day there, I left Fifi in my room while I took a swim. When I came back, she was gone. Clare Luce was staying next door, so I went to ask her if she had seen Fifi— and there was my little poodle sitting on the bed with Clare, snuggling up to her. Clare had heard the dog crying, had come in to comfort Fifi, and Fifi had followed her. When I got Fifi back into my room, she started barking and acting naughty again.

After two weeks at Maine Chance, and with Fifi still misbehaving, I decided to go to California. I took a suite at the Beverly Hills Hotel and put Fifi in Frances Hartsook's obedience school in the San Fernando Valley. At the end of three weeks, she had become a perfect lady. When I went to pick her up and take her back to the hotel, Miss Hartsook suggested that it might be a good idea for *me* to come out to the school and take some lessons in how to get along with a dog. Fifi's bad disposition was thought to be just as much my fault as it was hers. I was indignant at Miss Hartsook's suggestion. Perle Mesta could get on with people all over the world but couldn't manage a poodle?—nonsense!

The first few days back at the hotel, Fifi behaved beautifully, proving me right. All the fault had certainly been hers. Then she tore up the dressing-room carpet and was soon back to all her old tricks. That little scamp knew she could get away with absolutely anything with me. I put her back in obedience school, and this time *I* took some lessons, too. Before I returned east, Fifi and I had learned how to get along with each other, and she has been my constant companion ever since. I bred her the next year and after that she was much more gentle.

One of the litter was a beautiful toy we named A. M. (though I called him Tony). I sent Tony around the country with a handler, Maxine Beam, of Fort Worth, Texas, and the dog became a champion. Now retired from shows, Tony lives with Fifi and me.

Early in 1957 I gave a big party that in some ways was not too successful. I had been asked by the Sheraton Hotel Corporation to help open its new fifteen-million-dollar hotel in Philadelphia. Ordinarily, I never give a party unless it is my own and I have complete charge of everything, but when my friend Ernest Henderson, the Sheraton president, promised that his company would donate a large sum to any charity I might name, I agreed to put on one of my parties for him. I named the International Rescue Committee, which Angie Duke headed, as my charity, and the Sheraton Corporation's contribution went directly toward helping the Hungarians who had fled their country after the uprising of 1956.

I had a difficult problem in the matter of unexpected guests. In addition to the eight hundred I myself invited, the Sheraton people invited their own five hundred to a three-day opening festival, and many of these decided to come to the party. So we were hopelessly overcrowded. We had hired the orchestras of Meyer Davis and Xavier Cugat to play, but the waiters kept bringing in more tables until there was hardly any room to dance. Things went wrong in the kitchen, and the first course wasn't served until a quarter of ten. And most of the food was cold when it finally arrived. But being the daughter of a hotel owner, I could sympathize. Things nearly always go wrong at an opening.

In spite of the difficulties, almost everyone had a good time. Ernest Henderson donated ten thousand dollars to the Hungarian relief fund for one dance with Ginger Rogers, and Sheraton vice-president Robert Moore gave half that sum for a dance with Zsa Zsa Gabor (Zsa Zsa was a little miffed about the price differential). And Anna Maria Alberghetti, Ella Logan, and Eddie Fisher sang, and Gene Nelson did a dance.

The biggest moment of confusion—and the outstanding news event for the press that night—was the appearance of Mrs. Morris Cafritz, a Washington hostess whom the newspapers have sometimes called my "archenemy." Mrs. Cafritz and her husband, a prominent Washington builder, had been invited by the Sheraton people to attend their opening festivities.

While I was in the receiving line with the Anthony Drexel Biddles, I noticed that the photographers were beginning to cluster around our position near the door, and I sensed that something was coming. A moment later, Mrs. Cafritz came through the door. Just as I extended my hand to greet her, Mrs. Cafritz dropped the contents of her evening bag. Flash bulbs went off all over the place. The attention of the whole room was centered on us, and the photographers had a field day.

The newspapers—which for years have been mentioning a so-called "Mesta-Cafritz feud"—built up this encounter to enormous proportions. Actually, I have never taken part in this so-called feud and all I know about it is what I have read in the gossip columns. A few years ago one writer reported that, "Mrs. Cafritz said her feud with Mrs. Mesta started when she asked Perle for some Inaugural Ball tickets for some friends and Perle wouldn't give."

Now I don't know how the columnist arrived at his information, but I do recall that when I was co-chairman of the Truman Inaugural Ball in 1948 I received a request from Mrs. Cafritz for some box seats. However, they had all been spoken for by the time she got in touch with me, so I really didn't have a box to sell her.

On another occasion, after I had returned from my four years in Luxembourg, columnist George Dixon wrote that he had asked Mrs. Cafritz just how she felt about my return. "I was so happy with the status quo," Dixon reported Mrs. Cafritz as replying. "When she left Washington I couldn't have been more pleased. I thought Mrs. Mesta was out of my life for good, but it seems I just gave her up for Lent."

I bear no resentment toward Mrs. Cafritz, however. What she chooses to say and do is her own business.

In my earlier days, I did enter into a few good feuds. And I still get into scrapes now and then because I sometimes speak my mind when it would be more prudent to be silent.

One of the most publicized disagreements I had was with Lady Astor. I was attending a meeting of the Women's National Farm and Gardening Association in Washington in 1948. Lady Astor was the principal speaker. In her speech, she started criticizing

American women and said they were not interested in anything but "clothes, liquor, and brassière ads." I felt that she had no right to talk that way, so I got up and walked out of the banquet room. The next day Lady Astor called my walking out a publicity stunt, and for a while we had a first-class row going.

In 1953 I met Lady Astor when I was in England for the coronation.

"We've had a lot of controversy, haven't we?" she said.

"Oh, I think it's all just a lot of newspaper talk," I replied.

"I think so too," Lady Astor said. "Let's forget it." And the next night we dined together and have been friends ever since. I have heard that she talks much the same way about English women as she did that day about us Americans, so I guess her criticism was not to be taken seriously.

Some of the press tried to get a battle going between Elsa Maxwell and me because of what she said about me in her book, *R.S.V.P.* No sooner had advance material from the book come out in *McCall's* magazine than I had a telephone call from Washington *Daily News* columnist Tom Donnelly. I'll let his column speak for itself about our conversation.

ELSA MAXWELL
BRANDS PERLE
INDISCRIMINATE!

By Tom Donnelly

As soon as I heard that Elsa Maxwell had accused Perle Mesta of being "indiscriminate in making up the guest list of her famous Washington parties," I phoned Mrs. Mesta, in hopes of getting from her a fiery rebuttal that would be flashed from coast to coast and launch a new feud to eclipse the one Elsa used to have with the Duchess of Windsor.

"Mrs. Mesta," I said excitedly, "there's this terrific attack on you in this magazine. Elsa Maxwell says you're indiscriminate. She says you've never learned to say 'no' when people ask you for an invitation to one of your parties."

Mrs. Mesta said, "I think she's got something there."

My heart sank.

"Doesn't this turn you white with rage?" I demanded. "This woman accusing you in the public prints of—"

Mrs. Mesta said, "To tell you the truth I really almost have to get

217

out of town the day before I give a party. But how can I say 'no' to anybody who's dying to come? That's my problem."

"Well," I said, "if Elsa is right, are you going to change your ways? Are you going to be more discriminate?"

Mrs. Mesta said, "How can I change my ways? You are the way you are, and that's all there is to that. I have my ways and Elsa has her ways. I've seen her put 'em out. Anybody she doesn't want."

"How does she put 'em out?" I asked. "Has she got a bouncer?"

Mrs. Mesta said, "She just makes 'em go. I don't have any crashers at my parties to speak of. People call me up and ask if they can bring a friend or two so naturally I say yes. What else did Elsa say?"

I said, feeling everything slipping away from me, "Oh, she said you had many talents as a hostess but you have one serious fault— you're too kind hearted. And she said you can get practically any Washington celebrity to appear at your parties. She says, 'Name anybody in the Capitol and Perle will produce him like a rabbit out of a hat.' "

Mrs. Mesta said, "I think that's very nice of Elsa. I always have fun at Elsa's affairs."

So the Elsa Maxwell—Perle Mesta battle never got started. I like Elsa and go to her parties and she comes to mine. We disagree on many things. She thinks political people are dull, and I don't. But such disagreements make the world go round.

For a few years I carried a grudge against Drew Pearson because I didn't like some of the unfairly critical things he had said about Mr. Truman when he was President. One evening recently, I was invited to a party given by Herb and Marjorie May, and found myself seated next to Drew. At first I was rather cool toward him. But then he happened to mention something that "Harry" had told him a short time before in Independence.

I looked at Drew in amazement.

"You mean you and Harry have made up?" I said.

Drew nodded and told me that when he had called Mr. Truman to ask some questions about the Truman Library, Mr. Truman had invited him to come to Missouri to see it, and then had personally escorted Drew through the Library.

"Well, for goodness sake, Drew," I muttered. "Here I've been mad at you for nothing." So now Drew and I are friends again.

This experience taught me a lesson: Don't stay mad at someone just because he or she happens to be quarreling with one of your friends. They make up, forget to let you know, and then there you are, left out on a limb. Of course it is even better not to get mad in the first place. And you can refuse to become a close friend of someone who differs with you on things you feel are important. You can be against what they stand for without being mad at them personally.

This is my strategy with the Russian diplomats I occasionally encounter at Washington parties. When I came back from Russia in 1953, I figured that because of what I had written, I would be *persona non grata* at the Russian Embassy. This turned out not to be the case. I have recently been to receptions there, especially the one for Soviet Premier Khrushchev during his trip to the United States. A few hours before the reception, Mr. Khrushchev had visited the Mesta Machine Company in Pittsburgh. When I went through the receiving line at the Russian Embassy, Ambassador Menshikov explained to Mr. Khrushchev who I was. Through an interpreter, Khrushchev told me he had enjoyed seeing the Mesta plant and hoped we would allow Russia to buy some of our machinery. Since I had resigned from the board of directors some years before, I explained to Mr. Khrushchev that such matters were out of my hands. I took the opportunity to add that my husband had come from an immigrant family and had started with nothing and built up that tremendous plant. I wanted Mr. Khrushchev to know that this was another example of the opportunity available under a democratic free-enterprise system. He received my little lecture with a big and amiable grin.

Although the officials I met in Russia in 1953 and all of the former Soviet diplomats in Washington wore grim expressions, it seems that the new look is a smile. At a recent social event, I kidded Soviet Ambassador Menshikov about this thaw. "Why do you smile all the time, Mr. Ambassador?" I asked. "Oh, I'm just naturally congenial," he replied. And one afternoon when I was seated next to him at the International Day Races at Laurel racetrack, I tried to talk him into splitting a two-dollar bet with me. At first he refused.

"What's the matter with you?" I gibed. "You come out to the races, but won't even bet a dollar." He relented then, and gave me a dollar to bet on the horse I picked, Bombeau.

Bombeau won, paying $7.20. I returned from the cashier's window and gave Ambassador Menshikov his investment back, plus $2.60 profit.

"Now, you see—you're taking capitalistic money," I said. The Ambassador grinned, thanked me, and put the money safely in his pocket.

So you see, I don't really tangle with the Russians in Washington even though I don't agree with them. I have never invited any of them to a party. If I had an official position representing the government, of course, I would invite them. But since I no longer represent the government, I see no reason for trying to put on a façade of great friendship.

I keep the Skirvin temper in check pretty well these days. But there are exceptions. Shortly after the start of the first session of the Eighty-sixth Congress in 1959, I received a phone call from Republican Congressman Bill Ayres of Ohio asking me to lunch with him at Washington's La Salle du Bois restaurant. Ayres, I discovered then, was one of the group trying to oust Joe Martin from his post as Minority Leader of the House of Representatives.

"You are a great friend of Joe Martin's, aren't you?" Congressman Ayres asked me.

I admitted I was. "I'm a Democrat," I said, "but I'd do most anything to help Joe Martin."

"Well, if you are such a good friend of his, you should go and tell him he had better resign as Minority Leader," Ayres said bluntly. "I know you wouldn't want his feelings hurt. If he doesn't resign we are going to put him out, and we have the votes to do it."

I told Mr. Ayres I thought he was wrong, both in what he wanted to do and the way he was doing it. I said I never had tried to influence Joe Martin, even in the days when I was a Republican, and that I certainly would not be a party to any of their behind-the-scenes intrigue.

I was furious. I love Joe Martin. He is one of the best friends I have in the world. His word is gold. No Minority Leader and Speaker of the House ever worked better together than Joe Martin and Sam Rayburn, because they had implicit confidence in each other's word. I did not mince words with Mr. Ayres, and I never have reconciled myself to the shabby way in which he and his

220

group ousted Joe Martin. However, now that it is over, I hold no personal grudge toward Mr. Ayres.

A sense of humor is indispensable in Washington. I learned that long ago. Recently Speaker of the House Sam Rayburn got peeved at me for opposing his plan to face-lift the front of the Capitol. I usually approve of all of Mr. Sam's decisions. But not this one. What got him riled was a question I threw at Vice-President Nixon during a conference on foreign aid. At a public session, I asked the Vice-President why he approved the ten-million-dollar expenditure for tearing down and changing the east front of the Capitol when the money might better be used where it was really needed, for instance, in the Foreign Aid program.

A couple of days later I sat next to Mr. Sam at a dinner and he berated me for calling unfavorable attention to his pet project.

"I always thought you were pretty smart, but this time you were stupid," Sam said to me. "I'm going to stand up now and tell all these people how foolish you were and why you are wrong."

"Oh, you wouldn't do that, Sam," I said, as sweetly as I knew how.

"I certainly will do it," he growled.

I picked up a book of matches from the table. "See these matches?" I waved them in front of his nose. "If you stand up, I am going to light these and hold them under your coattails."

"You wouldn't dare," Sam said, not quite sure whether or not I was serious.

"Oh, wouldn't I?" I answered, glowering just as fiercely as he was. That did the trick and he burst out laughing.

Although Sam wasn't really mad at me, he still insisted I was wrong. At last, when I met Roscoe DeWitt, one of the excellent architects working on the Capitol remodeling, and received a full explanation of why the work was necessary, I changed my mind and became a supporter of this project.

EIGHTEEN: *Bigwigs, Littlewigs,*
and No Wigs at All

IMMEDIATELY AFTER the Sheraton Hotel party in Philadelphia, I flew out to Hollywood where a television dramatization based on my life was being prepared by Playhouse 90. Shirley Booth played the title part of "The Hostess with the Mostes'" and little Evelyn Rudie of "Eloise" fame played me as a little girl. Some of the scenes weren't exactly as the events of my life really happened, but I realized that producer Martin Manulis was trying to deliver the most entertainment he could in his space of ninety minutes. And when I saw the scenes so effectively played by Miss Booth, I forgot whatever objections I might have had. Hedda Hopper appeared in a guest-star role that closely resembled Evalyn Walsh McLean. I think Hedda would have liked to have had the Hope diamond to wear, but I tried to make up for the property department's inability to produce it by letting her wear my own diamond necklace.

Returning east, I went to New York for a couple of months, then to Washington. Marguerite and George, who had moved out to Nevada several months earlier, suggested I use their Washington house whenever I wanted. One of the first parties I gave there in 1957 was for Judy Garland. I had planned it as an after-theater supper party and my two hundred guests arrived at eleven-thirty. At midnight, Judy had not yet appeared. Unknown to me, she had decided to take a nap after her rigorous performance at the Capitol Theater. When she hadn't shown up by twelve-thirty, and my guests were eyeing the buffet table hungrily, I gave up and we started our supper without the guest of honor.

When Judy finally arrived at 1:00 A.M., with a great big smile for an apology, the party really began. After she had some supper and visited with the guests, we all gathered around her and the musicians. At three o'clock Judy was still going strong, singing the

222

songs she was planning for her act at the London Palladium. We thought she was wonderful. What had threatened to be a social disaster turned into one of my most enjoyable parties.

In the spring of 1958, I gave a party in honor of Dr. and Mrs. Wernher von Braun. The press had been reporting some differences of opinion on the nation's missile program between Dr. von Braun and some of the members of the Administration, and there had been controversy in Congress about this. I decided it wouldn't do any harm to bring the principals together, so I invited Secretary of Defense and Mrs. McElroy; the President's science advisor, Dr. James Killian, and his wife; Undersecretary of Commerce Walter Williams, Assistant Attorney General Malcolm Wilkey, and Secretary to the Cabinet Bob Gray; Senators Karl Mundt, Leverett Saltonstall, John McClellan, and their wives, and Senator Henry Jackson and a number of other official and nonofficial guests.

A few hours before the party, as luck would have it, the Senate got involved in a debate on taxes, and an hour before dinner I wasn't sure whether or not any of the Senate group could come. Senator Mundt couldn't make it at all. Senator Saltonstall brought his wife, had a quick cocktail, and then went back to work. Just before dinner, Senator Jackson found that he also had to return. Senator McClellan was able to stay, but only because he had already arranged to pair his vote on the tax bill with another Senator who was out of town.

I had decorated the table with ornamental satellites which seemed to soar over sprays of flowers. And because Dr. von Braun was originally a German, I used my rose-bordered white K.P.M. service from Germany—and he recognized it immediately.

Much of the table conversation that night was way over my head, especially when Dr. von Braun tried to explain the intricacies of space. As I remember it, he said that if an astronaut who had a twin went out into space for several years, he would return younger than his twin brother who had stayed on earth. What I *did* understand was the missile expert's views about the Russians. Dr. von Braun said we were moving 30 to 40 per cent more slowly on our missile program than were the Soviets. Knowing what I did about the Soviet methods of getting things done, I was not really surprised, but it was certainly startling to hear our country's backwardness spelled out by a top authority.

On Thanksgiving Day, 1958, I gave a party for some of the foreign ambassadors and a few Washington people, some of whom could not be home with their families on that day. I invited fifty-six in all and held the party at a private club because I couldn't seat that many at Les Ormes. For once we threw protocol to the winds and drew numbered cards to determine our places at the eight round tables. General Carlos Romulo gave a toast on behalf of the six ambassadors present: "However some of us may disagree with the United States' foreign policy, we always can follow America's heart." After dinner we tried to dance off all the extra calories we had just added. Argentine Ambassador Hurtado showed us how a tango should be tangoed, and Cuban Ambassador Arroyo proved the expert at the mambo and then led a conga line that wove all through the club and on to the porch.

One of my most pleasant gatherings in 1959 was a luncheon for Mamie Eisenhower. I invited the wives of four ambassadors—Senhora de Esteves Fernandes (Portugal), Countess Knuth-Winterfeldt (Denmark), Madame Alphand (France), and Lady Caccia (Great Britain)—as well as Señora Mora, wife of the Secretary General of the Pan American Union. I also asked four Senate wives: Mrs. Lyndon Johnson, wife of the Majority Leader, and Mrs. Everett Dirksen, wife of the Minority Leader, and the wives of Senators Hubert Humphrey and Barry Goldwater—two Republicans and two Democrats. Among the other guests were Mrs. Nathan Twining, wife of the chairman of the Joint Chiefs of Staff, and Mrs. James Douglas, wife of the Secretary of the Air Force; Mrs. Livingston Merchant, wife of an undersecretary of State; Alice Roosevelt Longworth, Mrs. Wiley Buchanan, Mrs. Struve Hensel, and Mrs. Philip Cox.

I worked out the menu with Augusta, my cook, about a week ahead and we did some experimenting in the kitchen. I knew Mamie liked egg timbales; we made these our first course. The main course was breast of chicken, fresh asparagus, and hominy au gratin. The latter is a dish Augusta and I made up ourselves. It's just grits fluffed up and topped with cheese. We ended with orange soufflé—another favorite of Mamie's—and fruit and coffee.

Our table conversation ranged over many topics, including the visit of the President of Ireland, who had been entertained the night before at the White House. Mrs. Dirksen commented on the beautiful table decoration at the White House—the hearts made of green carnations for St. Patrick's Day—and asked Mrs. Eisenhower what florist made the White House's arrangements. "Why, we make them!" Mamie exclaimed. Mamie knows exactly what is going on in the White House. Mrs. Truman was also very good about that.

Mamie seemed to be having a good time and she stayed until almost four o'clock. Before leaving, she went into the dining room and shook hands with all the help—even those who had just come in to assist for the day. She complimented Augusta especially on the orange soufflé and asked her for the recipe.

At the door, as Mrs. Eisenhower was leaving, I said, "Tell Ike I'm going to get him out here before he leaves the White House." Mamie replied, "All right, we'll try to get him out."

Every once in a while I try to think of something a little unusual for a party. Last summer, for instance, I chartered a yacht, the *Diplomat,* for a moonlight cruise down the Potomac. The party was in honor of Lee Walsh, the outgoing president of the Women's National Press Club.

Nine foreign ambassadors were aboard and also Chief of Protocol Wiley Buchanan, but we had no protocol. Lee Walsh's husband, Harold, commented that if the boat went down, Wiley would have to decide who would get off first. We had a buffet supper at small tables and the guests got their own groups together. But no one stayed put at a table for very long because Frankie Tam and his orchestra kept lively music going all evening.

The French Ambassador, Hervé Alphand, did a frenzied jitterbug with Betty Beale, mimicking the deadpan expressions that teenagers put on for this kind of dancing. Argentine Ambassador César Barros Hurtado and Mrs. Loy Henderson, wife of the Deputy Undersecretary of State, did a *paso doble.* Senator John McClellan told me it was the first time he had been on a dance floor in two years. Norma McClellan seemed to be having a wonderful time, and for once she got to stay all evening. Her husband seldom accepts a party invitation and when he does, he leaves early. But that evening there was no possibility of his leaving early. He didn't seem to be in the mood to swim ashore.

The *Diplomat* carried a wide geographical representation. Luxembourg Ambassador Heisbourg, Finnish Ambassador Seppala, and Danish Ambassador Count Knuth-Winterfeldt—all summer bachelors at the time—were aboard, as well as Nicaraguan Ambassador Sevilla-Sacasa, Greek Ambassador and Mrs. Liatis, Iranian Ambassador and Mme. Ardalan, and Philippine Ambassador and Mrs. Romulo. Another shipmate was the wife of the Korean Ambassador, Madame Yang. From Philadelphia came Dr. Anthony Sindoni, and from Oklahoma came my dear friend and prominent Republican, Mrs. Pearl Sayre; from Kentucky, the Honorable Pearl Pace, Chairman of the U.S. Foreign Claims Settlement Commission.

The White House staff was represented by the Homer Gruenthers and Robert Gray, and Congress by William Hull, Jr., and among those from the fourth estate who helped honor their colleague were the Leslie Carpenters, Hazel Markel, Marie McNair, Hope Ridings Miller, Patricia Wiggins, and Esther Van Wagoner Tufty.

Almost every time I am interviewed, the question is asked, "What is the secret of your parties?" Really, there's no secret. I'm willing to work hard at the preparations, that's all. When it comes to business affairs, I loathe details, but in organizing a party, I enjoy seeing to even the smallest detail.

Once I have decided to have a party, the first step, of course, is to set a date. And that isn't always as simple as it sounds, especially if I am planning a spring or summer party on the terrace at Les Ormes. Some of my friends laugh at me when they see me studying my *Farmer's Almanac* and *Hagerstown Almanac* to help find a day that is the least likely to have rain. I don't think this is so silly in Washington, where the weather is so unpredictable. I usually consider two or three dates and then let my guest of honor choose the most convenient date. Important people are busy people; they usually have to fit parties in when they can.

Then I start making up my guest list. I like to get just the right blend of guests—to mix Republicans and Democrats, and the bigwigs, the littlewigs, and the no wigs at all. As I have said before, I have found that bringing together people of differing positions and opinions gives a party a kind of chemical reaction that makes it interesting.

If I am planning the party several weeks ahead, I always send out written invitations. But most of the time these days my parties spring up on short notice, and then I telephone. It may not be proper according to some of the etiquette books, but I see nothing wrong with a telephoned invitation. It is in keeping with the present speed-up and informality of our lives. And with a telephoned invitation, I always know immediately whether or not my guests can come. A few days after I have telephoned, I mail a reminder card giving the date and time and place. Even when I invite my guests by mail, I like to send reminder cards to those who have accepted.

Once the guest list is completed, I arrange for the extra help that will be needed, work out a table decoration plan, call the florist to make sure the flowers I need will be available, and engage the music. If the party is to be at Les Ormes, I then get together with my cook, Augusta France, and we plan the menu. I also talk with my No. 1 party helper, Jean Anderson, about the china and linens to be used. Next, I work out the seating arrangement and have my secretary make place cards and escort cards. I do not use escort cards at all my parties. Occasionally, at small affairs, I just go around and tell each gentleman the name of the lady he is to escort to the table. When it is a larger or more formal party, each gentleman is given an envelope containing his escort card. And on a table in the foyer I have a chart which shows where everyone is to be seated.

The seating at a formal dinner party or luncheon is different in Washington than any place else in the nation because of the observance of protocol. Anywhere else you can seat your guests where you please. But in Washington, practically every American and foreign official has a fixed ranking determined by the position he holds. The rankings are determined by the State Department and the White House, although no official list is ever published. As might be imagined, the placing of officials is often a troublesome business. Some of the basic plan is mysterious enough, and then occasionally positions are shifted.

For instance, during the Truman administration, when Fred Vinson was made Chief Justice, the place of the Chief Justice was elevated to the No. 3 spot, just below the Vice-President. This put him above ambassadors, the Speaker of the House, and former Presidents. When President Eisenhower took office, governors were ranked ahead of senators, but at an early White House dinner where there were both governors and senators, the senators were seated above the governors. From then on, Washington hostesses adopted this change. And in 1957, the position of Assistant to the President (then held by Sherman Adams) was boosted over both senators and governors to a place just below Cabinet members.

This is the way the ranking goes today:

The President
The Vice-President
The Chief Justice
Former Presidents
The Speaker of the House of Representatives
Ambassadors of Foreign Powers
Widows of former Presidents
The Secretary of State
United States Representative to the United Nations
Heads of Legations with rank of Minister
Associate Justices of the Supreme Court
The Secretary of the Treasury
The Secretary of Defense
The Attorney General
The Postmaster General
The Secretary of the Interior
The Secretary of Agriculture
The Secretary of Commerce
The Secretary of Labor
The Secretary of Health, Education and Welfare
The Assistant to The President
Chairman of The Atomic Energy Commission
Director of The Bureau of The Budget
Director of Defense Mobilization
United States Senators
Governors of States
Acting Heads of Executive Departments
Former Vice-Presidents
Members of the House of Representatives

The list goes on and on. If I am ever in doubt about seating a table, I consult with Wiley Buchanan's protocol office at the State Department or with Carolyn Hagner Shaw, whose *Social List of Washington* (always called "The Green Book") gives a complete Table of Precedence. Sometimes, when having more than one ambassador, it is necessary to find out when their credentials were

228

presented, since this is what determines precedence. The Dean of the Diplomatic Corps is automatically the ambassador who has been in Washington the longest. It is also necessary, when inviting two or more military men of the same rank, to find out which was given this rank first, as seating depends on this.

Whenever Washington talks about precedence, someone is sure to bring up the well-known story about Dolly Gann and Alice Longworth, which was supposed to have started in an argument about who preceded whom. Alice herself once told me it was all a tempest in a teapot. When Charles Curtis became Vice-President, he designated his sister, Mrs. Dolly Gann, as his official hostess. Alice's husband, Speaker of the House Nicholas Longworth, disapproved because he felt it was a discourtesy to seat the sister of the Vice-President above the wives of the representatives of foreign nations and, incidentally, above his own wife. According to Alice, the legendary feud got its start when she and her husband accepted a dinner invitation at the home of Eugene Meyer, the publisher of the Washington *Post*. To begin with, Alice's husband was not very anxious to go to the dinner because the Meyers did not serve liquor. When he heard that many high officials and foreign ambassadors were going to be there and that Mrs. Gann would be seated next to the host, Mr. Longworth refused to go. The combination of the precedence situation and the dry dinner was just too much for him. The press pounced on the incident and blew it up out of all proportion. Alice says that she and Dolly Gann remained good friends all along.

Under certain informal conditions, the hostess can dispense with protocol if she so desires, as I did at my Thanksgiving Party. Or if there is some unusual protocol problem, a hostess can have several small tables, designate a host and hostess at each table, and work the protocol around that host and hostess.

On the day of a party, I always help the florist in making the arrangements, talk over the music with the leader of the orchestra, and go in and out of the kitchen seeing how Augusta and her assistants are getting on. Just before the arrival hour, I try to check and recheck every single detail. By the time the first guests have arrived, the running of things is entirely in the hands of wonderfully capable Jean Anderson and Day or Domenic, who are my favorite head butlers. I keep the cocktail period short. An eight o'clock dinner means eight o'clock arrival, and by eight-thirty we are in the dining room. In Washington, it is definitely not fashionable to be late.

From the moment my first guest arrives, I play the party by ear, and my byword is "flexibility." Sometimes at the table, I try to start the conversation going, but I never attempt to direct its trend. And contrary to advice in the etiquette books, I like to bring up controversial subjects at the table. An excellent way to keep a party alive is to seat political opponents near each other.

Once I invited Senator Alexander Wiley and the late Senator Pat McCarran to a dinner party, knowing perfectly well that they were not even on speaking terms. I had seated Senator Wiley at my right and Senator McCarran at my left. During the first course, Senator Wiley leaned toward me and whispered in his gentle way, "Why have you got that McCarran here?" Before long, Senator McCarran nudged me and said, "What in hell have you got Wiley here for?" For a while things remained pretty frigid. Finally I looked straight ahead and said good and loud so that I could be heard the length of the table, "Well, Perle, I guess you'll just have to talk to yourself all evening." And do you know?—at the end of the evening those two men left the house arm in arm.

Another time a few years ago, I placed Democratic Speaker Sam Rayburn next to Alice Longworth, knowing she was firmly opposed to most of Sam's policies. The two of them were arguing politics all through dinner. At one point, Alice started in on the Democrats' proposed twenty-dollar across-the-board tax reduction plan. When she took a twenty-dollar bill out of her purse and started waving it in front of the Speaker, he grabbed it.

"Give me back my money!" cried Mrs. Longworth.

"A Republican shouldn't be carrying around a picture of Andrew Jackson, anyway," chided Sam, and proceeded to put the bill in his wallet, where he carried it all evening before finally giving it back to Mrs. Longworth just before the party broke up.

As a dinner is ending, I generally rise and propose a toast to my guest of honor. At dinners outside of Washington, I seldom do this unless I feel the situation really calls for it. But in Washington it is the custom and seems appropriate, since my guest of honor is usually someone who deserves to be commended for his or her achievements.

230

After dinner, the men go into one room and have coffee and liqueurs while the women go to another room. I have no set length of time for this to go on. After a while I take a peek into where the men are gathered. If I find they are in deep conversation, I let them alone, but if it looks as if nothing much is going on, I send the butler to ask them if they would please come in and join the ladies.

From then on, the party is on its own. I never know just what turn it is going to take. If I see that my guests are interested in talking, I signal to my musicians to keep the music soft and low. If I sense that they are in a dancing mood, I choose one of the men and start dancing in the foyer, and all those who want to dance follow suit. Those who want to continue their conversation can go into one of the smaller rooms. Sometimes one of the guests will start to sing, and then maybe the whole group will join in. Or sometimes, when expert dancers like Betty Beale and playwright Speed Lamkin, or Mrs. Dale "Scooter" Miller and Jack Logan start a mambo or a Charleston, everyone gets off the floor to watch them and clap in time to the music. If some of my guests want to play canasta or bridge, they are free to go up to the library where a table and cards are always available. It's their party, really, so I let people do as they please.

Ordinarily, the guest of honor at a Washington party leaves around eleven, because many of the guests dine out nearly every night of the week and have to arise early to be at their offices. After the guest of honor leaves, everyone else is free to go. Often, though, the dignitaries who leave early miss the best fun when we little-wigs and no wigs start cutting up. Sometimes we gather around the piano and sing old-time songs. Or we may square dance or put on impromptu entertainment of one sort or another. I always keep my music until the last guest has left, which sometimes is early in the morning.

Another question interviewers ask me is how much my parties cost. Though I am aware that my style of entertainment is doubtless out of the reach of numerous party givers, I would like to point out that I have been to many parties—and indeed have given them myself—where the cost has been comparatively small. Whether it is a lavish party at Wakehurst, the magnificent Newport home of Mrs. Louis Bruguiere, or a simple party like one I attended recently in a tiny Georgetown apartment, it is the atmosphere of warmth and friendliness more than the elegance of the food and service that spells success. If the details are worked out systematically and thoroughly beforehand, the hostess can then greet her guests calmly and graciously. On the other hand, if she is fretting and worrying over things, and has a pained expression on her face, the guests immediately feel her tension and the party is off to a bad start.

I am often asked to list my basic rules for party-giving. Though I fear there will be no sensational disclosures in the following, I offer these few points. Most of them apply to any kind of party, no matter the size or the underlying purpose.

1. Like the people you invite.

2. Make every one of your guests feel wanted. Don't let anyone stand around looking lost.

3. The quality of the food served is more important than the quantity. Be sure that the hot food is hot, and the cold food is cold.

4. Do not urge people to eat more than they desire. Some may naturally have small appetites; others may be on diets.

5. Try to have some kind of music, even if it is recorded. If there is a lull in the conversation, music fills in the gap.

6. Do not ask your talented guests to perform. If your entertaining has put them in a good mood, they undoubtedly will.

7. The hostess should always look her best because it is a compliment to her guests.

8. Don't fret. Tell yourself before the first guest arrives, "I've done all I can—now let's enjoy things and see that everyone has a good time."

NINETEEN: *Memos to Myself*

WHENEVER I WANT to remind myself to do something, I scribble a few words on the nearest scrap of paper and then pin the note to the front of my dress or apron. Those fashion experts who three years ago nominated me as one of the nation's best-dressed women would surely have thought twice if they could have seen me at home, walking around with scraps of paper pinned to my favorite red apron (I love to wear aprons because I can stuff things into the pockets). Often I look like a walking bulletin board, but I don't care—my system for not forgetting has proved effective. To give an idea of some of the things I get involved in, I'm going to reproduce some of my recent memos to myself, and then explain what they mean.

MEMO: Get Mattie pinchin' scissors.

Mattie, my maid, just can't stand for anybody to have any gadgets she doesn't have. The other day, just before a party, she saw one of my extra helpers using pinking scissors to make plate protectors.

"Mrs. Mesta, I need some pinchin' scissors too," said Mattie.

I asked Mattie what on earth she expected to do with the scissors.

"Oh, my, there's lots of things we could do with 'em," she said vaguely. That's all the satisfaction I got, but she talked me into it. Now I will have to go downtown and get them for her.

Sometimes Mattie thinks she owns me. I really can't get mad at her because she is always so happy and is such a good worker, but I sometimes pretend to be angry, especially when she uses my nail polish, noses into some of my personal business, and tries to get me to buy things we really don't need. In New York recently, she even made me take little Tony up to the Saks Fifth Avenue dog salon and have a complete winter outfit made for him, just because Fifi had gotten some winter togs the year before, and Tony didn't have any.

233

Mattie is always worrying about me, and no matter how late I get in at night, she is always waiting up for me. And when the newspapers published stories recently about my purported romance with the Argentine Ambassador, César Barros Hurtado, Mattie came to me just before bedtime. She looked worried.

"There's something I've got to tell you, Mrs. Mesta. I've been reading about that man, and if you marry him I wouldn't even know where the country is we'd be going to."

I assured Mattie that I had no plans for marrying anyone. I also heard from Marguerite that Edna and Garner Camper had been on their vacation when they saw the same newspaper stories, and Garner had called Marguerite long distance in Nevada to check on the seriousness of the situation. When Garner and Edna returned to the Tysons' I happened to be with them in Nevada. Garner told me of how he had heard about the romance.

He had been in Wichita, where his daughter works for a doctor, and the doctor had showed him a newspaper with the headline, WEDDING IN THE AIR FOR PERLE MESTA? The doctor asked Garner what the chances were.

"Think no more about it," said Garner. "There's nothing to it."

"But it says in the story that he's a very rich man," said the doctor.

"That doesn't mean a thing," replied Garner. "We've [Garner also thinks he owns me] run into a lot of rich men, but they don't have as much as we've got."

The newspaper stories were a bit premature. I had been going out with Ambassador Hurtado, yes, and I enjoyed his company very much, and he was not married. But nothing serious was in the air. We were and are only good friends.

MEMO: Plan trip to see foreign students.

This is to remind me to find time to go to Fairleigh Dickinson University, at Rutherford, New Jersey, to see my scholarship students there and also to talk to the school's president, Dr. Peter Sammartino, about future scholarships. I'll never cease to be grateful to President Truman for that idea he had back in 1950 when I asked him what I could do to improve American-Luxembourg relations, and he answered that I might consider sending a young Luxembourger to the United States for a college education.

234

Harry Truman's idea has grown a bit since then. In the past few years I have had a great deal of satisfaction in having materially assisted in the education of eighteen young people from thirteen countries. Besides those from Luxembourg, the students have come from France, Iraq, Korea, Canada, Liberia, New Zealand, Japan, Australia, England, Lebanon, Afghanistan, and Greece. The schools they have attended or are now attending include Purdue, Fairleigh Dickinson, the Fletcher School of Law and Diplomacy at Tufts University, the Sherwood School of Music in Chicago, and Yale University.

One of my scholarship students now at Fairleigh Dickinson is Basir Younoszai from Afghanistan; he is studying dentistry. I was happy to learn recently from Dr. Sammartino that Basir had been selected as one of the students to represent Fairleigh Dickinson at the 1959 University Model United Nations held in Montreal. Also at Fairleigh Dickinson is another of my students, Isaiah Bara-Hart, a young Liberian who is studying journalism.

Although the countries or the universities select the students who will come to America on these scholarships, I have two requirements of my own. The first is that the winners do not have to be straight-A students. Straight A's don't necessarily make a successful engineer or businessman or diplomat. There are many capable youngsters who, for any number of reasons, may have only average grades but great potentialities. My other requirement is that when the students have completed their education, they must return to their own countries so that they can put into practice for the benefit of their own people whatever they have learned. It is certainly part of my hope that they will take home a helpful understanding of our American way of life.

When I look at the accomplishments of these young people who have returned home, I know that my program of support must continue. Mohammed Tahir Al-Shawi is now principal of a high school in his native Iraq and has written a textbook on bookkeeping which is used in the secondary schools there. Robert Nettheim, who graduated from Fletcher in 1957, is now Program Director of the Canadian Broadcasting Company. Bryce Harland, another Fletcher graduate, went into the diplomatic service for his native New Zealand and is now back in the United States as a member of the New Zealand Mission to the United Nations. And Mr. and Mrs.

Pierre Reiff, the one outstanding example of my success as a matchmaker, are both active in Luxembourg. Pierre is today an engineer, while Evalyn, whose father has become the Duchy's Prime Minister, teaches music in the moments she can spare from raising her family.

A short time ago, I received a letter from one of my scholarship students that gives a good idea of the caliber of the young people I have been assisting:

Dear Madam Mesta:

It has already been nearly three years since I had the privilege of meeting you toward the end of my stay in the United States. As a former recipient of your Fellowship at the Fletcher School of Law and Diplomacy, I wish to take this opportunity to inform you of some of my activities here.

Since my return to Japan in July 1956 I have been working with the Foreign Exchange Department of the Bank of Japan, which is the central bank of this country. Having studied at the Fletcher School, I am very happy to say that my experience in the United States has proved to be very helpful to me in carrying out my duties in the field of international finance.

In addition to my work with the Bank of Japan, I have been very active in helping your Embassy here and the Fulbright Commission in Japan in their orientation program for the Japanese students going to the United States. Already three times I have talked to those students about my experiences in the United States, and I will do it again next week at the panel organized by the College Women's Club for this year's outgoing students.

At present there are more than ten Fletcher graduates in and around Tokyo, and it has also been my task to arrange the meeting of those alumni from time to time. Twice in the past, we on behalf of the Fletcher School interviewed Japanese applicants for admission to the Fletcher School. Because of variety in nationalities as well as professions of Fletcher graduates, my contacts with them not only enrich my life but also continue to stimulate my interest in international affairs.

At the moment I am applying, upon the recommendation of my bank, for the Training Program of the International Monetary Fund.

Hoping this letter will find you in the best of health,

Sincerely yours,

Shijuro Ogata

My helping to bring a few foreign students to the United States is of course only a small part of the over-all student exchange program that today is bringing many young foreigners here. Nonetheless, my participation gives me a feeling of doing something worthy, since I earnestly believe that international knowledge can be a decisive factor for world peace. The impression some foreigners have of America is based on the myth that America is a country without a soul. No amount of speeches made abroad will prove to our world neighbors that we do have a soul. But I believe that the firsthand knowledge gained by foreign students who are educated here will help replace myth with truth.

MEMO: Call Billy about bulls.

This note reminds me to phone my nephew out in Carson City, Nevada, and talk to him about the price of new bulls. The James Canyon Dairy was organized in 1958, and I was named a trustee. Billy Tyson (I probably should call him Bill, now that he has grown up and is a father) operates the James Canyon Dairy. Bill has his eye on a Guernsey bull in California that is priced at six thousand dollars. He has been talking about buying it. But I've seen some of those six-thousand-dollar bulls, and they don't look any better to me than bulls that sell for two thousand. Bill, however, will probably convince me he is right and quote me a long list of figures proving that one six-thousand-dollar bull is a better investment in the long run than three two-thousand-dollar bulls. Bill has proved himself a good businessman. By the end of the first year's operation, the James Canyon Dairy was distributing more Nevada-produced milk than any other dairy in the state.

The family is also proud of Bill for becoming the first one of our clan to run for and win an elective office. In 1958 he decided to run for the Board of Regents at the University of Nevada. These positions are filled by state-wide elections. Bill started campaigning, aided by his pretty blond wife, Jerry. I was in Nevada during part of the campaign, and attended a meeting of Democratic women in Reno. I gave a talk, but did not mention my nephew, because the regent's race was nonpartisan (and also because Bill is a registered Republican—although I hope to change that).

During the question period after my talk, Jerry Tyson got my eye.

"I know you are not out here on a political mission," she said, "but couldn't I interest you in my husband's campaign?"

Of course this gave me an opportunity to explain that my nephew was running for regent and that anyone with a wife as pretty and sweet as Jerry certainly deserved to win. I did not bother to mention to these Democratic women, however, that Jerry is the daughter of Mr. and Mrs. Livingston Merchant (he is Undersecretary of State for Political Affairs in the present Administration). Come election day, William Tyson won a four-year term on the Board of Regents. And several months afterward, he was appointed to the Nevada Milk Commission.

MEMO: Check battle plan with Alice.

This note means I am to go to the National Woman's Party headquarters for a conference with Alice Paul about planning our strategy to get the Equal Rights for Women amendment to the Constitution through Congress. A lot of my friends are still wondering why I have worked for the last twenty years in the Equal Rights movement. I remember when I first started lobbying for the amendment I paid a visit to Senator Hamilton Lewis of Illinois. He was a great charmer, and as I earnestly lectured him about our movement in the Senate reception room, he picked up my hand and gallantly kissed it. Then he held my hand up to the light and chuckled.

"Imagine you, with all those diamonds, sitting around here lobbying for women's rights!" he said. Nonetheless we got his vote.

Many of my good friends disagree with me on the subject of Equal Rights for Women. Roberta Vinson insists it is wrong to try to get more rights for women. "I don't think there is anything women can do that men cannot do better—except having babies," says Roberta when she wants to get into an argument. And Sam Rayburn likes to tease me by saying, "You women have all the rights in the world now. What do you want with more?"

Despite their quips, both Sam and Roberta are sincere in their opposition to our program. And I am equally dead set that equal rights for women is one of the great needs for the whole world today. I feel it is more than a matter of principle that the many gross discriminations which now exist should be eliminated.

Most people are unaware that approximately fifteen hundred

laws and regulations in the United States today discriminate against women, even though the situation has improved greatly in the last twenty years, largely through the efforts of the National Woman's Party. Twenty years ago, for instance, twenty-five states barred women from service on state and Federal juries. Today, women are eligible for Federal jury service in all states and only three states bar them entirely from state juries. This can be quite important. Some years ago, a Massachusetts woman who was charged with a law violation requested that there be women on the jury, and her lawyer challenged the all-male jury before which she was brought. The courts, including the United States Supreme Court, denied her the right to have women on the jury.

In some states, women are still denied the right to control their own property after marriage; in more than half the states they are denied the right to make contracts on an equal basis with their husbands; and in some states they are restricted in the right to control their own earnings as they desire. In six states, the father but not the mother is entitled to the guardianship of a minor child. And even in Federal employment or in defense industries holding government contracts, discrimination in hiring and promotion is permitted with regard to women, although such discrimination is forbidden on the grounds of race, color, creed, and country of origin. This means that the Federal Government or a firm with government contracts cannot refuse to hire or to promote a Negro, a Jew, a Buddhist, or a naturalized Japanese just because he happens to be a Negro, Jew, Buddhist, or Japanese. But don't be a woman! It is all right to refuse to hire or promote a woman solely because she is that—a woman.

Many people assume that women are protected by the Fourteenth Amendment to the Constitution, which forbids any state to deny any person "the equal protection of the laws." Unfortunately, the Supreme Court has decided that while the guarantee of the equal protection of the laws applies to Mexican wetbacks, the Southern Pacific Railroad, and General Motors, it does not apply to women.

If our Constitution had been written in the last twenty years, women automatically, in all probability, would have had all the rights of men. But, as most of us know, ours is the oldest written constitution in the world today, and at the time it was written, women were merely chattels of their husbands, as based on British common law. That is why it was necessary to enact an amendment to the Constitution to give women the right to vote.

The solution to the situation I have just presented is simple. All we need is a twenty-third Amendment which will provide that: EQUALITY OF RIGHTS UNDER THE LAW SHALL NOT BE DENIED OR ABRIDGED BY THE UNITED STATES OR BY ANY STATE ON ACCOUNT OF SEX.

Actually, our amendment will protect men as well as women. It is known as the "Equal Rights for Men and Women" amendment. Legislation to enact this amendment has been introduced in every Congress since 1923, and every time, pressure groups keep it from being submitted to the people of the United States, through their state legislatures, for a vote.

The opposition comes from several sources. Much of organized labor opposes the amendment because many union leaders are afraid women will take jobs away from men. There is another group, including some women's organizations and the United States Department of Labor, which argues that passage of the amendment would destroy the so-called "protective" legislation now in effect for women.

Katharine St. George, the New York Congresswoman who is leading the fight in the House for passage of the Equal Rights amendment, points out that there always has been special legislation for various groups of citizens and yet this does not deprive them of equality under the Constitution.

"Veterans have special legislation that applies only to them," says Mrs. St. George. "The sick, the aged, the poor, the blind— all have special legislation applying only to them. Today students are the recipients of many benefits under special legislation. Yet none of these groups are deprived of their rights under the Constitution for this reason."

Alice Paul, the leader of our women's rights crusade, founded the National Woman's Party in 1913, and several times in her early days as a suffrage leader, went to prison on behalf of women's right to vote. After the Suffrage Amendment was adopted in 1920, Miss Paul led the National Woman's Party to take up the battle to gain complete equality for women. She now helps direct the campaign from our party headquarters at the Alva Belmont House, situated only two blocks from the Capitol.

240

In the last several Congresses, the resolutions to submit the Equal Rights amendment to the state legislatures have made good progress. In the Senate, where a majority has announced as being in favor of the amendment, it has three times gotten to the floor after approval by the Judiciary Committee. Once it received a majority vote, but not the two-thirds required for Constitutional amendments. On the other two occasions, a rider was attached that would have made the amendment practically worthless, had it passed.

In the House of Representatives, where we also have nearly enough strength to pass our measure, it has been kept bottled up in the Judiciary Committee since 1948.

In an effort to help arouse support for passage of the amendment in the Eighty-sixth Congress, I recently gave a party at the Alva Belmont House. Senators Karl Mundt, Sam Ervin, Henry Jackson, Dennis Chavez, Frank Carlson, Wayne Morse, Theodore Green, Ernest Gruening, John Carroll, and Howard Cannon attended, as did several representatives—even Speaker Sam Rayburn. And in a fruit-punch toast, Mrs. St. George sounded our rally call: "Equal rights for men and nothing more! Equal rights for women and nothing less!"

Today, in addition to my work in Washington, I am spending much time in New York at my new post as accredited representative to the United Nations for the World Woman's Party and the National Woman's Party. In the worldwide situation the United States has lagged behind such countries as Egypt, Burma, Greece, Japan, Pakistan, and Western Germany, all of which have written equal-rights-for-women provisions into their constitutions. I will do everything in my power to see that the United States will be the next nation to do so.

MEMO: Pay A.N.W.C. dues.

This is to remind me to get a check into the mail to pay my annual dues to the American Newspaper Women's Club. A number of years ago I was invited to join the club as an associate member. I don't know why they asked me unless they needed someone who was good at pouring tea. I quickly said yes, before they could change their minds, because I didn't want to miss this opportunity to associate with women of the press. All my life I have had a secret

www.ingramcontent.com/pod-product-compliance
Lightning Source LLC
LaVergne TN
LVHW021911100225
803330LV00002B/261